ELIZABETH BEST's first book, *Eli's Wings*, was published in 2002. It became an inspirational bestseller, and appears on high school reading lists across Australia. She has written for film, and her articles have appeared in newspapers in the UK and Australia, including the *Herald Sun*, *The Age* and *The Australian*. She is an ambassador for the Butterfly Foundation and is currently writing her first novel.

COLIN BOWLES is the bestselling author of over thirty books, including *When We Were Gods*, *Anastasia*, *My Beautiful Spy* and *Pearls* (under the name Colin Falconer), and *The Naked Husband* and *The Naked Heart* (as Mark D'Arbanville); and has won awards for his young adult fiction. He currently lives in Adelaide.

**For more information on Eli and Colin's journey, go to
theyearweseizedtheday.net**

the Year We Seized the Day

A true story of friendship and renewal on the Camino

ELIZABETH BEST & COLIN BOWLES

ARENA
ALLEN&UNWIN

This edition published in 2010
First published in 2007

Arena Books, an imprint of
Allen & Unwin
83 Alexander Street
Crows Nest NSW 2065
Australia
Phone: (61 2) 8425 0100
Fax: (61 2) 9906 2218
Email: info@allenandunwin.com
Web: www.allenandunwin.com

Cataloguing-in-Publication details are available
from the National Library of Australia
www.librariesaustralia.nla.gov.au

ISBN 978 1 74237 295 2

Text design by Lisa White
Map by Ian Faulkner
Set in 11/13.5 pt Goudy Old Style by Midland Typesetters, Australia
Printed in Australia by McPherson's Printing Group

10 9 8 7 6 5 4 3 2 1

This book is dedicated to El's grandfather, Bob. And to Col's father, Joe, who died while the book was in final edit.

Two old soldiers and gentlemen.

We hope we made you proud.

Contents

N

BAY OF BISCAY

PORTUGAL

Finisterre
Santiago de Compostela
Monte do Gozo
Santa Irene
Melide
Gonzar
Sarria
Triacastela
Alto do Polo
Perefe
Ponferrada
Astorga
Hospital de Orbigo
León
Reliegos

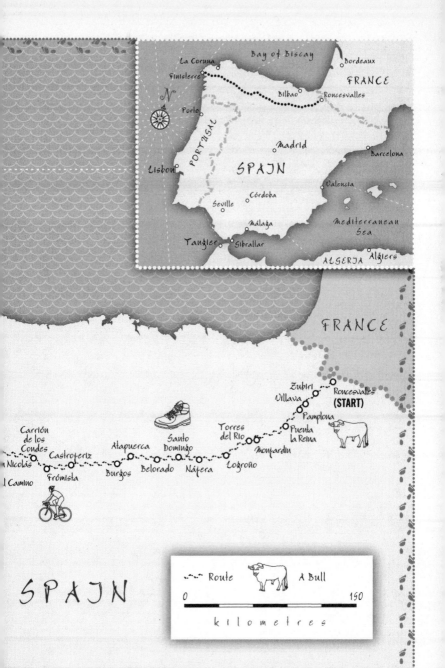

Eli: Shadows don't lie

I turn to find Colin on the trail. Head down in thought, he wanders along, never looking more than a few paces ahead as he goes.

They say the Camino is like life; however you have lived you will walk, and in your time here, all will be returned. In that sense, for many the Way is a penance, a succession of past karmas reflected on request. For others, it's a stepping stone, a progression toward something more beautiful than what they presently are.

The first time I heard the Camino described that way, I thought the people who believed it took the business of walking far too seriously. Paul, the Canadian volunteer in Roncesvalles who issued our pilgrims passports; Yoski and Petra, the young Swedish couple in love with the gentle nature of the Way; Mathew, the young Italian student; Elisabeth, the French-woman walking with her dog; all with scallop shells and all with similar views. There appears to be a connection; those who know the history and know what it is they are here to find wear the scallop shell like an emblem of honour. The more naive among us mosey along bewildered, guided not by history or a cause but by a cruel guidebook. For some reason, I thought *they* were different from Col and me, as if they belonged out here and we were merely visitors to their world—house guests who arrive unannounced and stay longer than they should.

I look around again at Colin ambling along and watch him kick at the dirt, occupying his mind with thoughts, then turn back to study my own shadow. Every bump and bulge, angle, edge and line of the jagged silhouette is familiar. I've watched it now for hours and days. The peak of the cap shield-ing the sun from my face, the curve of my pack eclipsing each shoulder, cargos rolled to the knee encouraging a breeze, heavy, weathered boots already worn from the one hundred and twenty kilometres trudged so far, and water bottle at the ready.

It's taken a week but—aware now of my solitary purpose— the urgency has finally left my feet. There are no bills to pay today, no calls to make, errands to run, traffic to battle, friends to meet or appointments to keep. But there is much work to be done. And it all revolves around the same four threads woven throughout every day: food, water, health and shelter. The life of a pilgrim is a life stripped bare, reduced to the essentials and nothing more. It takes time, effort and energy to get lost in the modern world.

Gazing down at my shadow, the prospect of walking back through my life frightens me. It is a journey I wouldn't wish to reverse, yet it's not one I'd particularly wish to endure again. It's becoming more obvious each day that what they say is right: the Camino is life. It's like stumbling into a scene from *Alice in Wonderland* and learning the rules as you go. No one really 'belongs' out here, and that's the point. We are all visitors, all equal, all trying to reach our destination, as best we can. To do and be better in some way than we were the day before.

Eli: So you wanna be a pilgrim?

My mother will tell you that walking a pilgrimage was something I first spoke about as a child, not because I was particularly pious but because I dreamed about, one day, being the sort of person who would. As a kid I never knew what I wanted to do when I grew up but knew exactly who I wanted to be.

Having said that, I also imagined a pilgrimage would be something I would undertake much later in life. A journey of reflection, to look back upon fifty or sixty years' worth of experiences. I'd certainly not planned on this.

Colin and I met two years ago at a literary festival. I was invited to speak about my first book. An author of twenty years, he was there to represent one of thirty-five he had published internationally. Feeling somewhat out of my league among the twelve other 'real' authors, Col and I became friends first. Though we'd not seen a lot of each other since, we had kept in touch via phone and email and, with time, he became somewhat of a mentor within the publishing industry. He had read my work, believed in my ability and often suggested that we should write something together.

The Camino came about randomly in conversation. Something I simply suggested one night over the phone. 'We'd need time to research, of course,' I said, estimating three months to be long enough, 'and it's a bloody long way, we'd have to train for it. How about we aim for next November?' I suggested.

'I have commitments in November,' he said. 'How about the week after next?'

'Are you serious?' I asked, shocked.

'Yes,' he replied calmly. 'Are you?'

I wasn't sure. It was a big decision.

It had been two years since I'd written my first book. I wanted—more than anything—to get back to writing full time but lacked the confidence to do so. Embarking on a project with Col felt like the perfect opportunity. A step in the right direction, encouraged by a friendly nudge. Physically, I wasn't sure I was capable of completing a five hundred-mile hike, not after being so ill six years before; the health repercussions had plagued me ever since. But I was tired of feeling fragile, and needed a challenge, both personally and professionally.

The Camino de Santiago appeared to be just that: a test of faith, courage, strength, physical and mental toughness. It was perfect. With Col there for support I was, at the very least, hopeful. And regardless of whether we actually made it or not, I expected to gain much out of taking the risk. After all, it was something I had always dreamed I'd do. If not now, when?

So, less than three weeks later, there we were, in Spain, in a bus heading northeast toward the French border, on our way to Roncesvalles, the starting point of our pilgrimage along the great Camino to Santiago de Compostela.

It was at that very moment, amidst a busload of boisterous Spaniards deep in the foothills of the Pyrenees, that this naive pilgrim wannabe realised one of life's greatest ironies: dreams seldom coincide with reality.

My moment of truth had finally arrived. And I freaked out.

Eli: Days like these

An hour and a half from Pamplona, and already the congested highway has become a single-lane road. As we wind into the hills, the view from my window grows more breathtaking.

The purple haze of the surrounding hills turns darker shades of grey. Sweeping valleys lean deeper and the distance between farmhouses along the roadside grows longer. We'd been told the trip would take forty minutes. The temperature drops, fog settles on the windows and I wonder how much further it could possibly be.

The Camino trail runs east to west along the north of Spain. There are several preceding trails entering from France, all of which converge near the small Spanish town of Roncesvalles just west of the border. This is where Colin and I have agreed to begin our journey. Yet, ironically, the only bus to Roncesvalles leaves from the Spanish city of Pamplona, where we had arrived from Paris the previous night. Pamplona is also to be our second day's walking destination and we now find ourselves travelling east—the opposite direction. We have scheduled just nine hours to retrace on foot the terrain our bus covers in an hour and a half. And with each passing minute of remaining daylight, my concern grows.

Nothing but hilltops and mountains now in every direction: exposed cliff faces, steep shale descents. My concerns turn to fear as I realise that from this point on, Colin and I will be on our own. Anxious, I turn to my companion. *Why does he look so bloody calm?* Oblivious to my pending mania, he continues to gaze thoughtfully out the window.

Time slips into slow motion, my vision tapers to a narrow tunnel and my mind begins to race with disconnected thoughts. My palms grow clammy, throat jams shut, mouth is dry like stale carpet, my teeth chatter and the ability to breathe all but deserts me. Suddenly, all idealistic fantasies about personal challenge and achievement career into a brick wall of present reality, bringing with it a sick sense of dread that settles in the pit of my stomach like wet cement.

I sit in my seat wide-eyed and stunned with terror. *What have I done?* My tongue grates against the roof of my mouth like chalk on a board. I try to swallow.

Colin looks across. 'El, you okay?'

The blood races to my cheeks like needles piercing the skin. The laughter of Spanish pilgrims behind us, joking amongst themselves, sounds like the echoed screams of an amusement-park haunted house. *What are they saying?* There they are in their state-of-the-art hiking gear, backpacks the size of my bum bag; professional trekkers, laughing at the two hapless tourists both with backpacks the size of bar fridges.

'El,' Colin repeats. 'What's up?'

I am unable to speak and simply shake my head.

'Well, say something. Are you homesick?'

Homesick? I'm not homesick. *I am angry!* Furious! *Whose idea was this anyway?* They used to offer this pilgrimage as a substitute for jail time when sentencing hardened criminals. Who on Earth, with my history, would walk it for fun? What insane act of lunacy has driven me here, on a bus full of singing Spaniards, with a guy I haven't seen for over a year, about to walk eight hundred kilometres across a country whose language I speak not a word of? I've never even been camping!

'No!' I snap, through clenched teeth. 'I'm not *okay*. Okay?'

His eyebrows jump up his forehead like someone has just poured a drink over his pants in a bar. I turn back to face the seat in front, nostrils flaring with each deliberate breath. He drops the subject, leaving me to sort things out for myself.

It is probably for the best.

Later that night, in Roncesvalles, I take some time alone to write and think, and calm down. The bottle of red wine with dinner has helped and, although I'm still not happy about the situation, I am at least speaking coherently again.

I'd suffered anxiety attacks briefly when I was young. I clearly remember the first hitting out of the blue when I was seven. It was the final day of the school year and, awaiting my school report, I had convinced myself I was about to fail. I hid under the table in a corner of the room, devising an elaborate plot to run away from home that night, once my parents were asleep. My classmates laughed as my sixty-three-year-old teacher hitched up her skirt and lay on the floor to read my report out loud to prove I'd passed before I finally agreed to come out.

My teacher told me then, as many have since, that I 'think too much'. What a thing to say to a child. The mind is the most powerful tool we have. It dictates our entire lives, our thoughts can make or break us. It was my own mind that almost killed me once; now it has brought me here. To the Camino. And why? Only time will tell.

I wonder what Colin makes of all this?

Day 1
Roncesvalles to Zubiri

Colin: *The violence of the lambs*

The first long walk I ever went on was during a school trip to Scotland and Wales when I was twelve. It was where I learned the wisdom of travelling light. The first day we set out to climb Ben Lomond, one kid got as far as the first knoll, threw down his pack in despair, and collapsed, crying: *Leave me here to die!*

Okay, I thought. If that's what you want.

But our geography teacher wouldn't do it; no backbone. Instead, he lifted the kid's pack himself and found that it weighed more than Saturn. Inside was a hardback copy of *War and Peace*, three empty bottles of Lucozade—which the kid had drunk on the bus before we even reached the foot of the mountain—and a radio the size of a microwave oven that could not work without mains power.

Our teacher's name was Mr Alves. I watched a blood vessel pop in his temple like a varicose vein as he threw the lot on the ground in despair.

'Why did you bring all this . . .' I think he was about to say 'crap' but restrained himself. '. . . this rubbish?'

'Well,' the kid said, 'you never know what you might need on a rainy day.'

This is not the attitude to take on a hiking trip, because what you need—whether it rains or not—is as little as possible. All you need for a rainy day is a poncho that you can fold into a matchbox. I thought I had learned my lesson.

We start our walk at 7.15 am, heading downhill through the woods. The air is chill and bright. There is an unspoken tension between Eli and me. We have finally realised we might be a tad unprepared and if we don't make it through the first week—the first day seems only an even-money bet— we're going to look like a real pair of tossers.

That morning before we left we stole surreptitious glances at the other hikers and their intimidating array of equipment. They have sleeping bags that weigh less than a neutron, collapsible walking sticks that look like ski poles and water bottles made of new compounds discovered by NASA just the previous day.

For food they have hydrolysed green Madras curry with prawns and chapattis in a silver foil packet so light it floats if they take it out of their backpacks. Me, I have some leftover *churros*—a kind of Spanish doughnut that looks like a sausage—and a warm bottle of Coke. The thing about having *churros* for breakfast is that you can make them last, because they are indigestible in one sitting. I bought them yesterday and today they are the consistency of biltong. They are chewy, sweet and sit in the stomach like shit on a shovel.

For me, this journey is not about distance. I am confident I can make it without losing a limb. It all seems so easy: I am the accomplished author going along to co-author a travel book, provide a bit of the humour and technical expertise, while Eli writes the serious stuff. I am the rock, the mentor. And this will distract me while the woman I love is in Italy working out her future and, by extension, mine. Though in truth, I know what she will decide, I always have known. There was never any question where our affair would lead, never any choice. But my heart is breaking. As wrong as it sounds, perhaps even is, she is the only woman I ever really loved, for reasons I am unable to explain. Needless to say, that love was expressed in ways impossible for her, or for me, to fathom.

There is also, at the back of my mind, though unexpressed, the hope for a miracle, some evidence or proof that there is something out there worth believing in that might make me a better man.

For all practical purposes, this venture is insane. I hardly know Eli and she hardly knows me. I could be Ivan Milat for all she knows—and as it later transpires, she might have preferred it if I *was* Ivan Milat. We had met at a writers' festival and intuitively felt an overpowering connection. But we lived three thousand kilometres apart and almost all our contact before this trip has been by phone or email.

We descend into a valley within the crinkled folds of the Pyrenees. I look back at Eli. She is struggling already. I admire the risks she is taking, professional and personal, in doing this. Being brave is a courageous thing to do. It starts with a decision; the hard part is getting your body to follow you into your battles.

She stops when we reach our first incline. 'No,' she yells. 'I don't do hills!'

But we do do hills. We do several before making another long descent. Our guidebook has already become a study in bathos and understatement; 'an undulating path' is in reality a tortuous series of ascents and descents that has the thigh muscles creaking like wet rope on a rusting freighter; 'a long and winding ascent' is an endless climb that squeezes sweat out of you so that your mouth turns as dry as a vacuum cleaner bag; 'a rapid descent' is a scramble down shale so broken and loose that every step feels like someone shoving tent pegs through your knees and into the little hollows of your thigh bones so that the marrow oozes out through your hips.

At last the walk becomes a little more pleasant; we roll through woods trilling with birdsong and wide pastures with red-roofed chalets. There is the sound of cowbells; it's like being in Switzerland. There is the smell of pine and cow shit. Heidi is going to come skipping round that corner any minute. Or maybe Julie Andrews. The hills are alive.

We run into a shepherd and his large herd of black-faced sheep with tiny curved horns. Our choice is to move to the side of the laneway or run away. Bravely we stop to face them.

The horns are at a strategic height; one wrong move and one of these little buggers will be wearing my testicles as earrings. It is like the running of the bulls, only in miniature. The running of the lambs.

Hemingway would have loved it.

At a village called Burguete we congratulate ourselves on walking three kilometres and stop for a coffee. There is a television above the bar and we watch the running of the bulls live from Pamplona; men in white tunics and white trousers with fetching red scarves and sashes around their waists are having their rectums rearranged by tons of angry hamburger.

We talk to a young guy from Sweden, Victor. I ask him where he is from. 'Norrköping,' he says.

'I've been there.'

'Well, it's not the town. It's a little village about ten miles away. You won't have heard of it. It's called Skärblacka.'

This is like an alien meeting someone in a bar in Reykjavik and finding out they too are from Alpha Centauri.

'I know it! I lived there for two months!'

He stares at me and shakes his head. 'No one ever goes to Skärblacka.'

Many years ago, before I was even shaving, the first girl I ever loved came from Skärblacka. It was a village with a population of seventy-nine, half of whom were goats. I lost my virginity to her. All I remember is it didn't take me long to do it. Echoes of other kisses, other embraces, a comet shower across a pale sky; of a more innocent time when a broken heart meant only a bruised ego and feeling sad for a few weeks. How times have changed. I wonder what she is doing now, how her life has been. We parted acrimoniously, but now I wish her only good things.

We walk until lunchtime, a total of eighteen kilometres, until we reach Zubiri, an industrial town that looks like Bhopal and smells like cement. Our pilgrims passports allow us entry into a bombed-out school gymnasium that is the town's *albergue*, or hostel, for weary pilgrims. We are exhausted. We have another seven hundred and eighty-two kilometres still to walk. At this rate I will be two and a half weeks late for my flight home.

I am sick of this already.

Day 2
Zubiri to Villava

Colin: *Feeling like death by the afternoon*

We set off next morning in a mist of rain. It is a cool grey dawn, the air heavy with the smell of wet hay and pollution from the magnesite factory that is the only reason for Zubiri's existence.

Today is even harder than the first; the adrenalin has been burned off, and all that remains is the lactic acid that settles like salt into leather. I can feel every muscle and tendon in my legs.

Eli, I notice, is not in good shape. She has been throwing up all night. Or so I find out from other pilgrims. I snored through it all apparently.

We cross a river and follow the blue and yellow *peregrino* sign that marks the path of the Camino here in the region of Navarre. On the other side of a medieval stone bridge that pilgrims have trod for six centuries is a bright red Coke vending machine. I imagine pilgrims from the fifteenth century stopping here for effervescent sweetened drinks. It encourages me to go on.

My backpack is heavier than it was yesterday. It felt like a rabbit in a sack at Roncesvalles, now it feels like a large wet bag of cement that is bending my spine out of shape like a stick of liquorice with a potato tied to the end. I am sure every time I turn my back some bastard slips another brick in the pack.

I begin to suspect that we were not as severe with our packing as we might have been. The Trangia camping stove now feels like a real stove. What can I say? It seemed like a good idea at the time. Today there is no geography teacher to hurl the Trangia on the ground and tell me to wake up to myself. On this walk, as in life, I am on my own, and any weight I have to carry, I have to carry alone.

In the next village we stop for a coffee and find our friend Victor, the Swede, already sitting in front of the television with a *café con leche*—coffee with milk—and toast, waiting for the 8 am running of the bulls from Pamplona. His mother was Swedish, but his father was from Pamplona and he loves to watch the *encierro*, as the Spanish call it.

'Have you ever run?' Eli asks him.

'Many times. I don't like bullfighting. But the running is different. The bull does not get hurt. It's the man that gets hurt, if he is unlucky, if he makes a mistake.'

'A mistake?' To me, it looks like volunteering to stand in front of a machine gun. If it gets pointed at you, you get mown down.

But Victor shakes his head. 'My father ran every year, he still does, when my mother lets him. He taught me how to do it. He walked the course with me, showed me which sections to run, the sections where it was not so dangerous, where you had a place to shelter if the bull came too close. The worst place is near the end of the run, at the entrance to the Plaza de Toros. Here you have nowhere to go if the bull hunts you.'

If the bull hunts you. Sounds brilliant.

'There are important things to remember. If you go down, you must stay down, stay down and do not move. Some instinct will make the bull jump over you. But if you get up he lowers his horns and puts you down again. The ones who get hurt are mostly foreigners. The Spanish know the rules and they respect the bull.'

He explains what it is like; first, there is the waiting, he says—the waiting brings out something primal in a man, something only a man can understand. There is the fear, the adrenalin, the men slapping their rolled newspapers against their thighs, the same newspapers that carry the body count from the day before, different columns for those injured by hooves or by horns.

When the bulls come there is an explosion of excitement and terror. His eyes grow bright as he describes it; the fear, he says. This is what the *feria* is all about. The two minutes in the whole day when you discover what it is like to be a man, or crazy, or both.

Suddenly he falls silent and his eyes go to the television. The run has started.

Every year San Fermin attracts tourists from all over Europe. You sometimes see the images on the evening news, men dressed in white with red sashes, holding rolled-up newspapers with which to taunt the bulls. Some people say it is not as much the running of the bulls as the chasing of the idiots.

The bulls are driven through the narrow cobbled streets of the old quarter, sliding around the corners like three-year-olds in an ice rink, slipping on the wet cobblestones and thudding into the wooden barricades. Confused and more than a little pissed off, they occasionally trample over the top of some testosterone-crazed unfortunate and occasionally a liver or a set of testicles is removed by a stray horn.

Which seems to be what has happened right now. At the bar two old men grunt and shake their heads as one of the foreigners goes down, then immediately rises to his knees.

This does not mean he is not already badly hurt, Victor says. It is just the adrenalin.

As Victor warned, as he gets up he makes himself a target. He is hit again by a second bull. He bounces over the cobblestones like a rag doll hurled from a train. And then everyone in the bar groans, because he starts to get up again. The third bull hits him while he's still on his knees, and he hurtles back like he's been sprayed with an Uzi machine gun. Three-nothing to the bulls.

Victor shakes his head. 'Idiot,' he mutters. 'Probably an American.'

As the lead bull charges through the street, the runners look like the foam spraying from the bows of a motorboat. 'If the bulls stay together,' Victor says, 'everything will be okay. If one of these bulls get separated, he will get confused and start to look for targets. Then it gets really dangerous.'

And this is just what happens. Outside the entrance to the plaza, one of the bulls decides that a certain Spaniard, lying prostrate on the cobblestones beneath his hooves, is the cause of all its troubles. It gores him not once, but three times, finally tossing him aside like a used Kleenex.

Thirty seconds later, the run is over.

Victor grins at me. 'That was fun!'

I wonder if the used Kleenex being hurried away on a stretcher by the Spanish paramedics thinks that was fun. Possibly not. But as a combat photographer mate of mine used to say, it's only terrible if it happens to you.

Colin: Eli gets a wobble on

We descend into the valley of the Rio Arga. The road takes us down through the pine forests beside cool running streams where Papa Doc Hemingway once fished for trout and where local Basques still do. There are chalets built entirely of stone and white farmhouses called *caserios*. This is Euskal Herri—Basque country.

I find I have become very conscious of my body, as a working piece of machinery. Already the twinge in my lower back that I have had for ten years has become a steel scalpel softly inserted and then withdrawn with every step. The once interesting clicking of my left knee is a stabbing pain that raises a patina of sweat on my forehead. This body consciousness is a new thing for me; I normally ignore it except when I have an erection or the flu. But now I am becoming as attuned to my body as a camel driver to his camels, a cowboy to his horse, a lawyer to his BMW. Every twinge is a potential disaster.

'Did you know,' Eli slurs, 'did you know it takes seventy-two hours for lactic acid to settle in the muscles?'

I calculate we started walking twenty-six hours ago. At least forty-four more hours of pain to anticipate.

'Thanks, El.'

'No worries.'

Right now she is stumbling ahead of me, head down, legs and arms waving about like a crayfish but everything else perfectly tuned. There is a chamois towel the size of a baby's fist attached to the side of her pack, maps of Spain tucked into a little flap, and a funky top she bought yesterday on the way through Pamplona that says *San Fermin 2004*. Top-of-the-range hiking boots and a headscarf complete the picture. She may look the goods but she does not feel it. In fact, Eli is seriously fucked.

She is the colour of wall putty, and acting very strangely, walking backwards down steep hills and talking about catching a tram to St Kilda. Her eyes are moving independently in her head. You could fry eggs on her forehead. She has only needed to stop for a pee once in the last half an hour, so by her normal standards she must also be seriously dehydrated. She is a tough girl, and determined, so she keeps staggering on like a drunk out of a bar at closing time. But it is clear she is not going to get much further. This is not looking good. We are only two days into the walk.

Eli gets a serious wobble on. We are edging along a cliff face, there is a sheer drop on one side, a stumble will see her over the edge and my workload for the book immediately double. I wonder what I'd tell her mother if she takes a tumble. Stopping to ship a body home for burial will mean I may have to walk an extra ten or twenty kilometres a day to finish on time. Perhaps I should just keep walking and let the foxes and the ants sort her out. Except she still owes me a beer from last night.

An hour from Pamplona she collapses against a wall, stiff as a bit of two-by-four. I lay her out on the ground, legs raised on her backpack, while she mutters incoherently about going to a funky bar in Brunswick Street for brunch and a glass of red.

Uh-oh.

Victor, the Swedish Spaniard, offers to carry some of her pack—the hair dryer, the easel for painting watercolours, the three million muesli bars. Two Irish nurses stop and give Eli their supply of rehydrating powder.

After half an hour I help Eli stumble back onto her feet. We can't stay here. An Australian called Simon and a Spanish girl called Mercedes—pronounced MerTHEDis—stay with us the whole way to the next *albergue*.

When we get to the outskirts of Pamplona Mercedes negotiates with the *hostelero* of the *albergue* to let us into the dormitory three hours before it is officially open for the day. Eli passes out on the bed, saying she'll buy the next round, let's wait for three-quarter time.

It's clear to me that the trip is over before it has begun. Eli is stuffed. As soon as she's well enough, I'll put her on a plane back to Melbourne.

There is a part of me that is relieved. I didn't really expect her to make it and I didn't really expect to find my miracle; yet my naive soul is still disappointed. I've spent the better part of the last three years travelling. The constant movement has become a welcome distraction from my life. Without something else to focus on, I am as restless as a caged animal. We all have things we don't like to face; with me, it's myself.

Colin: A few unassuming reds

While Eli is recuperating, I head into Pamplona for San Fermin. Take a look at the famous *feria*—festival—before we head home.

As I walk into Pamplona, there are graffiti and posters everywhere, written in Basque, for this is the heart of Basque country. Basque is an intimidating language, with lots of Ks and Xs and Zs. A typical Basque slogan reads something like *KXAZIXK KXEKLE XXXZWQ!*

The ETA is Spain's IRA, a ruthless terrorist organisation that has been fighting for an independent Basque state for decades. But many Basques don't like them and rich Basques despise and fear them because the ETA kidnap them for money. Most Basques I spoke to are quite happy with the autonomy they already have. Independence won't change anything; most importantly, it won't make Atlético Bilbao play any better. But on the way into the city I see a lot of ETA propaganda posters on the walls and light poles with pictures of young Basques currently in prison for heroically blowing up an unsuspecting policeman plus a few women and children who happened to get in the way.

Today, though, Pamplona is unconcerned with the ETA. This is the *feria*. By the time I complete the long climb into the old city, it is going off like a frog in a sock. There are young men, white tunics torn, knees bloodied, faces hollowed by the terrible things they have seen, staggering all over the square. And that's just from the drinking. Wait till they run with the bulls tomorrow.

San Fermin is a little bit about bulls and a lot about drinking. The bulls only run for two minutes every day; the drinking goes on for twenty-three hours and fifty-eight minutes. An unassuming bottle of *tinto* with the texture of chainsaw lubricant and a kick like aviation fuel costs just three euros.

The *feria* is important to Spanish society, MerTHEDis has explained to me, because most sons stay at home until they marry, perhaps at twenty-six or twenty-seven. If they don't party on the street, they don't party at all.

Any hour of the day or night during San Fermin you will see people staggering around the plaza drinking *tinto* out of clear plastic glasses the size of a plumber's bucket. There are buskers painted like gold cowboys or silver pirates, and Africans move about the crowd holding out trays of cheap sunglasses with more hope than expectation. There is no pitch; they just shove the tray in the middle of a conversation and wait for someone to tell them to fuck off, and they do.

Everyone has a red scarf; old women, babies, even a chihuahua.

The square is packed with people, all kinds of people: mothers kick footballs to their sons, punks vomit, babies fall asleep in prams, lovers smooch. Three young Spaniards, reeling drunk, attach themselves to a mariachi band busking around the square. What has been a slow day so far for the crooners turns into a bonanza. The boys are a movable party. Soon a crowd of about a hundred has gathered. Bottles are broken, middle-aged Spanish women tossed in the air. No insults are traded, or punches thrown. These are hopeless happy drunks.

I like the Spanish and I love San Fermin.

Behind the square the alleyways reek of urine and stale wine. There is more broken glass than spilled blood. I go into a bar and order a *tinto*. This is my kind of pilgrimage.

I remember thinking: I hope Eli's all right. Half an hour later I can't even remember who she is.

Day 3
Villava, and we're not going nowhere . . .

Eli: *Are we there yet?*

I wake to an empty room, disorientated, and look for a clock. A note sitting next to a small pack of teabags on the bedside table reads: 'Manzanilla Infusion'. It smells like chamomile. I know I am in Spain but don't know where or how long I have been asleep. I can't even remember how I got here—it feels like days have passed.

I kick back a cocoon of blankets and sit up on the edge of the bed. I feel weak, light-headed and sore all over. Each breath is hollow and moving sparks flecks of tiny stars before my eyes. Despite the heavy throb in my head and chest, I can feel the fever has left my body. Whatever it was, I am through the worst of it.

My digital watch reads 12:15. I pull back the curtain to see if it is midnight or midday. Light pours in. Squinting, I count back and realise I have been asleep for twenty-five hours.

A priest finds me standing in the kitchen getting water. Unsure of who he is, I begin to apologise but before I can finish he rushes towards me, placing his hand gently on my forehead.

'*Bien!*' he says. (I'm trying to learn three new Spanish words each day; '*bien*' was one of Monday's words.) I offer him a smile.

He pinches my cheek. 'Very much better,' he says in fractured English, explaining that he'd been in to check on me earlier and changed the blankets, which were soaked with sweat.

'You eat now,' he insists, bunching his fingers together and raising them to his mouth.

Yes, please. I haven't eaten since dinner two days before and I soon lost that.

I ask the gentle priest if he's seen Colin.

He raises both index fingers and places them either side of his head. 'San Fermin.'

We must be close to the city, the monastery is within earshot of festivities. I think back and remember Colin mentioned heading into Pamplona for the day. Hearing the Swede, Victor, talk about the bull run has appealed to some primal male instinct. Then again, he also suggested staying close to make sure I was okay. But maybe I imagined that—my recall is questionable. I started that conversation by asking him if it was yesterday today.

The priest uses the numbers on his watch to explain that he'll open the doors to the day's new wave of passing pilgrims at 3 pm. Until then, I am confined to the small refuge and its modest courtyard garden, which is enclosed by a twelve-foot stone wall. He leaves.

Wrapping a notepad, pen and a bottle of water in a blanket, I wander outside into the garden. The air is crisp but the sun is warm on my skin. Laying the blanket out on the grass, I sit cross-legged beneath the branches of a solitary tree and let the situation settle in. With Colin gone—presumably for the day—and just three stray cats for company, I have time and space to think.

We've already been forced to take the first of only five rest days allocated for the entire journey. Great start. Though he hasn't said it, I know Colin questions my ability to complete this trek or, at this rate, to make it through another day. I don't blame him. I warned him before we came; my mind is both my biggest weakness and my greatest strength. It's created havoc in the past and has the potential to ruin everything. It is obvious that what happened on the bus to Roncesvalles has taken its toll. The sudden sickness and fever were little more than physical manifestations of doubt and fear. My head and heart were locked in battle and my body paid the price.

I came to the Camino with a purpose; to find the part of myself that remembers what it is like to feel strong and confident. Simon and Mercedes, the young couple we had met, seemed as determined and certain of their destination as I hoped to be. I hated appearing weak before them. But I've grown to distrust my body. It's unreliable. There's a certain pain that lingers close to death and once you've felt it, nothing else seems to register. I tend to break down now long before I realise it's time to stop.

I take my pilgrims passport from around my neck and unfold the concertinaed pages, laying it across my lap. Your pilgrims passport is your badge of honour on the Camino, issued to you at the start of your pilgrimage. It contains numbered squares that represent the towns and villages you pass through on your way. Every establishment and *albergue* from Roncesvalles to Santiago has their own unique stamp. Presenting a passport full of evidence at your final destination authenticates the completion of a pilgrimage and you are awarded a certificate—still written in Latin—called the Compostela, marked with the official seal of the Sacred Church.

There is one catch, however: in order to qualify for a Compostela—your first-class ticket to the afterworld—you must state, when asked, that your official motive for journeying the Camino involved some spiritual purpose. If not, your Compostela is demoted to a measly *certificado*, and there's no getting into heaven with one of those. This makes your pilgrims passport on the Camino the equivalent of a CV in the corporate world. Mine, to date, wouldn't land me a job as tea lady in a call centre. Just three of the forty-eight squares contain stamps; the first from Roncesvalles, the second from the *albergue* at Zubiri, and the third here, from the monastery. We still have so far to go. Forty-five squares. Four weeks.

My challenge now is to convince myself—despite evidence to the contrary—that I am actually capable of completing the journey. If I can make myself believe it, then we at least stand a chance of reaching Santiago sometime this year.

Opening my notepad to a fresh page, I write an affirmation that I hope can become my new truth. Then repeat it until I've filled the next three pages, front and back.

Each and every step makes me stronger; without and within.

Later that evening, Colin returns and sits down beside me on the bed.

'So, how do you feel?'

'Good.'

'Okay,' he smiles, 'now tell me how you *really* feel.'

I laugh. 'I am good. Better anyway. Thanks.'

He explains the bus schedule to Paris and begins to run through options for a flight home. But I've already made up my mind.

'We can't give in this early in the trip. Let's get up and start walking again tomorrow. If something happens further down the track, at least we'll know we gave it everything.'

Colin looks concerned and hands me a note.

Colin & Eli,

Good luck & safe travelling. A pleasure to meet you both.
Simon & Mercedes

PS If we don't see you along the way to Santiago, send us a quick message to let us know you're both OK.

The note makes me even more determined to get going again. I ask Colin to promise: no matter what happens between now and Santiago, he will not stop believing in me. And even if he does, he can't let it show. I don't always trust my own judgment but this way, when I doubt myself, I'll trust him. If he thinks we can, then we will.

Day 4
Villava to Puente la Reina

Colin: *Never say Navarre again*

By the next morning Eli has her smile back and is ready to walk again. I suppose I will never really understand what this walk means to her. Two days ago she was doing the funky chicken down the mountainside, legs wobbling like jelly on springs. Today I expected to be putting her on a plane back to Melbourne. A part of me does not think she is physically strong enough to do this. But today she is not only talking about going to Santiago but walking the rest of the way to Finisterre as well, another eighty kilometres.

Eli's physical struggles have as yet not permeated through my own pain, which I am doing my best to hide, even from myself. I have not treated her unkindly. If she is sick I will make sure she gets safely on a plane and I'll finish the journey and the book myself. Or I'll go home with her, if that's what she wants. Whatever provides the best opportunity for not thinking. Because I don't want to think about my life right now. It hurts too much. What I want is distraction.

As we eat breakfast Eli is her old self again. She has rediscovered her passionate appreciation of food. Ironic, really.

We eat scrambled eggs and brown rice. 'This is perfect for us,' she tells me, spooning a heap onto her plate. 'It's full of complex carbohydrates and protein. Carbs give you energy and protein is good for building muscle.'

'Yeah?'

'Did you know that Negro people have a higher proportion of fast-twitch muscle fibres than white people? Fast-twitch muscles are perfect for quick explosive action, which is why black guys win most of the Olympic medals in the one hundred metres, and also why white men can't jump. It's genetic. For thousands of years, their ancestors were hunting lions and elephants while ours were home, ploughing fields and burning witches.'

Wow. I love having breakfast with Eli. It is like doing a pilgrimage with your own personal dietician.

We get in to Pamplona soon after dawn and climb the hill towards the city, skipping around the pavement pizza. We pass a reveller on his way back from the *feria*, moon-walking home to Burlada. We arrive in the square an hour before the day's run; the bars are still open and revellers are rolling out in wine-stained shirts, reeking of sweat, alcohol and testosterone.

The less committed are asleep in the parks, at the bus station, at the rail terminus. Two *bravos* lie sprawled in the square, toe to toe, plastic cups of *tinto* still clutched in a death grip. *From my cold dead hands* as Charlton Heston once famously said. Fellow revellers pretend to perform CPR, rearrange their limbs, take photographs. They don't even stir.

I check the newspaper over our morning coffee. The *feria* is reported like an eight-day Test match, or a baseball series. There is a lift-out supplement inside the newspaper, with eight pages of pictures and stories from the previous day's run—typical headline: 'I was worried about my femoral artery'. Detailed statistics, including weather conditions, how long the run lasted, number of people injured, transported and gored, appear in neat columns with a running total for the entire week.

The paramedics have attended two hundred and forty injuries in the past five days and six people have been gored. The temperature yesterday was twenty-eight degrees Celsius and the wind was four knots from the southwest.

After *café con leche* we leave Pamplona to walk through fields of wheat and sunflowers, a patchwork of gold and dun. There are other pilgrims following the trail out of the city. I can tell because pilgrims are different from ordinary hikers; they have walking sticks, all kinds of walking sticks. For a pilgrim the walking stick is a fashion statement. There are ski poles, steel devices that fold up like collapsible telescopes, branches hacked from trees, or traditional wooden poles bought from pilgrim shops along the way. Most have individual flair, some are decorated with eagle feathers found on the path and almost all have the ubiquitous scallop shell attached to the handle.

The shell is the symbol of the Camino. Saint James is never seen without one, which he wears on his rather rakish hat, which maybe he got from Jesus as a Christmas present. You will see one of these shells on the walking stick or backpack of every pilgrim on the Camino.

The origins of this symbol are unclear but they almost certainly predate Christianity, or at least the Santiago tomb. One legend says that when James first arrived in Spain, a pagan wedding was about to turn pear-shaped because the bridegroom and his horse fell into the sea but James saved him from the waves. When the groom reappeared from the water, coughing and spluttering, he was covered in scallop shells.

What was the bridegroom doing on a horse near the beach on his wedding day? Was he rushing back from his buck's party? How did he fall into the sea? How did James get him out? I suppose he was a fisherman by trade. But a groom and a horse would have been very heavy. Did he have one of those special chairs they use for catching swordfish or did he trawl for him? What did he do afterwards? Did he take off the scallops and throw him back, try to catch some more? These are all good questions. The answer to all of them, of course, is that if you believe any of this crap you also believe the Easter bunny comes down the chimney every Halloween.

The real reason the scallop is emblematic of the Camino is less fanciful. In pre-Christian times the original pilgrim trail was to the temple of Venus at Cape Finisterre, and one of the icons of the religion was the scallop shell that served as a talisman against evil as well as a symbol of fertility and rebirth. This symbol was almost certainly appropriated by the latter-day Christians cutting and pasting onto existing beliefs to make their own more palatable to the locals.

Eli and I don't bother with either the stick or the shell. We refuse to try to pretend we know what we're doing.

We start to ascend the sierra. The climb flexes the buttocks and hamstrings like retuning a guitar. You feel the stretching and hope to God nothing goes G-sharp and then twang.

There are windmills on the ridge above us, huge, white and hi-tech. My idea of a windmill used to be a round clapboard house with a wooden blade on the front and a little Dutch girl in clogs standing next to it. But these are just like giant propellers. The whoosh-whoosh of the blades accompanies the gasps of our ascent.

At the summit the power company has constructed, at great expense, a crappy rusting metal sculpture depicting medieval pilgrims that says: *Where the way of the stars and the way of the winds meet.* Must have cost them all of ten euros.

We stop for a break. It was a big climb and I wasn't sure Eli would make it, not after almost collapsing just two days ago. It's not like there's much of her. Arnold Schwarzenegger shits bigger than her. She is tall and slender as an underwear model. But she has a heart like a football. A twenty-seven-year-old Elle MacPherson with feet like waterskis.

She drinks some cold sweetened tea and chows down on half a chocolate bar, then takes off like a frightened racehorse. Eli has some sort of weird sugar imbalance thing going on and the snack has set it off. I watch her sprint past mountain goats and cyclists. She overtakes a rabbit that's trying to get away. She looks like Road Runner on speed.

Eli: Back on track

The views are awash with colour: blazing yellow fields of sunflowers, patchwork crops and distant hilltops, the biggest of which lies before us on the far side of Pamplona. It is the first time I've looked up from my feet since we began. A sudden return of strength has boosted my confidence. The food and rest yesterday helped and before setting out this morning I loaded my pockets with a variety of snacks. Six pockets, six different delicacies: nuts, dried fruit, wholemeal crackers wrapped in plastic, boiled butterscotch sweets, gum and a mini fun-size chocolate bar.

In the last forty-eight hours, I have lost all of the weight I'd purposely gained in preparation for the walk. It's obvious food will play a vital role throughout the weeks ahead. I'm prepared to eat my way across Spain and arrive ten kilos heavier, if I have to.

Yesterday I met a woman from Barcelona who has the opposite intentions. She's dragged her husband to Ronces-valles in the hope a long walk might trim a few kilos from his waistline. She spotted me in the garden of the monastery in the afternoon, doing yoga beneath a tree, and asked me to show her and her husband a stretch that might help his back. They were a strange pair, the kind you're more likely to meet in a rowdy pub than on a pilgrim trail. The husband lit a joint while the three of us rolled, bent, stretched and laughed on the grass. Their pilgrimage holds no real significance, no great meaning. They say they'll stop when they get sick of walking. Their Camino will be measured by the kilogram not the kilometre.

Though it was a tough ask, yesterday I promised Colin that we would catch Mercedes and Simon within the week. I want to try to make up the day we've already lost. We left the monastery in the morning, planning to walk through Pamplona and thirty kilometres on to Puente la Reina, the same distance they'd walked the day before. Long days on the Camino mean that walking just a kilometre further than someone else at either end of the day could put you behind or ahead of them for the remainder of the entire journey.

The chances of us finding them aren't good but they aren't bad either. By doing so, we'd be back to our original schedule and back with friendly faces. I also want to prove something to Colin and restore his faith in me. So, side by side, we head straight for the summit.

Later that afternoon, following a chocolate-inspired dash down a mountain, Colin finds me in the main street of a deserted town slumped against a vending machine, grinning deliriously and sipping on a cold can of Coke Light, Europe's own Diet Coke.

'What the hell was all that about?' he laughs.

I'd pre-warned him about a childhood illness that had resulted in the condition hypoglycaemia. Over the years I've learned to manage my blood sugar levels using natural supplements and nutrition, but in a new environment, with new foods and increased exercise, it's going to take me some time to readjust.

For a guy who's never had to think twice about what he eats, Colin finds it fascinating that I have to. He immediately takes an interest, which is nice, in a weird kind of way. It's rare. I explain that I occasionally misjudge it and throw my blood sugar levels out of whack. If I don't burn up excess energy in my system, my body tries to compensate for the imbalance and my sugar levels plummet. If blood sugar levels spike it's manageable, but if they dive it could wipe me out for days. Thinking he's found the solution to tackling every hill we face from now on, Col stocks up on chocolate biscuits in the next town, offering them to me at the base of each mountain, to ensure I don't lag behind. He also gives me the green light to dart ahead anytime.

Later that day we reach Puente la Reina, thirty kilometres to the west of where we set out that morning. We check into the first of two *albergues* and gratefully take off our packs. We made it.

Taking your pack off is both pleasure and pain. Relieved from the strain, the muscles in your back, stomach and chest release like slack rubber bands. But the vertebrae in your spine don't cope as well. While supported they're kept aligned like a row of obedient soldiers. Slip off your pack and suddenly they stray, wandering off in different directions as if scattered by small-arms fire. Bend—*click, crack, click-click*. Stretch—*clunk!* That's better.

The differences between Colin and me are evident in many ways. The more we talk, the more ironic it becomes that we should find ourselves out here together. He's a father, I'm a daughter. He's an established author of twenty years' experience with a repertoire of over thirty books, I'm a novice of one published book, working on a second. He is the crusty professional, I am his trusty sidekick, Tonto. One thing we do have in common, however, is a love of food. This has become our bond. And after seven hours on the road today, I am less concerned about finding a shower than I am finding calories—thousands of them!

The shops are due to close in thirty minutes and will not reopen until after siesta at 5 pm, so we head into town and decide on a bar. Choosing from bars in towns that have more than one is a simple process. We don't go by reputation or recommendation as you might in your own country, because we lack local knowledge and our Spanish sucks. Nor do we select by the menu. We read Spanish worse than we speak it.

Instead, we walk in and check the floor. If there's no blood or offal, we stay.

Col and I do our best to decipher the menu and I accidentally order three meals! Fortunately, I am sitting opposite a man dubbed 'the human garbage can'. He tells me this was the affectionate nickname bestowed upon him by his wife and daughters. Despite the fact that he ate lunch just two hours earlier, Col generously offers his support. And before I swallow my first mouthful, the three plates piled with *carne arroz* (stewed meat and rice), *menestra* (stewed vegetables) and *lomo y patata* (stewed pork and potatoes) are licked clean. Colin doesn't eat food, he sucks it down like an industrial strength vacuum cleaner. On the odd occasion he does chew, his jaw gapes and slaps like a fish out of water. Col obviously enjoys eating and already I've learned that any conversation you might attempt is wasted until both the plate and bread basket are empty.

Satisfied, we return to the *albergue*. After a cold shower, I hand wash the day's walking clothes, hang them to dry and sit out on the grass in the afternoon sun near the clothesline to start writing up the day's notes. It is there I meet Ben and Emily, a couple from France who might be lovers or siblings. Hopefully not both. It's anyone's guess and no one is game to ask.

Seeing me alone, they come over and ask if they can join me. They are both young, attractive, very friendly, and speak fluent Spanish, French and English. As proud as I am to be Australian, it is at these times I feel slightly inadequate. The flip side of casual is laziness. I'd never needed French or Spanish because, unlike Ben and Emily, my country is not bordered by eight others. It's no excuse.

'I would like to learn Spanish,' I explain, showing them my little blue notepad marked with pages of scrawled translations.

'So you are not from England?' Ben asks. 'English people think everyone should speak English and won't even try.'

I reassure them I am not English and for the next two hours, Ben and Emily teach me a few new Spanish words. By nightfall, I have made two new friends and filled three more pages of my pocket pad.

A good day.

Colin: Using the bath with normality

The *albergues* are also known as *refugios*. These are the hostelries where you stay as you make your way along the Camino. We will encounter all types: some are school gymnasiums requisitioned by the church for the Holy Year as the army might requisition your home as a barracks during a war; some are privately run, like bed and breakfast establishments; there are half-ruined monasteries run by monks or nuns, but most are church properties run by volunteers. Like the box of chocolates in *Forrest Gump*, you never know what you're going to get.

At the beginning of our journey we were issued with a pilgrims passport, which allows us to stay for just one night in one of these places as long as we move on early next morning. The cost is humble. Sometimes five euros is way too much; but it can be way too little.

The smell of the Camino is the smell of rancid cheese. By late afternoon in every *albergue*, hiking boots stew on balconies and under beds, steaming like fresh turds on a steel shovel. A hot day in Castilla y León and a pair of hiking socks go off faster than a blue cheese in a Balinese urinal. Even if I can't remember how a particular *albergue* looked, I can still remember what it smelled like.

There is a star system for ranking the *refugios*, and this is my attempt to demystify this grading.

FIVE STAR: Has a garden, a modern kitchen and a washing machine. Is situated in a sixteenth-century monastery with moss-covered stone walls. Run by a pleasant middle-aged Christian gentleman with a kind disposition and silver hair.

FOUR STAR: Has no garden. The kitchen has no microwave oven and the laundry has no clothes dryer. Is situated in a chalet with a russet roof and flower box. Run by a fruity twenty-year-old university student who failed his English exams at his last two attempts and is now studying to be an exotic dancer in Biarritz.

THREE STAR: Has a flower box. The kitchen is in the laundry and the oven doubles as a clothes dryer. Is situated in a former army barracks and run by a surly middle-aged priest with halitosis and a signed photograph of Franco above his desk.

TWO STAR: Has a concrete yard, a Coke vending machine and a cement wash trough. Is situated in a disused *jai-alai* court. Is run by a thirty-something lesbian nun with hairy knuckles and a suspiciously prominent Adam's apple.

ONE STAR: Found in a darkened alley smelling of urine and boiled turnips. Has no garden but there is vegetation growing inside. You can only wash your clothes on the nights they are boiling cabbage. Is situated in a medieval monastery with crumbling stone walls and no roof. Run by a former member of Franco's secret police.

Every *albergue* has a set of rules posted prominently. I found the following posted on the wall of a crumbling hostelry near León.

- In the shelter they will have the right to pass the night the travelling ones that seasoned credentials bring.
- Fry will be due to cook with water.
- The sweeping containers will be due to use and the

rest of the food in the shelter will not be able to be left.

- The connx to the Internet will be at the most of one hour and its act will be the own will.
- The baths will have to be used with normality.

We have already established a routine, and this is mine: when we get to an *albergue*, I use the baths with normality, wash my T-shirt, underwear and socks, find a bar. Find somewhere for dinner. Write up my notes. Complain about how sore my feet are. Go to bed. Wake up at 2 am to the sound of a Spaniard swallowing his sinuses. At 4.30 get up and start walking by the light of a half-moon.

Do this for about thirty-five to forty days and you've done a pilgrimage.

Eli: *The hapless pilgrims*

Colin and I agree over dinner to wake at 3.30 am and hit the road by 4 am, ahead of the other hundred or so pilgrims who will spend the night in Puente la Reina. I am buoyed by our day's performance and after several one-euro bottles of local celebratory Spanish red, it seems like a great idea.

The next morning, we both spring to attention at the sound of the alarm on Colin's mobile phone. We crawl from our bunks, slide our packs outside to the dimly lit corridor, passing a handful of less dedicated pilgrims still sleeping in their bunks.

Colin crouches on his haunches stuffing his sleeping bag into his pack, while I duck back with my torch to scan the room, making sure we've not left anything behind. When I re-emerge, Colin has already made his way down the hall to the meals area of the hostel. I tiptoe quietly, conscious of the fact we are the only two awake.

But as I get closer, the noise coming from the end of the hall suggests otherwise. There Col stands, in the middle of the dining room amidst a group of twenty—*more* dedicated— pilgrims, who are loudly chatting amongst themselves in several languages. Brows raised, I turn to Col, confused. *What the hell are they doing up at this hour?*

They are a breed unlike any I've seen in our five days so far. Two French men with peppered grey hair and great legs are seated before a breakfast of doughnuts and pastries dunked in black coffee. Several Austrians are stretching as a team. Others are filling water bottles and packing the last of their things, while a group of four Germans stand around laughing over a map. *Sadists!*

As Colin and I sit at the table to begin our new ritual of tending to hot spots on our feet, I notice that none of these others has a bandaged blister, speaks any English or wears the same expression of dread that Colin and I share at the start of every day.

What the hell are we doing up at this hour? We're out of our league. It is obvious these are professional pilgrims who know exactly what they are doing. It is even more obvious that Colin and I do not.

Col ties the worn laces on his crappy leather boots, I rub the backs of my scrawny legs trying to wake them up.

'Hey, Crusty, we're not fooling anyone, are we?'

Day 5
Puente la Reina to Monjardin

Colin: *The armchair traveller*

We leave Puente la Reina in darkness, cross the bridge before dawn. Venus is bright under a half-moon, reflected in the dark patina of the river. The bridge here has seen the passage of pilgrims like us for hundreds of years: I wonder if their feet were as sore as mine.

As we climb out of the town I start to appreciate the term 'armchair traveller'. Reading a travel book allows you to get up and make a cup of tea whenever you want. You can enjoy the scenery without having to walk through it, and your attention is not focused on the pain in your back, your feet, everywhere except your eyeballs, and even they're starting to water. Armchair travellers don't sweat or have suppurating blisters leaking into their boots.

As we climb I see a statue of the Madonna by the roadside, arms outstretched. She inspires me on. It is only as I get closer that I realise my Madonna is actually a Stop sign. This is going to be a long day.

We march through fields the colour of chamois leather, patches of scrub and rock, islands of verdant green. To get to a village, to water, to coffee, to breakfast and to lunch, to find a bar or a *supermercado* or a restaurant, we have to climb another fucking hill. Why do they always put villages on top of fucking hills?

Eli's method of getting up a hill is to swing her arms and raise her knees. It works for her and I in no way wish to belittle her efforts. That she finds the strength to climb yet another hill two days after a raging fever is testament to her spirit and tenacity. But the walk cracks me up every time. It is like following the SS into Paris.

The guidebook is really pissing me off. The trail apparently 'snakes' for 2.7 kilometres: the term 'snakes' in no way prepares you for the thigh-busting, heart-breaking climb up a vertical cliff. By mid morning the pleasant winding trail has squeezed every drop of moisture out of me, like putting a bar towel through a wringer. I reach the top of another hill, fat deposits utterly depleted, stress fractured, blistered and wasted. The only thing in good working order is my teeth, and I am ready to use them.

By ten I have already consumed a plate of spaghetti, two packets of biscuits, a Coke, a coffee, an orange, an apple, a milkshake, a beer, two yoghurts, half a bar of chocolate, a Magnum ice-cream and a packet of sugared almonds. And I am still hungry.

The walk becomes a series of delirious cameos under a raging summer sun mingling with the smell of pine, eyes fixed on the blue ridge of a distant sierra. My Pamplona 2004 T-shirt, complete with screen-printed bloodstains, is soaked in sweat, my vertebrae are twisted and stretched like a wire fence after a hurricane and my feet glow in my boots like radium. My arms sting from the sun as I gulp down water staring over a vista of church spires, modern highways and wheat fields.

Under these pale blue skies, alone with the indifference of heaven, I have become aware of a gnawing pain in my gut. This is no longer just mental torture; the pain is physical, like a cancer, and it is getting worse. There is a coldness inside me, dry ice of the soul. I am scared.

Poor El. She trusts me, and believes that I will somehow help her get to Santiago. I am her rock. What happens if the rock breaks?

Eli: Morning mauves and red heaven

The novelty of a return to health has waned and today the Camino feels like military boot camp. First, it must break your spirit. The fallacious guidebook adds a touch of mental torture as our hopes are continuously raised then dashed. And Colin's relentless snoring last night adds sleep deprivation to the morose state of affairs.

It was nice of him to wait until we were on the flight to Paris to warn me about it. Even then, he did so in a way that suggested it would be my own fault if I heard it. Colin has no shame. He also tells me that his snoring, along with his table manners, have been contentious issues with many women in past relationships. But apparently that was their fault too.

The view from the top of the morning's first hill is disappointing to say the least. It barely seems worth the effort. We've spent nearly three hours navigating a steep ravine through shrubs, paddocks, roadworks and rubble and, looking back now, we've barely made any progress. The hamlet of Puente la Reina rests at the base of the hill like a discarded cluster of children's blocks. It is already a quarter to seven and we are just four kilometres from where we started.

We are both tired but Colin is particularly moody this morning. His energy noticeably shifted late yesterday. Something's bothering him. But the fact that he assures me everything is fine makes me nervous. I decide to keep to myself, in the hope he'll talk if he needs to.

Apart from a nagging sense of discomfort, everything from my waist down is numb. The fourteen kilos in my backpack has cut the circulation to my limbs and my hands have swelled. One of the other pilgrims told me yesterday that you are only supposed to carry ten per cent of your body weight when you hike. I have twenty-five per cent. Why didn't I know this before?

Though it doesn't hurt yet, my left knee has also started swelling, suggesting that it soon will. It is obvious we are both carrying too much weight. Some of the gear will have to go.

Already, I've come to appreciate that it takes at least forty-five minutes on the trail each morning before your legs decide they are going to work for you—and even then it's reluctantly, and only because you give them no other choice. You just continue to put one foot in front of the other and try not to think about it too much.

If I was to think, I'd be a bit concerned about a blister forming beneath the little toe on my left foot. It started two days ago and has begun migrating to the right. It is growing by the hour and appears to have taken on a life of its own now.

I wanted to pop it last night, to relieve the pressure and allow it to heal, but Colin protested, reminding me that he has twelve years' experience as a volunteer ambulance officer.

He assures me he knows what he's talking about, so naturally I believe him.

We stop at the first 'café' on the west side of Puente la Reina. Actually it's a house belonging to a family who are capitalising on the passing trade, establishing a 'help yourself to our pantry and we'll charge you triple what you'd pay in the store, just because we can' type enterprise. It's rustic, novel, and mischievously innovative. And right now I don't care about the price hike.

Colin chows down while studying his guidebook for the fourth time this morning. He's developing an addiction. I eat in silence and watch him riffle back and forth between pages, reading and re-reading everything he already read minutes before. We continue.

The last three kilometres into Estella drag like days. We make our way past an open air sewer; human excrement gently simmering in the heat. It's thirty-three degrees at one in the afternoon. We've walked twenty kilometres since daybreak but it feels like two hundred.

The harsh start of the morning has taken its toll. Colin leads a few paces ahead, looking sullen. Old locals, strolling by, stop to offer words of encouragement as we pass along the outskirts of town.

'*Un poco más!*' they say—*just a little further*—their faces brimming with sincerity, as if willing our every step. I smile, showing my appreciation. The gesture is sweet and it helps.

Spotting the township brings relief. There is a refreshing river below, lined with trees that droop and lick at the water's edge. It looks inviting but the colour of the water is suspiciously similar to that of the sewer we've just passed and I can't lose the lingering scent. The promise of cool drinks and shade keeps my legs moving along the steep decline into town.

We shuffle along the main street. A teenage boy kicks a soccer ball with his younger brother, their laughter echoing off the stone walls. Behind them, a sign bearing a scallop shell hangs from the wall above a door. An *albergue*. Colin makes a beeline for it.

Dropping our packs, we slump together against the cool of the shaded wall. Colin begins removing his boots. We still haven't discussed whether we will continue past the town or stop for the day. Breaking the silence for the first time in hours, I pose the question.

'You wanna stay or push on?'

It seems such an easy decision. You're hot, hungry, tired and just metres away from a cool shower, food and a clean bed for the night. But it's not that simple. Setting out each morning is the hardest part of every day. That first hour on the trail demands a wholehearted effort of physical and mental discipline. It's the most crucial time of the day as it dictates your mood, energy level and enthusiasm for the long hours ahead. If you don't bound out of bed at the first sound of the alarm, you don't get up at all. Your body doesn't want to move in the mornings and nor does your mind.

But as with all great struggles there are rewards. Any incentive at all is welcome and without our customary coffee stop at the end of that first hour, I doubt I'd make it through. Already, that first break has become my favourite part of our day. Sitting opposite Colin and chatting over coffee is special. It's the first victory of every new beginning and reminds me of home, Sunday brunch with friends, sitting in the morning sun outside the hidden cafés of inner Melbourne, the city I love.

So here lies the dilemma. Do we grant ourselves a much easier day tomorrow by going on a further nine kilometres in the heat of the day, across a notoriously barren stretch to Monjardin, or do we stop here, knowing that same tough nine kilometres waits for us first thing tomorrow morning—two hours with no coffee stops in between?

'You call it,' Colin says, uninterested, turning back to his guidebook.

Wary of his mood and fearing responsibility for any potential repercussions, I insist: 'No. I'm good either way. You call it.'

Our silence continues, the mercury crawls higher with every passing minute and my knee continues to swell. Colin is in no mood to discuss the situation. Eventually I cave.

'Right then, let's go.' And on we trek to Monjardin.

Leaving Estella, the sun grows harsher with every step and the tension between Colin and me builds with it. A few kilometres on and we have reached the point of no return. There is nothing ahead or behind and on either side lie open fields of vineyards, olive trees and wheat.

Practising Spanish from my notepad, head low, dripping beads of sweat and melted sunscreen, I reach down into my pocket to find some gum to break the monotony. Gum's great for keeping a tortured mind occupied.

While rummaging through the leg pocket of my cargos, I find a pen. Knowing my own is zipped away in the front of my pack, I pull it out to take a closer look. It's identical to my four-coloured Bic with one defining difference: the side of the top reads *Made in France*. Immediately I realise I have mistakenly picked up Ben's pen—Ben was the boy who taught me Spanish words on the lawn in Puente la Reina. The French couple were sweet; young and free spirited. I admired their affection for each other. Whether siblings or lovers, it was clear they were having more fun than Col and me. I tuck it back into my pocket where I know I can find it, when or if we see Ben and Emily again.

And we arrive at Azqueta.

It can't be. It can't possibly be! Oh . . . but it is!

By now a freshwater fountain would have been reason enough to celebrate but a fountain flowing with free local shiraz, compliments of a nearby winery, is almost too much. A mirage. Only it is actually there.

The Bodegas Irache Fuente del Vino is just that, a wine fountain. When Colin references his guidebook he tells me the fountain is renowned throughout Spain. Colin already knows this because in the last week he has memorised every word of the 416-page compilation. I would've known this if I'd used what short notice we had to prepare, by doing more research, instead of spending days and nights down-loading songs to an MP3 player bought cheap on eBay and shopping for a funky pair of hiking boots. A girl has priorities.

I would also have known this if Colin had mentioned it. But he hasn't mentioned much all day and the fact that it is completely unexpected makes it even sweeter.

Apparently, pilgrims consume thirty-five thousand litres of the free wine each year and by mid afternoon in a remote area of a barren plain, Col and I are prepared to down our share. We race toward the fountain half expecting it to disappear. When it doesn't, high-fives and water fights soon follow.

Twenty minutes later, Colin and I are sitting on the ground, legs sprawled, backs against the wall of the fountain, facing front. I offer Col another round. He passes me his green plastic camping cup. I feel above my head for the tap and pour until the cup sounds full.

We repeat the process, again and again. Soon Col's on his feet setting the timer on his pricey SLR camera (which weighs more than his boots, by the way). It rests precariously atop his backpack, which in turn rests precariously upright in the middle of a concrete slab. One wrong move and—

'You ready?' he yells.

'Yep!'

'On the count of three.'

'Yep!'

'One, twooo . . .' He rushes back to the wall to grab his cup, the pack begins to tip, we lean with it. 'Threeeeee . . .' The flash snaps and we collapse on top of each other in a screaming heap. I roll to my side in fits of laughter and look up to notice a small surveillance camera perched in the corner directly opposite us.

'Shit, Col, look. We're on candid camera!'

The Bodegas Irache webcam can be found at www.irache.com. Check it out whenever you're in need of a good belly laugh.

An inscription above the fountain itself reads: *Pilgrim, if you want to reach Santiago with strength and vitality, drink this great wine and toast to happiness.*

I'll drink to that!

Colin: Faw-west, life is like a box of chocolates

The wine fountain should have been a high point, something to marvel and chuckle over for the rest of the day. But I'm schlepping my own dark cloud around with me today. Too much thinking. In my life I organise distractions so I don't have to listen to what goes on in my head. It's worked until now. Out here there's nothing else to do but think.

Heartbreak is not just a word; if you have it, you know it—it's like a toothache, only all over your body, and it won't let you be. Thus far I have lived a semi-charmed kind of life. But here, I am suddenly stalked by demons from my past, and we have only just begun. They say time heals all wounds; the people who say this to you mean well but they have clearly never been wounded. Or perhaps time can heal wounds; but can it heal disillusion?

For all my cynicism about religion, I suspect I am here looking for spiritual redemption. I am not alone in my search. An Irish couple we meet tell me they are doing it for penance. A dumpy blonde Austrian is doing it as part of her grieving; after her mother died she walked out of her house and just kept walking. So far she has walked nearly three thousand kilometres. When she gets to Santiago she will turn around and walk all the way back. We have nicknamed her Forrest Gumpenberger. Walk, Faw-west, walk!

There's a Swiss-German from Basel who's doing it as a physical challenge. Simon and Mercedes are not sure why they're doing it; they are searching for something, but they don't know what.

At the *albergue* in Monjardin I meet Leslie, a *hostelero* from the States. She walked the Camino three years ago and now she is back as a volunteer, manning this sleepy *albergue* in a quiet hilltop village somewhere between Pamplona and Logroño.

'I did the Way because friends of mine in the States had done it and were so taken with it. There was no transformation, at least not for me. I got back after my walk just before 9/11. I lost a lot of friends there. Things like that make you realise you are not in control of anything. I guess that's what you learn most of all. You really are not in control. You plan to walk the Camino but the Camino walks you. Nothing ever works out the way you plan. You can throw a knee, get sick, a thousand things can happen.

'And in a way this is what spirituality is: the realisation that you are not ultimately in control of life. Friends die in car accidents. Family members get sick or someone you love falls in love with someone else. Life itself is a humbling before God.'

Humility. Perhaps it is what this is all about. I suspect I have always been an arrogant bastard, behind the smile. Life has finally caught up with me.

I don't want to lead a spiritual life; I just want this pain to go away. Find a healing from the knowledge of being both betrayer and betrayed, and from the loss of my illusions. They may not have been real, but they were comfortable and they were safe. And being comfortable and safe, ask anyone— isn't that what life's about?

Be comfortable and safe from life? *Now, Faw-west, how you gonna do that?*

Colin: I'll learn to say mañana tomorrow

Spanish is a wonderful language. It makes even the most banal objects seem exotic. Puente la Reina is actually only a town called Queensbridge. And take the word *cornada*, for example; a *cornada* is the word they use when you are wounded by a bull's horn. A horn up the ass is a *cornada*. When the bull runs off with your pancreas skewered on its horns like a scallop en brochette, it's still just a *cornada*. Brilliant.

Eli has been attempting to teach herself Spanish. She is convinced she is a linguist, despite all evidence to the contrary, and will not be daunted. She has a sheet with useful French and Spanish phrases on it, and a notepad for new words but she doesn't always read the right line. She tells a Japanese pilgrim her name is Melbourne and she comes from Ham Sandwich. She tells fellow pilgrims my name is Happy Walkings. It is impossible not to love her.

That evening in Monjardin she practises her Spanish some more at the local bar. The owners outnumber the locals three to two. There is Mama, a short, squat, garrulous woman with a laugh like a witch sucking helium; her husband, a taciturn grey-haired man with teeth like tombstones in a rundown municipal graveyard; and their daughter, who has a weight issue, tends bar and eats peanuts like she is feeding logs into a mulcher.

Eli orders beer in Spanish—they pretend not to understand even though the only thing they have to drink is fucking beer—and then we are offered the set menu. The *menú del peregrino*, the pilgrim's menu, consists of soup, main course and *postre*—egg pudding—bread and a bottle of wine. They must know all pilgrims are hopeless booze hounds.

'I'll have the chicken,' Eli says.

Peanut Girl leans over and very deliberately puts a line through the chicken with a ballpoint pen.

'I guess the chicken's off,' I tell her. 'That leaves pork, pork chops, or pork balls. Or rice. With pork. Do you like pork, Eli?'

'No, I hate it!' But Eli's blood sugars are screwed from the day's climb. She needs food and she needs it now. N-O-W! So she orders pork.

An hour later Mama is still cackling like a Cornish fishwife, Papa is teetering on the edge of his bar stool, completely wasted, and La Mulcherina is still filling her face with nuts. Eli is getting very testy. She looks pale, her teeth chatter and her speech slurs, but it's not the beer. A hypoglycaemic coma seems minutes away.

'Oi, I need food!' Eli shouts.

Chiquita shrugs her shoulders and looks at Mama. Papa puts his head on the counter and starts to snore.

Everything will happen when it happens.

Have another beer.

Have another peanut.

Mañana.

Fuck off.

Day 6
Monjardin to Torres del Rio

Eli: *Under a Spanish sun*

We sleep until 7 am and rise to face a gentle twenty-kilometre day, compliments of yesterday's efforts. I never thought I'd see the day when twenty klicks seemed like a walk in the park. But although the distance is short, it's by no means easy. An hour out, the sun burns, the sweat seeps through the singlet on my back and this vast landscape offers no shade. Every day is getting hotter.

We walk along a dirt trail cut through olive and asparagus plantations framed by distant fields of wheat, broad emerald strokes against a beige canvas. It is flat but the early heat eliminates any potential advantage offered by a generous terrain. It's hard to believe that both the landscape and conditions can change so much in such a short period of time. I look around at the view—compared to yesterday it feels like I've woken in another country.

I pass Colin, offering a line—one of those useless facts no one needs to know—then pull out in front in search of some space.

Though he's not been himself, he's not alone. I too woke feeling low, down about nothing in particular, just flat. Mood reflecting the landscape, perhaps? With three more hours of heat and haunted by the sound of my feet timing across the coarse sand, I pull out my MP3 player and, for the first time on the trail, settle in to some tunes.

I've missed music. The first song brings with it a wave of emotion and a flood of memories that threaten to break my stride. Of all the one hundred and thirty songs set on random, it has to be this. My favourite band. Once my favourite song. Our song. About running, searching, building unnecessary walls—setting challenges—in order to prove your worth. Trying to leave behind shadows of the past in the hope of becoming someone better, or new.

Someone special once said that song was written just for me. He was right then, he's probably right now. It's times like these I wonder whether this relentless quest, to challenge myself, to break down walls, to walk across countries, to do and be more than I already am, might be fuelled by fear. Fear of not being enough. Or perhaps, fear of being too much like everybody else.

I wonder if by the end of this trip, I might feel as comfortable with myself as he did?

There's not a day I haven't stopped to wonder why I'm out here. Today more than before, the question lingers, refusing to fade.

Colin: *You don't mess around with Jim*

All roads do not lead to Rome. In this part of the world they lead to Santiago.

In the Middle Ages Santiago was a sort of Mecca; Rome was too political, and too closely involved with papal corruption and meddling in state politics. (Thank God those days are behind us!) For a medieval pilgrim, making a pilgrimage to Rome became a dangerous political statement, identifying the supplicant as a papist, a hazardous label in a world tortured by the power struggles between Rome and the European kings.

Jerusalem was dangerous too because of Muslim hatred of unbelievers. It's good to look back and see how far we've come in the last five hundred years. Instead, to demonstrate their piety, the medieval Christians chose to visit the grave of St James and revere his mouldy old bones.

It is impossible today to comprehend the value of relics to the medieval mind, what it meant to see or touch a fragment of the Holy Cross, for example, or a bone of one of the martyred saints. In doing so, one acquired some of its sanctity. Relics became important accoutrements then to any church with ambition. By the Middle Ages there were so many prepuces of Christ scattered around Europe that if they had all been genuine the Blessed Saviour would have been hung like a horse.

These relics were believed to be the conduits of divine intercession, the link to an authority greater than man's. Faith in such reliquaries derived from a dread of life, and the conviction, encouraged by the church, that personal and perhaps total destruction was imminent.

Hell was merely an extension of contemporary life. Heaven promised a final benevolence against all the odds, like winning the lottery. It was the only spiritual nourishment afforded in a world of torture racks, plague, feudalism and open sewers. Medieval man was indoctrinated with the urgency of obtaining divine favour against damnation and the surest way of doing this was by obtaining the intercession of the saints. He undertook his journey to view these reliquaries as caveat over the Second Coming, the Day of Judgment and his own eternal damnation as preached relentlessly by the clerics of the time.

But relics ain't just relics, and saints ain't just saints. There was an A list, like in Hollywood; the holier the saint, the more powerful the redemption afforded by their bones. So a martyred saint was more virile than one who had died of natural causes (not that many do) and the more gruesome the martyrdom, the more powerful the saint's relics. The *primera liga* therefore was the dried-up bits of the martyred apostles.

Which brings us to the curious case of Jimmy the Fish.

According to the Gospels, Santiago, St James, was one of Jesus's twelve disciples, one of the fishermen he called to ministry while they were mending their nets at Lake Genneserat. After Jesus's death, the disciples spread out, like Mormons without bicycle clips, to disseminate the Word.

St James went to Spain. Like David Beckham, he had a great pedigree but didn't really perform over there. Not such a hot evangelist in fact. Obviously wasn't paying much attention at the Sermon on the Mount. In fact he was evangeless. Five years knocking on doors brought just nine converts. The rest slipped through the net, as it were. Disillusioned, he returned to Jerusalem where Herod further disillusioned him by chopping his head off.

His body was then taken to Spain by his followers—there were barely enough to carry the coffin and arrange the flowers in the church—in a stone boat. The body was buried on a hillside eighty kilometres from the coast—another obvious move—and forgotten for about eight hundred years. These are the bare bones of the story.

Then, in the ninth century, a hermit called Pelagius had a vision after seeing a shining star over a deserted spot in the hills of northwest Spain. The local bishop was moved to investigate the incident and a tomb containing three bodies was found in the spot indicated by Pelagius. These were immediately identified as those of St James and two of his nine followers.

It would be reasonable to ask how, in the absence of a qualified forensic technician, the bones could have been identified as those of a Hebrew fisherman who died a violent death a thousand miles away centuries before, but that would spoil a good story.

News of the discovery was later promulgated by the arch-bishop of the town that had grown around the tomb. His name was Diego Gelmirez and he was anxious to promote Santiago as a pilgrimage centre, for the funds it would inevitably bring to the church coffers, much as a modern shire council cashes in on a good surf beach or a waterfall. When the Muslims seized the Holy Sepulchre in Jerusalem in 1009, Santiago became increasingly popular, as there was less chance of being murdered by Muslim fanatics in Spain.

The site was visited by none other than King Alfonso II, who consequently and conveniently declared James the patron saint of Spain. He built a church and monastery at the site. It was known as Campus de la Stella, or place of the star. This was a smart tactical move. The Moors, as Al Qaida was known then, had invaded Spain back in 711 and overrun most of the country, except for pockets in the mountainous north. The Spaniards, unable to turn to George Bush, did the next best thing and turned to God.

In fact, James had showed up just in time. What he lacked in life he made up for in bones. He failed as a human being but succeeded brilliantly as a corpse. Despite being a headless fisherman with just nine conversions to his name, he appeared to the Spanish army as a heavenly warrior at the battle of Clavijo in 844, when Ramiro I of León defeated the Moors. Our hero had major spin applied; Jimmy the Fish became Santiago Matamoros, the Moor-slayer, a sort of Donald Rumsfeld in holy orders.

For God and St James! became the battle cry that for centuries gentled the consciences of generations of conquistadors as they burned, raped, trampled and slaughtered their way through millions of indigenous peoples across the Americas.

The impact of the discovery of Santiago's tomb is almost impossible to comprehend today by the thousands heading off on a journey towards the setting of the sun and the end of the Earth for personal salvation. There was no one 'official' route then. Most people in the Middle Ages just followed the Milky Way south. The most important route extant from the Middle Ages is the 'French way', the *Camino Francés*, through the Pyrenees. But there was also the Portuguese way (coming from the south), the Greek way (coming from behind) and the English way (getting drunk on the ferry over, complaining about the food and then starting a fight with the locals when you get there).

The church cultivated and profited from the pilgrimage trail by offering pilgrims 'indulgences'—absolution from sins committed in this life. So pilgrimage became a form of celestial superannuation.

The Inquisition later mushroomed the numbers; the most minor infractions were punished with the burden of pilgrimage. A whole industry grew up around the Camino; there were professional pilgrims who made their living by walking to Santiago and back for those too busy or too uninterested to do it themselves. Hospitals, bridges and hostels sprung up along the route. Whole towns grew up with their own distinctive town planning and architecture. Later merchants came, looking for business opportunities.

Many medieval celebrities such as St Francis of Assisi and St Bridget of Sweden made the pilgrimage; the first European travel guide was written by a French monk called Aymeric Picaud, an advisory on the holy pilgrimage route. *Let's Walk! Santiago de Compostela on one copper coin a day.*

The tomb's popularity brought money pouring into Santiago and these funds were used to finance the Reconquista, the reconquest of Spain. After the defeat of the Moors and the Protestant reformation, the pilgrimage lost some of its cachet. The reputation of the Spanish Inquisition also detracted from its appeal, some of the more squeamish discouraged by the prospect of having a hot iron inserted in their rectums because their distant cousin owned a black cat.

By the time of the Renaissance, pilgrimage had become associated with the dodgy element. The sort of people who might, five hundred years later, appear on *Ricki Lake*.

But there is also a subtext to this whole story, as there is with so many aspects of the Christian church, for Santiago's hold on the popular imagination was more complex than might initially be thought. For instance, it was extremely fortuitous that the bones of one of Jesus's disciples should have been discovered where they were, for pilgrims from all over Europe had been walking this route for hundreds of years already. The *Camino Francés* actually followed the ancient Roman road, the via Triana, which also tracked the Milky Way. In Roman times these stars, like a render of dust tossed across the night sky, were believed to point to the edge of the known world.

The belief must have persisted, for even in medieval times many pilgrims did not stop at Santiago de Compostela but walked on through a pagan landscape of woods and water to Cape Finisterre. In Latin, *finis terre* means, literally, the end of the Earth. Why did they do this? Having paid obeisance to the church, perhaps it was a spiritual longing of a different nature that led them another fifty miles to the chapel of Nuestra

Señora at Finisterre, a peninsula that crooks into the ocean like a finger pointing west.

There is a tradition of pilgrimage of much earthier provenance here than the church would ever acknowledge. Could these medieval pilgrims have been searching for a pagan goddess, the spiritual aspiration of the Mediterranean people who lived here long before Jesus was born? It is possible. Historians have long speculated on the origins of many of the floral motifs found in churches along the way and believe they may be a sun icon of Celtic origin.

After all, Santiago is not Spain; it is Celt, as we were soon to discover.

Eli: Snapshots

Walking puts you into a trance-like state, induced by the monotony of such a natural movement and the deafening silence of a barren land broken only by the rhythm of your feet: *crunch, crunch, crunch* . . .

Pain becomes a welcome distraction, as does the sound of a bird, a song that pops into my head and just won't leave, or the sight of an eagle soaring above. There's the occasional random memory as well, flashbacks that spring from nowhere to surprise me: a girl I knew in high school but haven't seen since; a verse of a poem I wrote years ago; a childhood Christmas; the girlfriend I had coffee with three weeks earlier; my best friend's wedding; a car accident; someone I loved and lost. Eight hours is a long time to spend in thought, day after day. It's strange, the things you find when you are tortured by time.

Recently, I've thought more about things that happened just days ago. The Spanish term for hard-boiled eggs; Colin's conclusions about his life, his comments about mine; the fact that I still have Ben's pen; the little Spanish lady in the *tienda* I played charades with for a bag of almonds. We're just five days in and already I feel like I'm losing pieces of the experience, as if it's slipping through my fingers like sand. I'm conscious not to take a single thing for granted, yet there's simply too much here to process all at once.

The Camino lies directly under the Milky Way. Some say it reflects the energy of the star systems above, that it rises up beneath your feet to change you in some way. Whether you believe that or not, there's something uniquely moving about the Camino. When you walk, the pain, the heat, the thirst, the monotony and the loneliness take most of your focus, most of the time. But eventually, hours in, your body turns numb, your mind switches off and your feet continue to march on regardless: *crunch, crunch, crunch.* And it's there, somewhere in the emptiness, that the essence of all who've gone before still remains.

After spending most of the morning walking alone, Colin and I arrive at Torres del Rio around one in the afternoon. The village, like most towns throughout the region, surrounds a church and rests atop a hill.

We follow the maze trail of scallop shells painted on the walls at every turn. Colin spots a privately owned *albergue* and we go inside, parting the coloured plastic strips hanging from the architrave. We sigh in unison as we're engulfed by a wave of cold air.

The woman behind the counter is deliriously happy to see us and immediately begins gibbering frantically about her *fantástico* facilities. When there's more than one *albergue* in town, a sales pitch comes standard on arrival. We're obviously the first customers she has seen for a while.

She shows us around, presenting a guided (and extremely detailed) tour. I explain that we don't speak Spanish but she's not easily discouraged. She continues, taking time to explain that the sun is at its most severe this time of day as it reflects off the tiles of the patio but by afternoon, the shade creeps across the courtyard casting shadows beneath the umbrella and the sunset is the best you'll find in the region.

Uh-huh.

I translate this to Colin.

'How do you know she said all that?' Colin asks, slightly peeved.

'I don't know,' I tell him, equally surprised.

The look on his face suggests he doesn't believe me. The silent theme of the day continues.

Colin: A cameo of the Camino

Today it is too hot to walk much past noon. We stop in Torres del Rio and I head off to find a bar, like a bird returning to its nest. I order a very unassuming *rioja* and read the newspaper.

Yesterday was the worst day of the *feria* with three *cornadas*. The events of that morning are replayed endlessly on the television above the bar, middle-aged Spanish men having horns shoved up them by enraged bovines with balls like porn stars. Afterwards they happily chat to TV reporters as they lie in hospital beds, intravenous lines going in and out while a nurse rummages around under the sheets trying to find somewhere to put a loose bit of small intestine. It's like folding a map really: once you get disembowelled you can never get everything back the way it was. Thirty-four runners were treated by paramedics and three transported; not a bad day's work for the bulls.

I put down the paper. The pain in my gut is still there, nagging away. Hard to sit still with it. I order another *rioja*. It works like morphine on a trauma; another couple and the pain will be gone. It will come back, of course, but the important thing, as any alcoholic will tell you, is it's not there *now*.

I have no idea what is happening to me. I treat Eli as if she is a minor inconvenience. I have no idea, really, why she wants to finish this walk so badly, and have no idea, really, why I have come. I have become as insensitive to other people as I have to myself. I am vaguely aware that people around me may find me brusque, arrogant and even rude, but I don't really care.

I have no idea that I am slowly coming apart.

If you'd asked me, I would have told you.

Everything's fine.

Eli: Postcards

The *albergue* in Torres del Rio is nice, relatively new, fresh, clean and we seem to have it all to ourselves. In usual fashion, Colin leaves to find a bar and I head off to find food. When I return, I take a long shower, pull on a clean set of clothes and wrap a towel around my wet hair. Craving company, and perhaps a familiar voice, I find a pay phone in the reception area to call home.

After the call, I sit on the patio with my feet in a bucket of sea salts, an ice pack on my left knee and a damp towel draped across the burnt skin on my arms and neck. A giant red sun sits low on the horizon. As I settle in to watch it slip below the yellow fields, the cast-bronze church bells of Torres del Rio toll the angelus, echoed moments later by the dance of the bells in the next town, a kilometre across the valley.

Alone, I feel sore, sorry and confused. And there, at the sight of the sunset, I begin to cry. The *hostelera* was right—it is beautiful.

Day 7
Torres del Rio to Logroño

Colin: *Moonrise over Navarre*

A shadowed quarter-moon dips over the hills. Venus hangs just below, in a star-fallen sky. The air smells of red earth and wheat. Dawn is still an hour off.

As we walk, the trailing tendril of a hawthorn brushes the skin of my arm. Already the wind is warm and there is a patina of sweat on my back trapped under my cotton shirt.

It's a difficult day for Eli and me: we walk apart, largely consumed by our own thoughts. I have realised through my latest introspection that although I come across as an easy-going and affable sort of a bloke at first, in reality I'm moody, complicated and self-obsessed. I'm not proud of this, but it's the way it is.

The worst part is the rest stops. I spend an inordinate amount of time with my head in the guidebook. It may look like I am profoundly interested in the local history and places of interest but it's basically to avoid eye contact. I am trying to hide what's going on here.

I have developed a certain charm over the years, I've noticed; it helps keep people at bay. If they discover what I'm really like—and no one has so far, not even my former wife, and I was married to her for twenty years—I'm afraid they'll leave me. So I never let anyone too close.

Someone once said of me that I was the sort of man who would definitely go to heaven but that I probably wouldn't like God. I think what they meant was, I was a personable sort of guy who privately considered he could run the world better than his own Creator.

This is completely true. I am not at all accepting of speed humps in my path, let alone complete reversals. I have constructed in my mind my own map of my life and I take any deviation from it as a personal affront from the Universe and proof that there is no God. This might be construed as a slightly arrogant way to view one's life, even by me.

In the unspoken contract between Eli and me, it seems that I am to be the mentor, the strong, silent type. But already I can feel myself arcing up. Why? Isn't this what I want, what I try to set up in every significant relationship in my life? Why do I feel so angry about it?

Eli has a history with controlling, possessive men. Not me though, surely? Then why are we starting to get so badly on each other's nerves? And we still have to spend almost another month living, eating and sleeping together. Yesterday she strode ahead, head down, listening to music. She has what Ali G would call the well head gear; some sort of iPod-style thing with every song she's ever heard on it.

It is a pleasant morning and the green hills are lovely but someone is digging a set of car keys into my left heel and their second knuckle into my neck muscle on the same side, and this takes some of the joy out of it.

Eli walks past, her boots crunching on the gravel.

'There's more sugar in a banana than there is in a Mars bar.'

We keep walking.

'Just thought I'd mention it.'

And she puts her headphones on and walks on.

In Los Arcos we are welcomed by a dog carrying his mate's turd across the street in his jaws. We stop at the church for a quick drink of water and hurry on.

We pass the cemetery outside the town; the gated archway dates from 1814 and bears the cheery inscription in Spanish: *I was once what you are now: you will one day be what I am now.*

Eli looks at me: 'What's that s'posed to mean? One day I'm going to be a gate?' Her attempts to humour me are benign.

Some of the stones inside are ancient, some of these people have been dead two hundred years. One of them might be Shirley MacLaine by now.

I remember soon after I left school I got a job in an office in London. I had to catch the train to the city with the rest of the great unwashed, as they were known, the inhabitants of my little commuter-belt town. To get to the railway station I would take a shortcut through the church cemetery. I remember looking at the gravestones as I look now at these moss-covered markers of lives come and gone, and thinking: *Jeez, you're dead longer than you are alive.* I promised myself that I would live before I died and that I would risk, even if I failed, to make sure that happened. *You've got one go at this, son. Better give it your best shot.*

The Camino is part of my best shot. I have travelled the world, known what it is to love with every ounce of passion in my soul, written over thirty books. These are all things I have hoped and wanted to do. For all my failures and shortcomings, and they are many, I gave it my best shot and I do not think I let down that geeky teenager in the ill-fitting suit as he walked, head down, in the rain through that solemn grey Essex churchyard on his way to the 8.11 Fenchurch Street train. Yet recently something has gone wrong with the plan. The perfect picture fell down, leaving behind just the stain of

where it had been on the wall. It was a fake, an artful repro-
duction. Someone else's life, not mine.

I don't want to think about this. The pain in my gut is
getting worse. It's like walking with a stomach ulcer, but it
takes my mind off my feet. This is starting to scare me now. I
have never experienced anything remotely like it in my life.
I look at El and smile reassuringly.

Oh my God.

A cameo of the Camino: you are walking on hot coals with a
broken neck, your shadow lopes ahead of you, chased by the
sun, and the only sounds are the tramp of your boots on
the dirt path, the call of songbirds, the wind ruffling the
heads of the wheat like dried leaves. There are windmills on
the distant sierra. A monastery, ochre against a blue sky, rises
from a green and rounded hill.

It is a rolling landscape of jade and chamois, wheat and
asparagus. I can see now how the medieval pilgrims navigated
their way from town to town: they followed the line of church
spires from hill to hill. Once the village hovels crowded
around them, and in most the old quarters still remain,
narrow cobbled streets and window boxes and *bodegas* and
cantinas. Here in rich Navarre, the houses are grander, white
stone with affluent red roofs. In the seventies there was an
exodus from the cities back to the country as rich Navarrans
inherited granny's old cottage after she fell off the perch and
they renovated it with city money, working flexi-hours from
their rural retreats or using them as weekenders.

The sun rises and we walk on to the next village. I ask Eli
why it smells like Weetbix round here.

'Because the fields are full of wheat.'

Tramp, tramp, tramp.

'Right.'

We meet a man who has walked all the way from Marseilles to Santiago and is now on his way back again. He has been walking for four months; another month and he'll be home. Is he inspired, brilliant or crazy? The decision is split. But we both agree he has great legs. Brown, well muscled, and he has a French accent. I'm jealous. Women just love tight buttocks and broken English.

We look along the valley to the distant sprawl of Logroño. There are fields of asparagus and vines. And, of course, wheat. I should prepare myself. There's a lot more of the stuff to come.

Colin: *Cupid's little yellow arrows*

The Camino is extraordinary. It is almost impossible to get lost. All along the way you see a yellow arrow, painted on kerbstones, walls, culverts, trees, rocks, telegraph poles, bridges, dead dogs, everything that doesn't move, pointing the way to Santiago for the *peregrinos* that walk this route every year. Once I even saw a yellow arrow painted on a car. The car was abandoned and had been there a very, very long time.

The numbers on the pilgrimage have grown. I look back up the dirt road and today we have ourselves a convoy. There is one long line of teenagers, a youth group from Germany, also a few families, sauntering along as if they are at the beach. Most others are like us, travelling in pairs.

We even pass a woman in a wheelchair. Her name is Francesca and she has multiple sclerosis. She thinks she will probably die before she reaches Santiago. She is being pushed by an older man with cropped grey hair and a wiry frame. He never speaks. I wonder if he's mute. He is her lover, we learn.

Francesca has come from Rome to make her final pilgrimage and this is the way she has chosen to die. She is brave; her lover is incredibly strong. We have seen them several times, labouring along stone tracks. She wears a large brimmed hat and cradles a small dog. In the breaks he stands a little aside and smokes cigarettes.

We meet so many people and hear so many names that it is easier to call people by where they come from, or what they look like. Canada looks like Clark Kent; Bavaria looks like Harry Potter, though in a bizarre twist she turns out to be a nineteen-year-old girl from Augsburg. There is Norway and Ireland and Manitoba and Armadale and San Sebastian.

Strategic alliances are being formed already. The yellow arrow has become Cupid's dart and love has been blooming on the trail for some time. Ireland was on his way home, got as far as Bilbao, and came back for Canada. One day Dermot was standing on his own by the windmills outside Pamplona and the next time we see him, Dublin and Manitoba are twin cities. Meanwhile Australia has coupled with Spain and Norway has very smoothly invaded Germany, which is a nice change.

But this is all somehow appropriate; this is the ancient Way to Venus.

Eli: Whose demons?

Colin said something last night that's bothered me all day: *Your demons might seem real, Eli, but they're simply not there!*

In the same breath he told me he fights dirty when he's angry. He goes for the 'jugular', the hot spot he knows will hurt. He said this like a pro who's perfected the art of bare-knuckle boxing.

He returned from the bar to find me sitting alone as night fell gently on Torres del Rio. Within minutes, an argument had broken out. A disagreement about something trivial: *nada de nada*. Like new lovers, it was our first tiff. Something insignificant and pointless that we both knew would pass. It was over as soon it began and ended with his line, 'I know your demons might seem real, Eli, but they're simply not there!'

I still wonder what he meant by it. Without explanation, it was unfair and, like many of his opinions, patronising. But that's Colin; the ego often overshadows the man. I've never known anyone with as many demons as he has. He wears them like a monk wears a cloak. They hide a lot and it's hard to know what's really going on underneath. But this isn't about him, it is about me. And if his comment meant nothing at all, it would have left me by now.

I analyse his words with every step, trying to find grounds for them. And still I can't. I've fought personal battles as he has. Similar in some ways and different in others. What gives him the right to just discount any fear that remains?

Passing a large paper factory along the final stretch, we arrive on the outskirts of Logroño, a fairly substantial city built on a river's edge and consisting predominantly of stone causeways and century-old buildings. Neither of us has the spring in our step or the light in our eyes we had a week ago in Pamplona.

It's the first large city we've seen since then and we have allowed ourselves a rest day tomorrow to enjoy it. It will also be a chance to reflect on what's happened in the last week.

My mind now needs a break from the trail as much as my body does. I'm restless out here, sick of following my feet, being guided and directed by little yellow arrows at every turn. I'm craving independence. Do I wear lace or cotton under-wear today? I have one set of each, both black, and this is the current extent of my sovereignty, freedom.

We have decided to lighten our packs in Logroño, while we have the opportunity. I'm already down to two sets of everything: socks, pants, singlets. I am not sure how much more I can cull. But the promise of a lighter weight on your back is like finding room for pudding at the end of Christmas dinner—whether you think you can or not, you do. Let's start with the two litres of holy water I've been lugging since passing through Lourdes!

Albergue rules state that pilgrims can spend only one night before they must move on. This changes, however, if a pilgrim is sick or injured. Watching each pilgrim penny and facing the prospect of having to pay for a hotel for the following night, crafty Col returns to the *albergue* with a medical certificate from the hospital.

'Done!' he says, and sends me off to invent an 'injury' for myself.

I have several options. My left knee is a bubble of fun—a swollen mass of blended mulberry shades. My feet are full of blisters—fourteen at last count. And I've developed a rather suspicious clump of bruised tissue on the calf of my right leg. I'm not sure what that is. Like the blisters and the knee, it too is growing by the day but looks much worse than it feels.

I tell the doctor to take her pick.

Day 8
Logroño, and no place else

Colin: No bonking in the barracks

I head into the city on my own. Genteel buskers play violins under the colonnades and men in suits sit drinking coffee under the shade trees near the cathedral.

Inside the cathedral there is some impressive rococo architecture before the altar. But for me the real focus and power lie behind the altar in the curiously pagan mother sculpture and painting. On either side are various Madonnas and in the chapel, separated by modern plate glass, is one of the most ornate and imposing Virgin statues I have ever seen. It is huge. Here people pray in true reverence and there are no camera flashes.

The traditional hierarchy is reversed here. It is the Madonna who is head of the blessed triumvirate, before God and the crucifix. In fact in the entire cathedral her statues outnumber the Son of God four to one, by my count. Before Christianity the goddess was the heroic figure around much of the Mediterranean; an icon of sensuality, fecundity, kindness, nurturing and compassion. Perhaps Venus is not as easily forgotten or superimposed as the church wishes to believe.

In the evening Eli has a run-in with Obersturmbahnführer Manuel. 'Get out!' he screams at her. 'Get out!'

Eli's crime is that she is still using the internet at two minutes past ten o'clock when the stalag shuts for the night at precisely ten. It is, after all, an ungodly hour for a Catholic to still be awake.

'Get out!' he screams, flecks of froth forming at the corners of his hatchet mouth. 'Get out!'

She returns, shaken and bewildered, to the dormitory and slumps onto the bunk above me.

It is a restless night. I have to tell you, I hate snorers. No patience with them. People with inefficient sinuses should be shot. That night the snoring that goes on in the barracks-like dormitory is simply unbelievable. There is bass, treble and libretto; the guy next to Eli has a basso profundo with classic whistle in two/four time.

In the dark I hear the sound of giggling and snuffling in the corner and the telltale squeaking of love in bloom. There are pilgrims having a bonk in a bunk in the barracks. If Obersturmbahnführer Manuel finds out about this, there are going to be gassings.

So next morning Eli and I are both tired and bleary-eyed. Neither of us got much sleep. Eli is looking in the communal fridge for the yoghurt she put in there the night before when Obersturmbahnführer Manuel walks in.

'Get out!' he screams at her. 'Get out!'

There is a vein bulging in his temple like a piece of wet rope.

What commandment she has transgressed is not clear to anyone. Perhaps Commandment Number Eleven: Thou Shalt Not Put Yoghurt in the Fridge. Jehovah hates that.

It is a fine start to a rotten day.

Eli: Outside the comfort zone

The next day, Col and I lie in while the other pilgrims disappear into the cool pre-dawn. I feel curiously guilty. What is it about the Camino that makes simple pleasures feel like mortal sins? But whether or not we've earned this day's break is secondary to the fact that we need one. Col's boots are giving him grief and my body hates me.

Col leaves to find breakfast while I disembowel my backpack. I've been living out of it for over a week and don't even know what's in there anymore.

With the day to myself, I write some postcards over lunch and wander the ancient streets of Logroño like a tourist. There are coffee shops, fashion stores and restaurants, nice hotels, noisy traffic, buskers and many beautiful—and very clean—people; obviously not pilgrims. Even in a town like Logroño, European culture exudes elegance.

It is strange what you miss when you step outside your comfort zone. I miss the buzz of cities like this, the energy, the vibe. I'm a country girl turned city chick. I love them both and crave the freedom to bounce between.

I sit cross-legged in the sun, on the warm stone slab of the central plaza, watching thousands of birds wheel above the church. From here they look like sparrows, furiously flapping their tiny wings, circling the main belltower. They never seem to rest.

An old man in a tweed beret sits by me in the square. We share a smile and together we watch the small birds dance. He tells me my sparrows are *vencejos*—swifts. Throughout their life, they never touch the ground and only ever come down once. To die. Maybe our earth is their heaven.

I cross the plaza in search of a cold drink. Colin is seated outside a bar, taking notes, under the shade of a drooping maple branch. For a minute, I stand and watch him from a distance.

Colin's a fascinating man. When people heard I was leaving on this trip with a fifty-year-old single man about to release a book about his own infidelity, two questions inevitably followed.

1. *Why?* Eight hundred kilometres on foot is a long way and many were concerned.
2. *How well do you know this guy, Colin?*

In order to answer the second question you really need to ask another: *How well does Colin know Colin?* One thing is certain, you will only ever know of him what he wants you to.

Col's unique. He's a funny guy, a sweet man, a talented writer and a friend. If there are things you can tell about a person just by listening to them, I can also say he's a good father. His daughters mean more to him than anything else he has in life. He may exude an air of mystery, of strength, confidence and surety about everything he does, but there's more to Colin than what you see at first glance, much more than I presume to know. A vulnerability, a sadness.

The conversation we have over a beer that day in Logroño is completely unexpected, and changes everything between us. Suddenly our friendship takes on a new dimension, the game changes and so do the stakes.

'El, it's too much. I'm not sure I can do this.'

'Do what?' I ask.

'This. The walk. The Camino. It's bringing up all of this . . . *stuff*. I thought I'd dealt with it years ago and now . . . it's everywhere. I can't escape it, El. I'm dreaming about Helen, for God's sake!'

Helen was Col's wife. We've spoken about her briefly

before. He told me of the circumstances surrounding her suicide. But also that he has moved on. Watching him wince and grimace as he speaks, I realise this is real. And as raw as I imagine it has ever been. Colin, the rock, has just become human. I've not seen this from him before.

Tears fill his eyes—'And my little girls'—then fall as he speaks about the past.

I sit stunned, watching the man as he weeps, broken. I knew something was troubling him, but hadn't seen this coming. It's moments like these that you either ask why me, why now, or you simply say thank you. I can't help but question my ability to offer him any solace, comfort or support. What do you say to a man who's lost more than you've ever had? Yet I appreciate the fact that he's opened up and trusted me with it.

I reach across the table and take his hand. 'Col, it's okay.'

He looks at me, confused but not ashamed. He doesn't hide his tears, he is not afraid to cry. This is a man who knows pain too well.

'I'm not ready to look at this, El, not now, not here. It's too much. I don't know if I can go on.'

He isn't just referring to the Camino.

I don't even think before the words leave my mouth: 'Yes you can. We both can and we will.' I don't know if it is true. This is big. At a time like this, words alone seem futile. But I do know that one of us has to believe it. Just as I asked Colin to do for me, I want him to know that I also believe in him. And as we sit talking through the afternoon, I hope that for now, a caring ear and what little I have to offer will be enough.

Today I learn a valuable lesson about the Camino. Irrespective of your physical condition or your reasons for being here, the Way shows no mercy. Just as you have asked, it will rise up and meet you exactly where you are, assess your strengths and weaknesses, then set the task accordingly.

It has been obvious from the beginning that my greatest challenge out here is physical. It becomes clear today what Colin's will be.

Day 9
Logroño to Nájera

Eli: *Haul ass, troops!*

Late in the afternoon, Simon and Mercedes arrive in Logroño. It has been a week to the day since I promised Col that we would catch them. As it happens, we not only caught up, we passed them somewhere in a town forty kilometres back up the road.

That evening the four of us cook a meal together in the *albergue* and share stories from the past week. At the table, Mercedes is still brimming with excitement at having found us again. She is surprised I'm well and pleased to have someone to gossip with. Simon—a naturally reserved and laid-back bloke—is probably happy for the break. Colin puts on a brave face for the occasion and, for a moment, it feels almost 'normal'. But Simon sees straight through it and, following the meal, he takes me aside to ask if Colin is okay.

'He's not,' I tell him, 'but he will be.' What more could I say?

We agreed to set off at different times the next day, going our separate ways and meeting later in Nájera, twenty-eight kilometres west along the Camino.

I wake in the morning to find the swelling has almost disappeared from my left knee. The day's break has made all

84

the difference, though my blistered feet are still tender and squeezing them back inside my boots again is a process. Even with my sock full of soft skin ready to slip from my feet, I feel much better than I did two days ago. Colin's tendonitis is still troubling him but he's being a trooper about it. It will be interesting to see how our bodies react once we start over. We have between six and seven walking hours ahead.

As we prepare to set out, neither of us comments on our injuries. Col lifts the pack onto my back while I turn, slipping my arms through the shoulder straps. I posted four and a half kilos home the day before.

'It's supposed to feel lighter!'

The customary thump on the pack signals the start of another day. *Doof!* And we're on the road again.

Colin: How to win friends and influence people

You can walk with kings, you can walk with the angels. Or you can walk with tendonitis. I know which one I prefer.

As the day wears on my heels get so sore I am walking on tiptoe, as delicately as a prima ballerina creeping into her convent school dorm at four in the morning. Other pilgrims shake their heads when I tell them I have tendonitis.

'My friend had that,' they say.

'And what happened?'

'Oh,' they mutter, 'his foot had to be amputated.'

The one thing I learned very quickly on the Camino is that going down is much harder than going up. Going up just spoons lactic acid into your thigh muscles and makes your heart thump like an AM radio in a Louisiana redneck's pick-up truck on a Saturday night; but going down jars the cartilage in your knee joint, as if scraping paint off a wall, and turns your thigh muscles to gelatine. Get the shakes and you could go cartwheeling down the slope like a runaway round of cheese.

I tack down hills, a yacht into the teeth of a gale. Eli has slipped back, so, bored and sore, I pretend I am the master of a brigantine. I try to distract myself by shouting, 'Hard a-starboard, Mister Hardy!' and, 'Splice the main brace and bugger the cabin boy, at the double if you please, Cap'n Hornblower!'

Along the rocky trail that winds between the hills, pilgrims have created little cairns of stones, like a fairyland. It is a heartening and unexpected sight that makes me laugh out loud. But then a man reduced to shouting orders to an imaginary nautical colleague to take carnal advantage of an underage boy will probably laugh at anything.

Eli gets a second wind and slips past me again.

'Did you know there is more water in a banana than in half a watermelon?' Or something.

Silence.

And she forges ahead. From a hundred metres behind I watch her leaning forward to try to extract her water bottle that is hooked on the back of her pack. She looks for all the world like a turtle trying to scratch its own arse.

Ahead of us, Navarrete wraps itself around a hill like a cat wrapped around a fire. Swallows swoop and wheel in the square. Storks nest in the belltowers of the churches. It is the European white stork, the *cigüeña*. Some of the towers have as many as three or four heavy nests. Their call sounds like someone playing a funeral dirge on a castanet.

We stop for a coffee and this is the last time I see Eli that day. The previous day in Logroño I had bought her some impact absorbers for her boots, inner soles made of silicon rubber. As we reach the square she turns and shouts at me: 'Hey, Crusty, those silicon implants you bought me are just great!'

I can see the expressions on several faces. *You're old enough to be her father, you sick bastard.*

I am tempted to shout back at her: *Yes, but I wish I'd got you a bigger size now!* But I am not in the mood. Not a good sign. I left my sense of humour, which I admit I have used like body armour, back there in the square at Logroño.

How to explain what happened in Logroño? We met for coffee in the square opposite the cathedral. I was in the blackest of moods. For just a minute I dropped my guard; couldn't help it. Thanks to the Camino, I didn't have a guard left. Without distractions, this indescribable and unfathomable pain had free rein to gnaw away my defences. I literally did not know what to do with myself. I had to talk to someone.

I believe I may have told Eli that I wanted to die, but I couldn't do anything about that because I had two teenage daughters to whom that would cause incalculable damage and, besides, they still depended on me for money and support from time to time.

I watched Eli's face drop. I do not believe she saw this coming. How should she respond to such a declaration? It's not as if she hasn't seen enough hurt and death in her life, but she wasn't ready for this, and it wasn't part of the persona I had adopted.

Here is what you should know about me: I left my wife three years ago and she killed herself; but this is not just about guilt. This is sheer panic as well. I am only now starting to acquaint myself with the stranger who lives inside me. I left my marriage because my spirit felt it was shrivelling and dying. My wife was a beautiful woman, inside and out, but we had grown apart. This was not her doing or her fault. I am both devil and innocent, mugger and victim, stranger to myself and my family.

Across the square from where Eli and I had sat there was an antique shop called, of all things, Carpe Diem. *Carpe diem* is Latin for *seize the day*. It has a poignancy for me that perhaps I should explain because I realise only now how naive I have been in love with women. When a woman told me I was, to her, the most special man in the world I could not imagine that she might later be able to explain it away as an aberration or a mistake. Not that it would have made any difference to my utter inability to let *her* go.

I had met her just before I left my wife. I had never experienced anything as mystifying or as passionate or as profound as I felt for her.

A more circumspect individual might have replaced the lid on this Pandora's box. Would this have saved my wife's life? Was this the right and moral thing to do? But the prospect of living out my days as the man I was then, with so much kept inside, was an unbearable thought. I was no longer the man she had fallen in love with; I had become a reckless and unfathomable stranger she had fought a rearguard action against for the last dozen years of our marriage.

I could not have gone as far as I had in my career without my wife; with her, I felt only lost and trapped. Is it selfish or courageous to choose your own direction to the detriment of someone who has been loyal to you, and loved you? Do you instead stay with all that is safe and familiar, the devil you know?

Or when we reach such a crossroads, do we seize the day?

My lover once told me she had reached such a crossroads, and I had whispered to her, *carpe diem*. Seeing the words so unexpectedly, and so piercingly, there in the square, had undone me. It was clear to me that she would not seize the day, at least if that meant moving away from all she had known into uncharted territory.

Yesterday I told Eli I was at the point of complete despair. Today, how am I supposed to behave? I have no idea. Logroño has not been mentioned since this morning. I am no longer sure what the outcome of all this will be.

Eli: Hablo the local lingo

We make our first stop three hours into the morning, at Navarrete.

It's been a long wait on an empty stomach. Colin sits opposite me and in three bites devours a chocolate croissant. He's like a kid with an ice-cream on a hot day—can't eat it fast enough, then can't believe it's gone. Throwing back my first coffee as if it were water, I order another and prepare some food from my pack.

It's still early, just a quarter past eight, and already we've passed the halfway mark for the day. We're getting better at this. It's a pleasant twenty-five degrees but a sting in the sun promises a hot day ahead. It's important to take advantage of the morning breeze and push on. We can't stay long.

Looking out onto the dirt street, watching the procession of pilgrims, I realise my perspective has changed this side of Logroño.

Being back on the trail after time in a city feels strange. I feel caught between wanting to remove myself completely from the Camino crowd, and holding on to the small commercial pleasures that have come to mean so much. On the one hand, there are the *albergues* with line-ups and shower queues—the first-in, best dressed policies—the military-style barracks and curfews. The conformity is so rigid and suffocating it makes me want to dodge the cities, stick with the small *refugios* and monasteries or, better still, go it alone. On the other hand, Colin couldn't live without chocolate croissants and I don't function without coffee. After ditching my tub of cocoa butter moisturiser yesterday, coffee's one of the few pleasures I have left.

Occasionally, you hear of someone who's gone out on their own or you might see them from a distance. They have packed a tent and traded in their pilgrims passport. They don't sleep in crowded *albergues*, they sleep in fields beneath stars. They only enter towns when they need to restock food or water supplies. And they don't speak much, but when they do you realise that their intentions and their motives are clearly defined. Colin and I are among the greater percentage of pilgrims who stick to more conventional methods. We have both come to realise in recent days that there are significant personal reasons for our being here that run deeper than just the physical challenge. It's like an intuition you can't explain, yet know to trust. There are questions we must ask, conclusions we must come to and answers we both hope to find. But ironically, neither of us has a clue what they might be.

The number of towns and villages we pass through every day is convenient; one every couple of hours. They are not like the towns I'm used to. They range from villages with supermarkets, bars, cafés and shade to a gathering of dilapidated shacks where the only liquid comes from a water fountain bearing the warning *agua no potable*. But most at least offer some kind of refuge from thirst, hunger, heat and even isolation. Sometimes it's just nice to hear a voice after three hours of undisturbed silence, regardless of the language. The locals generally take very good care of pilgrims. It's a tradition they have nurtured for hundreds of years. In return, these small communities are rewarded with our tourist dollars.

Two days ago, the owner of the *albergue* in Torres del Rio explained that her family had sold their farm to build the establishment eighteen months prior to this Jacobean year. A Jacobean, or Holy Year, is any year in which the feast day of Saint James—25 July—falls on a Sunday, and as such is the highlight of the Camino's Christian calendar. To complete the Camino in a Holy Year is to earn plenary indulgence—a one-way ticket to the afterlife. It is, quite literally, a highway to heaven. As a result the number of participants in 1999 nearly doubled those of the previous year, and even more are expected this year. Following the earlier success, her family—along with many similarly entrepreneurial locals—hoped to cash in. Having such a popular pathway run through your back yard is a lucrative commodity. They're aware of the benefits and pilgrims are prepared to pay. This is the way it has been through history.

We are fed, sheltered and supported at a fraction of what it would usually cost to travel. We can walk into any café or bar in any town, village or city and use the bathroom, have our bottles filled with cold water from behind the bar, ask for directions or even a bag of ice for injuries. Most establishments have a set pilgrim menu consisting of three dishes, bread and a bottle of wine—*tinto* or *blanco*—all for around eight euros. If you are watching your pilgrim dollar, you can still sit at one of their tables while preparing a meal from your own food supplies. They may even heat it for you if you have the temerity to ask. If you're willing to put in a little effort, be polite and attempt to speak the local language, you'll find everything you need and it will generally be delivered with a smile.

Pilgrims are easily identified among the local bar crowd: ratty clothes, sweaty brow, backpack, scallop shells, walking sticks and the distinctive limp every pilgrim inevitably develops. Pilgrims are not your average travellers and besides, not many tourists visit these parts. There are few large cities and the attractions of rural village life pale in comparison to action-packed Barcelona or Madrid.

Struck with a sudden urgency to leave, I give Col the nod. He lifts his head from the guidebook, hoists the pack onto my back once more—*doof!*—and we're off.

Colin: One with all things except the French

I let Eli go on ahead and step inside the Iglesia de la Asunción. In the dark and musty interior I find a magnificent statue of the Madonna and child. I have a prayer to say, on a piece of card, but it is too dark to read it. But the moment I kneel down a light flickers on, on cue, perhaps the verger or the priest opening the church for the day. An aria of *Ave Maria* echoes from the vaulted arches. I say the prayer quickly and leave.

Call me hopeless, or naive, but I have with me, on a cord around my neck, a prayer for a woman I know is going to fracture my soul in the manner with which she will soon dismiss me from her life. I still thank God for having met her, and wish I never had.

The prayer is for her, and by her, and the bearing of it an act of obstinacy and healing. There is tenderness and anger in these supplications, for her, and for some God I cannot fathom, for touching me this way then leaving me with stark choices I feel inadequate to make. I have no defence for my actions but temporary insanity, for it is frankly a long time now since I have felt what other people call sane. My disguise has so far been impeccable.

I walk out again into the sun-warmed cobbles and as I leave the town the road is aswarm with butterflies. I find myself stepping over ants and snails. I feel a certain kinship with an ant trying to drag a dead beetle ten times its size twenty yards to its nest, a snail hauling itself and its Winnebago-sized home across the path. Some other poor bastard trying to haul his load up a ridiculously steep incline. There have been times in my life when I have stepped on snails and ants for no better reason than that they were there and I was bored. Now they feel like family to me. Crazy. But I wonder how I would feel if someone stepped on me right now.

Relieved probably.

Eli: *Enigma*

I fall in love with my place here today.

Walking alone, I suddenly catch myself realising I am the happiest I have been since first setting out along the Camino. Colin and I have been walking apart since breakfast, still with two hours to Nájera. Pacing to the sound of Enigma through my headphones, I approach the peak of a loping knoll. With the march of the Gregorian beat in my feet, the music makes the scenery surreal. Suddenly, I am stepping out of my own movie scene.

With the burnt yellow fields behind me, I reach the summit to find a valley sweeping down in a sea of green. On the horizon are a handful of distant hills with churches perched on top— possibly tomorrow's destinations—a towering communications antenna piercing the sky between them. It is stunning. And for a nice change, there's not a grain of wheat in sight. A gentle breeze sweeps through the valley and brushes against my skin, bringing with it a sense of freedom, and even belonging, that I've not experienced here before. It is one of those rare and precious moments when you realise that everything is perfect, all the pieces fall into place and everything fits. Such moments never last; they are not yours to keep.

A fellow Australian on the Camino told me a few days ago how the airline lost his baggage on the way to Spain. He arrived with nothing but the clothes on his back, a bottle of water, a Visa card and some change in his pocket. He started his walk anyway. When the airline contacted him via email to say his bag had arrived, he told them to return it to Sydney.

'I didn't want it anymore. There's a certain freedom in poverty, you know?'

Out here material things don't mean as much as they did at home. Letting go of them is like cutting a second umbilical cord. Expecting nothing, accepting everything, surrendering to each moment as it arrives, having the courage and faith to trust you have everything you need to be okay. I have less in my pack now than when I came. Tomorrow I will have less than I have today.

Every day so far, I have asked myself what the hell I'm doing here. But instead, before stepping off the hill this afternoon, I take a moment to say thank you.

Eli: *Cats, dogs and buckets of ... Colin!*

I love rainy days. But when you're caught in a downpour holding grocery bags under the narrow terrace of a *supermercado* that's just lost its power in the storm and the staff have locked the doors behind you . . . well, it takes much of the fun away. This isn't just ordinary rain, this is a torrent, with deafening thunder, an impressive light-show and flash flooding, all in the time it takes for me to make my way from aisle three to the checkout.

Nobody knows where I am. When I left, I wasn't even sure where I was going. Colin, Mercedes and Simon are all waiting at the *albergue* for me to return to prepare dinner. The streets are empty, cars have been abandoned by the roadside and I have nothing but a nearby sheet of cardboard to use as shelter. My satchel contains my most valuable possessions: passports, MP3 player, notepad and dictaphone. I am wearing my only dry clothes, and have just spent an hour cleaning and redressing my feet with fresh, *dry* gauze.

Minutes pass: five, ten, twenty-five. Stripped down to a singlet in the stifling humidity, I watch as the two checkout chicks from the *supermercado* are picked up and whisked away in waiting cars. The storm has set in. It is just five o'clock but already it is dark. Looks like I am here for the long haul, so I prop against a wall and drift off with the hypnotic drone of rain on the roof.

I think back to an old homeless man I used to pass on Swanston Street at 5 am each morning on my way to work in the city. Huddled in the corner of a dimly lit doorway as the rain beat down on a bleak Melbourne dawn. Jack lay curled beneath sheets of newspaper, with a filthy blanket and a piece of cardboard for a pillow. Every Friday I would leave home early to buy him a coffee and spend time there in his doorway. Jack hated the rain. Dreaded it, in fact. A particularly wet or cold winter for him could mean the difference between life and death. It occurred to me then as it does now, standing in my own doorway in Spain, that maybe I've always liked rainy days because I've always had the privilege to enjoy them: a warm shower, a fresh set of clothes and heating on the other end of a slow walk home. Not today.

My reverie is interrupted by the sight of a hooded, caped crusader bounding towards me through the dark. Splashing across an empty street and hurdling ankle-deep puddles, Colin has come to my rescue.

'Hey-a, Tonto,' he says as he slips beneath the terrace.

'What are you doing here—how'd you find me?'

'When I heard the rain, I asked directions to the biggest supermarket in town.' He smiles. 'It wasn't hard.' Passing me his plastic poncho, he takes the grocery bags from my hands. 'Here you go, mate, let's get you out of here, hey?'

Still stunned by the effort, and more than a little grateful, I stretch his plastic poncho above our heads. Huddled underneath, we venture out into the deluge. Dashing back through the empty streets, toward the *albergue*, stamping in puddles along the way.

Suddenly, the rain doesn't seem so bad again.

Colin: *Losing my religion*

I was raised High Anglican, but God or spirituality has never figured largely in my life. Out here on the Camino I am definitely looking for something. I have now come to suspect that a life is not lived on any meaningful level without an aspect of spirituality running beneath it, like an underground stream that gives the ground above its sustenance.

My underground stream is a trickle. I am losing my religion.

Every town, every village, has a church, and I go into each one, seeing them with new eyes, inquisitive, curious, questioning. Many, to my disgust, are locked; some you even have to pay to enter. Pay as you pray. There is something repellent in this: is this a church or a museum? If the Catholic Church has so much stuff they are worried about people nicking things, well maybe they should not have so much stuff. Is a church somewhere to pray or somewhere to store the loot?

One day as we are walking, Eli asks me: 'What would you do if you met God?'

And the answer comes back without thinking: 'I'd take Him by the shoulders, look Him right in the eye, and knee Him in the balls.'

This is how I have come to see God.

Thump.

That's for all the children starving in Africa!

Thump.

That's for my friend's kid who drowned in the bath!

Thump.

That's for the Inquisition!

I am not being flippant. I know the fault does not lie with whatever great intelligence created all this. The error is in my spiritual education. I was always taught to fear God and I did:

for most of my life I have been terrified of the bastard. He was portrayed to me as a sort of grim Father Christmas with PMT: rigid, judgmental, no sense of proportion, never did a thing wrong in his whole life, and sits up there tut-tutting every time I look like having a good time or a carnal thought.

People have told me I should love God. How do you love someone who has no sense of humour?

So what is God? Perhaps God is like gravity; just a force that works whether we believe in it or not, a law that just is. God is also a symbol, an image we carry in our minds—our GPS of where we are in the universe.

Sorting through this rich stew of Catholic and Templar churches, I am aware of a new God, and I actually like this one. This symbol does not make me feel guilty or afraid, and inspires in me compassion, warmth and humility. It is the Madonna. Not the Madonna, mother of God and archetypal virgin, the one who looks like Mother Theresa with a prune up her arse. For I have noticed that the Madonnas are all slightly different. The one I am drawn to is the other Madonna, the slightly edgy one who radiates a sort of sensuality and compassion; the pagan Madonna who looks like a real woman and not the National President of the Council Against Swearing on Television.

In some churches, especially the Templar ones, the images are pagan; compassion and human desire and frailty are depicted in these ageless statues. These other Madonnas touch me somehow at a primal level and it is here one Thursday morning in a small church after a coffee and a chocolate croissant that I experience for the first time the stirring of spiritual feeling. It is a sense of affection, rather than venal hope, for what some deity may be able to do for me in this world or the next.

But this is just between you and me. I would not want this sort of sentiment to become widely known. My mates at the footy club will think I've thrown a screw, or worse, joined a group in which they fondle crystals and do male bonding.

Having said that, it could just be that everyone feels like this after a chocolate croissant. They are really very good.

That afternoon when we reach the *albergue* in Nájera, Eli is still fretting about the *hostelero* who abused her in Logroño, so she decides to start preparing dinner for the four of us—her, Mercedes, Simon and myself—to try to take her mind off it.

'He hated me,' she mutters as she finally sits down.

'That's not true,' I tell her. 'How could anyone hate you?'

Just then a French pilgrim we have not seen since Puente la Reina walks in.

Eli smiles and holds out her arms for a hug. 'Ben!'

He steps back like she is a leper and points his finger at her head. 'You stole my pen!' he shouts. 'I hate you!'

Day 10
Nájera to Santo Domingo

Colin: *The secret of life—look after your feet*

Often, when people write on the Camino, they wax poetic about Romanesque churches and wheat fields and blue sierra. But if you want to know about the Camino, talk about feet that throb on the end of your legs like radio isotopes, knees pierced with slivers of steel, neck muscles taut as guitar strings from carrying a fourteen-kilo backpack, and thighs that burn like phosphorus. The Camino may be a spiritual experience but before long you will become less obsessed with the divine and far more concerned about chiropody. A week on the Camino and all anyone wants to talk about is their feet.

How can feet ever be important? They're just those odd-looking things on the ends of your legs. But out here they are much more than that; your feet are everything. If you have eight hundred kilometres to walk inside a month, you can't afford to damage them. A stubbed toe can be a calamity if it takes skin off inside your boot.

We pilgrims sit around at night in the *refugios* discussing whether sandals are better than boots, how many pairs of socks to wear while walking, and blister remedies. Should you pop your blisters or leave them be as protection?

I have become a foot fetishist. Mates had always said I would. That, or rubber. Let me recount the five stages of a Camino blister:

1. A hot spot appears, an angry red mark somewhere on your feet. It is slightly sore and throbs when you take your boot off.
2. A small blister appears. It hurts a bit when you walk. When you take your boot off everyone tells you to burst it with a sterilised needle. It will feel better. You ignore them. What do they know?
3. The next day as you walk, you know what it is like to be subject to the Spanish Boot, an instrument of torture used in the Spanish Inquisition, whereby the foot was placed in a steel boot and the boot was tightened by iron screws until it was the size of a toddler's welly.
4. The blister bursts inside your boot and turns into a patch of raw flesh the size of a fifty-cent piece. When you take off your boot the skin, flesh and raw nerve endings stick to the woolly parts of your sock and are all removed together. You take off your sock and ring out the pus and blood like a squeegee mop. Everyone asks you why you didn't burst the blister with a pin.
5. The next day you find on your foot a suppurating wound the size of a bath mat. You cannot stand on your foot. Even crawling is agony. You still have another month to walk.

Everything they once taught me about blisters in First Aid was wrong. I now realise there are two good reasons to pop your blisters when they appear: one, because no matter what the medicos say about blisters being Nature's natural protection, they hurt, and relieving the pressure is wonderful. They also heal better that way. You puncture them with a sterile needle, put on some antiseptic and a decent dressing and you're good to go. Otherwise they burst in your boot like a punctured water hydrant and spray serum everywhere and then leave raw pink meat to rub inside your boot all day and turn your feet into hamburger mince.

The other good reason to pop them is because it's fun. Last night Eli and I spent a happy hour with a needle from her sewing kit that we sterilised with her cigarette lighter, and popped each other's blisters.

Wow! Look at that one go!

Yay, straight up the wall!

Whoa, sorry, I got you in the eye!

I can even remember where we were the night Eli showed me the blister she had grown underneath the end of her little toe. It was vast. It had its own pulse and hung there like a tumour. When she popped it, it went off like a firehose and it took me and three other pilgrims to hold her foot down and direct the spray onto the garden.

If only that was the sole problem. Her knee has swollen dangerously. Her leg looks like a cocktail stick with a maraschino cherry stuck halfway down. But it is clear to me that she will not quit on this, under any circumstances. And that scares me a little.

She might have a better chance if there was an orthopaedic surgeon in her pack, but it's heavy enough as it is. She will have to send home more stuff or she just won't make it.

She is totally preoccupied with her body now, not in a vain way, but she's attuned to its workings and takes time to carefully tend to it, like a man nursing an ancient car through the desert.

It is humid leaving Nájera. The morning hums and steams like the tropics. Pine trees crowd in on us in the darkness. We climb a steep ravine that opens onto vineyards and wheat fields. Not yet dawn and my shirt is damp with sweat.

Things are strained between Eli and me. We don't walk together much anymore. I feel like I have exposed too much of myself and now I am embarrassed, and angry at myself. Men are not supposed to show any sign of vulnerability. I feel like a fool. *This is not why people love you. You are loved for being tough, and for having all the answers, and for being able to fix things.*

The tendonitis in my left foot is slowing me down. Suddenly the skin peels back off my heel. The shock of pain is electric, like I have touched a live wire. My foot buzzes and goes numb. I have no idea what is going on. I keep walking. Whatever has happened, the damage is done now: I don't want to look.

As the sun rises—or *also* rises, as we're in Hemingway's Spain—we look out over field after field of wheat. A week ago I stood and gaped. Now I look at the patchwork of grain and vine and think: *Jesus Christ, more wheat!*

This is where they grow the raw produce for Spain's national lunchtime snack, the *bocadillo*. You see them everywhere, mouldering under glass in every bar, in every back street. Put some cheese in them and it's like chewing an inner sole.

Over to the right is what looks and smells like a piggery, where they feed the stringy tasteless porkers they eventually slaughter, wind cure and piss on before they put them in the dry fucking tasteless rock-hard bread. *Bocadillo con jamón.*

I hate *bocadillos*.

I find an abandoned chapel by the roadside. All the statuary and religious paraphernalia have been removed. Only the pews remain. I sit down where the altar would once have been and think about the church I went to as a boy. I was christened into the Church of Suburbia in Essex. Instead of praying people gossiped about each other in the churchyard.

In Pamplona, I went to a mass, but sat at the side facing the congregation, instead of the priest. The service was spoken in Spanish but made as much sense to me as it ever did in my own tongue. I watched people at the back yawning and looking at their watches, just as they did in my church, as they do in every church I have ever been in.

But the alternative to organised religion is to search for the divine yourself, following signposts where you find them, and with no guarantees of heaven at the end of it, and that's pretty scary. But I have the growing conviction that to be a better man there has to be some sort of spiritual connection made; goodness is not the consequence of a litany of prayers learned by rote. Perhaps this is what pilgrimage is all about.

That and learning to look after your feet.

Eli: Freddy Krueger's face

By the end of the day, my knee has doubled in size and Col's blisters—or what is left of them—are hideous. The back of his heel is a raw mess of weeping flesh that looks intriguingly similar to Freddy Krueger's face. It's horrible to look at yet impossible to look away. He's being brave and says he's happy to keep patching them but, rather aptly, it's his Achilles heel letting him down. The injuries, along with our conversation in Logroño, have me wondering whether we'd have been better walking through without stopping to rest. It seems to have done more harm than good. Then again, without the day's break, our pilgrimage might well have ended by now.

I think about Col's words in Logroño each day. I ask if he's okay but he's more determined than ever now that he's 'just fine'. I drop it and keep my thoughts to myself. Is this what happens when we don't face fear? Eventually, it catches up. And typically, it's when we are least prepared and least expect it.

We arrive in Santo Domingo.

Colin: My Achilles heel

When we get to the *albergue*, which is inside a convent in Santo Domingo, I go into the boot room and sit down on the stairs. When I take off my sock, a large part of my foot comes away with it, like when you peel really old wallpaper off a wall and some of the plaster and brick sticks to it.

I stare fascinated at my sock and the stuff that is still attached: there's some skin, there's some meat, a bit of blister plaster, a major blood vessel, all in a sort of soft pink hamburger lump. At least the tendonitis is going to be better because the bit of tendon that was troubling me is there as well, I think. Now there is less of it to strain. What is left is a piece of bright pink raw flesh the size of a beach flag.

'That's got to hurt,' Canada says, but it actually doesn't. It's too numb to hurt.

It's a great anatomy lesson. Like the song says, the ankle bone really is connected to the foot bone. And what's left is still connected to my sock.

Eli: Santo Domingo—Catholic cocks and one crowing nun

Santo Domingo de la Calzada is a town best known for having chickens in the church. This odd attribute pretty much sets the tone of the place. Walking the grey-framed medieval streets reminds me of a family holiday in the US when my father took a wrong turn on the way back to our hotel in San Francisco and walked us through a dodgy part of town. The air was thick; I'd never felt anything like it. I was seven and my family were the only white people in a busy street. We'd just come from evening mass and tentatively edged along the footpath, dodging the glares, my father's vice-like grip crushing my tiny hand. When we returned, the hotel manager was visibly distraught when told of our detour and couldn't believe we'd made it out alive.

There are no ghetto blasters or street gangs in Santo Domingo, but there's certainly an uncomfortable air about the place. Maybe it's the high stone walls, the empty streets, or endless shades of grey. Maybe it's the fact that we have arrived in the middle of siesta. Or maybe it's the chickens!

Santo Domingo de la Calzada was named after the town's patron saint, Dominic, a hermit who lived in a forest nearby. After a vision he decided to dedicate his life to pilgrims on their way to Santiago. His first accomplishment was to single-handedly carve a pathway through the dense forest for pilgrims to pass. The very pathway we have just entered along. Santo Domingo de la Calzada in English roughly translates as 'Saint Dominic of the Road'.

Following this feat, he went on to build a bridge over the Rio Oja along with a pilgrims hospital. In time, the township grew around the hospital, providing complementary services and, as such, is said to be the world's first purpose-built tourist town. Domingo was later canonised for his efforts.

But about the chickens. The veracity of the story, as with all great fables, is debatable. But let's go with what we know.

Around the fourteenth or fifteenth century, a man and his wife, who may or may not have been from Germany, decided to make a pilgrimage to Santiago, taking their teenage son, who may or may not have been called Hugonell, along with them. They stopped overnight here at the inn.

Now the innkeeper's daughter, as in all good limericks, fell madly in lust with the strapping young Hugonell, who was quite generously endowed by all accounts—well hung, in today's parlance. But Hugonell was a good Christian lad on a pilgrimage so he refused her advances, believing she would understand. He may have known how to be good but he obviously did not know much about women.

By way of retribution, the young lass hid a silver goblet in Hugonell's sack as he slept, and next morning told her father she had seen him steal it. Dragged before the courts, Hugonell was well hung again, this time for good.

Hugonell's parents left their son's body to rot on the gallows—as all good Christian parents would—while they continued their pilgrimage to Santiago. Upon arrival at the Compostela, they prayed to St James for their son. Amazingly, when they returned to Santo Domingo the resurrected Hugonell was waiting to meet them.

The town's governor, who had himself condemned the boy to death, was enjoying a lunch of roast chicken when told of the miracle. 'Impossible,' he scoffed. 'That boy is as alive as the two birds on this plate.' With that, his dinner—a cock and a hen—jumped up off the plate and began to crow.

The town soon became famous for its clucky miracle and to commemorate the event—or to attract more pilgrims, which some cynics have suggested might have been the reason behind this improbable story all along—a polychrome hen-house was erected above the entrance to the cathedral, and a pair of live birds placed inside.

The custom continues today, although I assume with a different pair of chooks. It's a strange sight in a cathedral. It's also possibly the most interest I've shown in a church since visiting Notre Dame.

Medieval marketing at its best!

Eli: Something afoot in Chicken Town

It started with a boot. A very big boot.

Dan is a Canadian guy, 'Canada', who looks remarkably like Clark Kent; a tall, gentle giant with a backpack the size of my couch. Neatly cropped black hair, chiselled jawline, striking cheekbones and glasses to boot. Dan's a high school teacher and his nature suggests he's the kind of teacher his students remember. There's always one from your younger years, one who managed to reach through all of the angst and uncertainty to touch the part of you that actually cared.

It's only after taking his pack off at the end of the day that Dan realises he's missing a boot. After a particularly humid morning, he had tied them by the laces to the outside of his pack to allow them to dry while he walked. As soon as he notices, he quickly rounds up three local boys and offers them a handful of loose change if they head out on bikes along the trail and retrieve it. An hour later, the kids return empty-handed. Sitting on a patch of grass in the town square, nursing his left boot, Dan tells me about an article he read before he came away.

Written by a man who'd walked the Camino several years before, it told the story of how the man arrived in Spain with a backpack full of belongings. It was too big. Realising that his possessions served little purpose out here, he began to give random items away; a T-shirt in one town, a pair of shorts in another, a camera, a smaller bag and so on. By the time he reached Santiago, all he had left were the clothes on his back and his pilgrim stick. Standing outside the cathedral, taking a moment to enjoy his achievement, a beggar boy came up to him and asked him for his stick. When he refused to hand it over, the boy began to tug at the end and soon the two were embroiled in a bitter struggle for it.

'No, it's all I have,' the man insisted. His stick now represented the total sum of his external possessions.

As the two engaged in their tug-of-war, the man suddenly realised what his life had come to. He had completed a pilgrimage, a spiritual journey of humility, reverence and honour, and yet there he was fighting with a poor child over a stick.

Dan came to Spain with twenty-two kilograms in his backpack—twice what he needed and twice what he now realises he is able to carry. His heels, like Colin's, are bloodied and blistered. Someone suggested he post some of the backpack's contents home to Canada but, instead, Dan decides at that moment that as he walks he, too, will leave pieces behind until he has nothing left to give.

With that, he stands up, walks to the rubbish bin and places his single left boot inside. Then he calls across to the children who've spent their afternoon unsuccessfully searching for its mate and gives them the handful of small change, along with a T-shirt each for their trouble.

Eli: Is there a doctor in the house?

In classic Camino fashion, the trail grants an unexpected gift just as I need it.

Mercedes, our part-time translator, fellow pilgrim and local connection, spots me icing my knee outside the *albergue* and asks how it is. I lift the bag of ice to show her. She gasps, concerned, and demands I get it looked at, then tells me her aunt is married to a well-known doctor who specialises in high-impact sports injuries—*and she's not mentioned this before?* As it happens, the man lives on the outskirts of Santo Domingo and is bringing his family to town later that afternoon to meet with her.

'You hab to see him. He can hell-up.'

Following a phone call, the man generously offers to spare me some time.

As agreed, a few hours later Mercedes's aunt, her husband the doctor and their young daughter meet us outside the cathedral. Standing there in the street, the doctor examines the injury, poking at the textured clump of fluid around the knee, then asks a handful of questions. Mercedes translates my replies. Satisfied, he then takes a small notepad from his wife's handbag and writes out a makeshift script, initialling the bottom of the page. The man is apparently a very highly respected member of the community whose authority would not be questioned.

He then explains via Mercedes that the rainbow display of pastels surrounding the joint is the result of internal bleeding. He says that unless I empty the pack, I have little hope of making it through another week, let alone to Santiago.

I thank him for his time, say goodbye to his family, then return to share the news with Colin. His heel looks worse than my knee—it's a stew of raw flesh and skin adrift.

Realising we now have to wait for the pharmacies to open at ten the next morning before departing, Colin and I jump at the opportunity to sleep in.

Bliss.

Colin: Mother Mary Goebbels

I am having a nightmare. There is an incensed penguin wearing Adolf Eichmann spectacles leaning over me and telling me to *Get out! Get out!* Wait, I want to tell the penguin, you can't say that to me, I'm not Eli!

Let me introduce you to Mother Mary Goebbels, of the Little Sisters of the Piqued. This morning Mother Mary is mightily pissed off. Pilgrims are supposed to be out of the *albergue* by 7.45 am. After a week of getting up at 4.30 we have committed the mortal sin of sleeping in. We seem to be the last ones left in the *albergue*.

I get up, dress, and get my backpack organised. Eli takes a little longer. All I have to do is yawn and scratch my balls but Eli has this routine. And the routine drives the penguin crazy, like it used to drive me crazy before I got used to it. But Sister Goebbels goes off ranting in Spanish, on and on and on. Eli ignores her but I can't.

Finally I round on her and tell her, as politely as I can while she is screaming in my ear and spraying me with holy spittle, that she is an unholy Catholic Spanish bitch and will she please fuck off back to hell or wherever she came from because her ranting will not make Eli move any faster in the mornings and if it did I would have tried it.

And so, just for this, I get attitude. From a nun, for God's sake. Her eyes bulge dangerously like that cat in Tom and Jerry cartoons when the mouse connects his tail to the mains electricity supply. I am a mild, sweet-tempered man, as anyone who knows me will tell you, but I will not be hectored by an aged spinster in a penguin costume. So I yell back and soon we are screaming at each other in our respective languages. I hear her say something about *diablo*—the bitch called me Satan! In return I may possibly have referred to her as a crazy old Catholic shitbag.

The end result is that we are tossed out into the street like drunks out of a bar at closing time. A lifetime of charity and humility and Christian service notwithstanding, Mother Mary slams the heavy oak and iron door in our faces. I swear I saw her give me the finger in the instant before the door shut with a booming thud. It sounded like God closing the Book of Judgment after the last sorry case.

Until now my only experience of nuns has been Solving a Problem Like Maria in *The Sound of Music*, which my parents dragged me along to see three fucking times when I was ten. So the animosity is a bit of a shock.

Let me just say this before we consider the matter closed. If you are ever in Santo Domingo, Mother Mary Goebbels is Head Torturer and Flagellator at the first *albergue* on the left as you go down Calle Mayor. If you ever stay there, and I wouldn't wish it on a rabid dog, look her up for me. You can't miss her—she's the fat bitch with the wart on her nose. Please tell her from me to go and get fucked.

Day 11
Santo Domingo to Belorado

Eli: Karma chaos

Script filled, we leave Santo Domingo with a potent concoction of three different anti-inflammatories and two prescription painkillers, a handful of which I gobble down outside the pharmacy.

Suddenly, I can't feel my tongue. Bugger walking to Santiago—with these little gems, I could fly there.

Apart from a few fits of sporadic banter required to maintain sanity, Colin and I spend most of the morning trudging through the rising heat in silence, several metres apart. The incident with the nun this morning has set Colin off. He's had his head in the guidebook most of the day and hasn't spoken for hours. Except to himself, a new hobby he's developed over the past week. It started as muted chatter but has been worse since Logroño. He doesn't realise I've noticed.

Suddenly, there's an outburst of laughter behind. I look around. Colin and I are the only two in sight on a barren plain. I turn and watch as he wanders along twenty paces back, chatting away, shaking his head and gesturing with his hands.

I stop. 'WHAT'S THAT, RAINMAN?' I yell.

His smile drops away. 'WHAT?' he calls back.

I toss my arms out to the side.

'SHIT!—*mutter, mutter, mutter*—DID I SAY THAT OUT LOUD?'

'UH-HUH.'

'SORRY!'

Uh-huh.

Leading the way I pass a mechanic's workshop on the outskirts of a small town. A middle-aged man in grease-stained overalls is walking along the road toward me, presumably on his way back to his workshop.

Twenty metres out, I move slightly left, offering him the right of way on the narrow roadside.

He steps right.

Fifteen metres, I move right and onto the road, to allow him room to pass.

He steps to his left and bears down.

Ten metres out, he's lining me up.

Five metres, I hold my ground and keep walking.

Three metres, I greet the guy: *Buenos días, señor.*

Two metres, he spits a wad of green crud at my feet.

One metre, he grunts—something Spanish—then collects my left shoulder on his way past. *BOOF!*

Gracias!

He doesn't turn back.

As a general rule of thumb, small towns equal friendly people. But not today. Colin's run-in with the nun has brought consequences. He's danced with the devil and now we have a bad karma army seeking retribution on Sister Surly's behalf. Moments later, the store owner of a deli throws a block of cheese at my head. I duck, pick it up off the floor and then ask if she'd mind slicing it. I'm not a bad person, really. But this is the theme of the day and I'm developing a complex.

Colin: Seaman Staines

The scenery is fantastic, if you like looking at wheat. The hills roll away in neat little rectangles of baby *bocadillos*, the wheat bending and swaying in the hot wind around dirty green islands of scrub. All the houses have mossy russet-coloured half-moon tiles, and whitewashed walls.

We seem to have picked up some bad karma from our encounter with Mother Mary Goebbels. We get attitude all day. We ask the lady in the shop at Grañón for a tomato and she raises her eyes to heaven and shouts at us as if we have asked her to sacrifice her firstborn.

We go into a bar in the middle of nowhere, the only customers they have had all day, and the woman accuses us of trying to pass forged notes.

As we walk, we try to take our mind off our blisters by talking about TV programs from our youth. Eli tells me how Astro Boy was her favourite cartoon hero because he used to fire bullets out of his bum—how wrong is that?—and I tell her about a cartoon I watched on the BBC called *Captain Pugwash*. Years later I was in a pub in London talking to a friend about it and he pointed out some of the things that I missed when I was four; the names of two of Pugwash's crew were Seaman Staines and Master Bates. I later learned this was not true but typically I never let the truth get in the way of a good story.

We reach Castildelgado early in the afternoon, like John Wayne walking into Dry Gulch for a gunfight. It is siesta so the street is deserted, and breathlessly hot. Swallows swoop around the church tower. A dog lying on the stones raises its head but cannot summon enough energy to bark.

In the Plaza Mayor there is a table tennis table sitting drunkenly on the cobbles and a ruined building with an electric blue Pepsi machine chained to it. The vending machines are an attempt to replace the drinking fountains that are unfortunately—for the multinational soft drink companies—free.

We hear the sound of a man and woman arguing inside one of the houses. An old crone is reading a John Grisham novel on a plastic chair outside an abandoned building. Her legs are spread, revealing cellulite all the way up to the band of her orthopaedic stockings.

The cemetery has a wall around it and padlocked gates. So the living and the dead can't get mixed up.

Eli keeps going. I am so exhausted I slump down under a tree behind the church and eat lumps out of half a loaf of bread and some goat's cheese. After a while I become aware of the smell. I realise I am eating my lunch in the area reserved by local villagers to shit in. So it has come to this. Eating lunch in the shithouse.

My form teacher in Year 10 always said this is where I would end up.

Eli: As reel as life

Towns and refuges are further apart this side of Logroño. We have crossed the border from Navarre to Castilla y León where the terrain is flatter, the plains sparse and the climate significantly hotter. The daily temperature has leapt fifteen degrees since we began in the Pyrenees. By the time we make it to the next town, we're hot, hungry and exhausted.

Colin decides to stop and snack from food he has in his pack. His blisters are giving him major grief, the skin on the backs of his heels has worn away and they are bleeding through the wad of gauze padding he's covered them with. There's no *tienda* in town and I only have a few dried crackers, so I decide to chance it and walk on in the hope of finding another village further along.

Walking out of a town like this into the barren heat takes a degree of faith every time. You never know what's going to happen between now and the next village. But you do know it won't be pleasant. It will be hot and hard. You take as much water as you think you might need to get to the next fountain but no more. It's too heavy to carry.

Col and I operate on a buddy system. We both walk an average rate of 5.7 kilometres per hour on the flat. Uphill, we cover around 4.5 kilometres and, downhill, around 3.5 to 4 kilometres, depending on the gradient. If we separate at any stage throughout the day, we estimate each other's time of arrival in the next town, including rest stops, and the first to make it there waits outside the church (there's usually only one), until the other shows. I knew nothing of this when we set out. I'd not trekked or hiked before. In fact, my record to date was a twenty-minute stumble home to St Kilda after leaving a Port Melbourne bar. But after a few days on the road you get a feel for it and it becomes like a sixth sense. Despite how long we've spent apart, we're usually within a ten-minute window of each other.

Walking alone, scraping my feet, quietly singing and working hard on my suntan, I set myself in another—somewhat creative—movie scene. I—bearing a striking resemblance to Angelina Jolie—squint up towards a harsh sun. The camera pulls back to reveal a stark, colourless landscape. An unshaven Johnny Depp appears on the horizon. Tumbleweed rolls through the frame. The wind section of an orchestra swells in the background. Wiping a perfect lick of full-bodied hair from my face and a bead of Evian sweat from my brow, I check the time. Suddenly, I realise that there're still two hours to go. *Shit!*

In reality, there is no award-winning score, no luscious lips, no Johnny and no sign of life. Just dead wheat, stark vistas and a dense silence, broken only by the shuffle of tired feet across a long, narrow trail.

Cut!

Miss Jolie, we need you to go back to Roncesvalles and do that again, please.

I think about Colin a lot throughout the afternoon. Beneath the brash veneer, he is by nature a pensive man but, recently, his forehead is furrowed, creased with more intensity. He's in pain but these wounds can't be patched like blisters can.

It's natural to question a lot of things out here. But so far Colin predominantly seems to have questioned himself, his actions and the repercussions on his life. This has brought him face to face with a few demons of his own. It makes sense now. He's the first to admit he's run from many things in the past and always managed to keep ahead. But over the past ten days, all of those things left undone have found their way back. Out here, there's nowhere to run, nowhere to hide and nothing but time to remind you.

It's come as a surprise. More shock. I'm usually the one doing self-doubt. I've grown so good at it over the years that I've forgotten how to live without it. But Colin kept up such a convincing front until now and has done for as long as I've known him.

'The trail has brought up memories,' he said. Feelings, unresolved emotions that are haunting his every hour here. Most of them are related in some way to his wife, their kids, their former life together, the affair and his wife's suicide. I guess grief is a double-edged sword—you can grieve for someone you've hurt or for someone you've been hurt by. But whatever the cause, grief is loss and both are tragic.

Guilt, regret, fear, doubt, anger: independently they are heavy burdens to bear. But Colin carries them all. In the form of an iron cross that rests heavy on his shoulders, adding further weight to the strain of every day. By night, he says, it gets worse. But that's no surprise, things always do. Night is when silence couples with darkness and there's no one there to save you from yourself. I've not told him he's been talking in his sleep.

I think back to that day in Logroño and wonder if I could've done more. I listened as we talked and offered my support. I wasn't even sure at the time if that was what he needed. But I know now that it wasn't enough. There's something so profound about a grown man's tears. It takes great strength to admit vulnerability.

Eli: Sample some roadkill—it's tradition

I walk as far as I can without finding food then stop at the side of the road, unable to take another step. The sand is too hot to sit on. I unclip the strap around my waist, slip the pack off my shoulders and onto the ground, then buckle at the knees and flop down on top of it. The Camino trail now runs parallel with a deserted highway; ahead lies the sandy yellow trail, a strip of dead brown grass and a black bitumen road lined with white flecks that disappears into the distance. Still no sign of life.

My legs throb with the rush of blood having stopped. My spine clicks back into position from top to bottom like a row of falling dominoes. The blistered skin on my shoulders and neck has shrivelled brown and peeled away in patches. And what's left of my water feels like it's been poured from a boiling kettle. I lie back and close my eyes, squinting in the blaze of an angry sun. *Oh God, what am I doing?*

Dizzy and weak, I sit up and begin riffling through my pack in search of crackers. It isn't much but it is all I have and, as uninviting as dry crackers are right now, I hope they provide enough sustenance to get me to the next town.

'Hola, usted necesita ayuda?'

I look up to find a young man straddling a bike and leaning on the handlebars.

'Perdón. No hablo español.'

'Do chew speak Engleesh?' he asks.

'Sí. I mean, yes! I do.'

It suddenly occurs to me that my new cycling friend is an extremely attractive young Spanish boy. Quite stunning in fact: dark hair, olive skin and the most amazing green eyes hidden behind Arnette sunglasses, which he raises to his brow. There are also the beautifully sculpted, silky smooth legs typical of all cyclists. But then, a significant part of his appeal may be that he is the first life form I've seen in a while.

'Do chew need hell-up with sometink?' he asks.

'Ah, no. I'm just stopping to rest.'

'Is a strange place to be stopping, no? Is very hot.'

'*Sí* . . . I mean, yes, it is hot. But I'm not sure how far we are from the next town and I need a break.'

'Is a five minutes,' my knight in shining armour replies.

'Five minutes? You're kidding!' *Surely not?*

'No, no, here let me join chew, I will show chew on my map . . . unless chew want to be alone of course? Some pilgrims are strange, they don't like to speak, they wish to be left alone.'

'No, that'd be great,' I assure him, 'thank you.'

Observing my packet of crackers, the young Spaniard removes some food from a rucksack strapped to the frame of his bike, throws his shirt on the ground and sits down beside me in the sand. I admire his rippling abs and wonder if this might be the low budget version of my movie scene. He offers something to accompany my dry slices of compact wheat, handing me a small loaf of white bread and a rock hard roll of what looks like salami on steroids. He tells me this is *butifarra negra*, a traditional pilgrim food made of pigs' knuckles and blood, that 'all pilgrims *must* eat'.

Call me fussy, but a picnic of mouldy congealed blood sausage on a thirty-five degree day sitting roadside in the steaming dirt is about as appetising as the thought of a sardine smoothie after a night of heavy drinking. My Spanish prince has just become a toad. He's cute but as he sits before me carving slabs off the bright red sinew-speckled mass and joyously gnawing away on it like chewing on the tongue of a leather boot, my fondness for him quickly dissolves. Anyway, he's a cyclist. I'm not supposed to like him.

Cyclists cover in a day what takes us five to travel on foot. It's a cruel ratio that fuels a kind of 'us and them' mentality between the two factions. Their route is altered to better cater for wheels. While we're climbing shale-covered mountain trails, they bypass along scenic roads and smooth highways. Then when the paths realign, they boldly claim preferential position. Colin hates them. He groans every time they ding their little bells to bump us off the trail, then curses as they zip past.

Ding, ding.

'Cyclist cheaters!'

'Buen Camino!'

'Fuck off!'

I surmise any chance of happiness and children with the boy is not to be, and the cute cyclist toad rewraps his roadkill and treadles off. Within a few minutes, my knee has inflated like a hot air balloon. Comforted that the next township is—as assured—only minutes away, I slowly move out, chowing down on my handful of cardboard clippings as I go.

Further down the road I realise the cyclist was right. Belorado is only five minutes away . . . by bike. I, on the other hand, am still walking an hour later, with no sign of town in sight.

Cyclists!

Colin: Stop the Camino, I want to get off

By the time we get to Belorado Eli has more fluid in her knee than Lake Victoria. She bursts a blister on the side of her toe that is so huge it looks like a used condom when it's empty.

The wonderful woman who is the volunteer *hostelero* at Belorado is from Switzerland and her name is Sylvie. Of her own volition Sylvie holds a basic First Aid clinic every day at five o'clock, patching up the feet of the *peregrinos*. She takes a look at mine and shakes her head.

'You'll have to go to the doctor,' she says.

'But Eli will think I'm a wimp.'

'Who's Eli?'

'The girl I'm walking with, the one with no cartilage in her knee and blisters instead of toes.'

'You still have to go to the doctor. Yours are infected.'

She takes me to the local hospital where, as a pilgrim, you are treated free for anything except STDs, pregnancy and drug abuse. So my most pressing problems go untreated. Instead, the doctor looks at my feet and tut-tuts, shaking her head gravely.

'I'm not worried about the blisters,' I tell Sylvie, 'it's just the pain in my Achilles tendon that bothers me.'

The doctor laughs when this is translated.

'But she says that is your Achilles tendon!' Sylvie says, pointing to the hamburger mince on the back of my foot. 'She says you have to stop walking.'

'Forever?'

'Two days. If you want to get to Santiago. Your blisters are infected.'

I tell Eli the good news. She decides to keep walking, as I knew she would. She is taking painkillers and anti-inflammatories for her knee, and she has tendonitis and blisters, as I do, but walking the whole length of the Camino is an article of faith with her now.

Eli: Such is life

While Colin visits the doctor in Belorado, I sit in the street watching a funeral in the church next door. A small assembly of mourners, young and old, all dressed in their Sunday best, gathers outside the church as the coffin is loaded into a hearse. It isn't a sad farewell but, rather, respectful and routine. There are few tears among the crowd, the floral wreath adorning the coffin is plain and understated, and the presence of several generations leads me to the assumption that the deceased is an elderly man whose death was somewhat expected.

Funerals fascinate me. There's something about final goodbyes that inspires such rare sincerity. When I was young, I would read obituaries in the local paper before school and wonder why it was often only after loss that people found it within themselves to openly express their true feelings for each other. By then, it seemed too late.

I've attended funerals, said goodbye to people I have dearly loved. And naturally, I ached, hurt and wept at every one. Often, as much for those left behind as for my own sense of loss or grief.

Five days before I left Australia, a twenty-year-old girl from my home town lost all four members of her family when her parents and two sisters, along with a French exchange student who'd arrived in the country just days before, were killed instantly in a horrific car accident. In a split second, life as she knew it changed forever and without warning her entire family was gone. Days later, she stood in a cathedral packed with thousands and delivered four independent eulogies. One by one, she honoured their lives and said goodbye.

That young woman's courage moved me and many others beyond the scope of the tragedy itself, instilling an awesome respect for the capacity of the human spirit.

Death can be tragic, but life can be beautiful.

Day 12
Leaving Belorado apart

Colin: *Buddha sticks in Belorado*

The next morning I lie in my bunk in the pre-dawn dark listening to my fellow pilgrims schlump out of bed, haul on socks and boots and backpacks, their muted laughter from the kitchen as they throw down a hurried breakfast, and the click of their walking sticks as one by one they head back to the Camino for the day's twenty or thirty or forty kilometres. I lie there like a naughty schoolboy playing truant, pretending to be sick when I'm really not. Surely a little bit of pain never hurt anyone?

The frustration of not being able to walk is overwhelming. Today I should be sweaty, squinting with pain and hauling ass to San Juan de Ortega, not sitting around here reading a book.

This time last year I spent ten days in a hospital in Thailand when my ankle got infected—I was bitten by a Russian countess—and I know the dangers. Sylvie and the doctor are right. But it's like all the times I played sport. If you get injured you always want to be out there playing. I was never a good spectator. But I am hoping a couple of days away from the Camino will give me time to regather and regroup.

Once, a few years back, I shared a Buddha stick—dope laced with LSD—with three other backpackers. Later, after the gear had worked its magic, I remember stepping over a cow in the street and wondering if it was really there. I had this feeling that everyone in India was watching me, talking about me. I would say things and then wonder if what I had said made sense to anyone else.

My life is becoming one big Buddha stick. I am genuinely concerned. Might I be going mad? All my energies are expended now in trying to appear normal. This is not why I came to the Camino. But I admit it is possibly why life drew me here.

I won't give up, for Eli, or for myself. It's not blisters or heat or hills that will stop me. But what scares me is that in the process I will fall apart, from the inside out, without even noticing that it's happening.

Perhaps it already is?

Eli: *Comfort in numbers*

Leaving Belorado without Colin brings mixed feelings. Initially, I was feeling mighty brave about it. But as I step out of the *albergue* into a dark, empty street at 5 am, I might as well be naked.

Venturing tentatively into the unknown with the dim glow of a reading light strapped to my wrist, I take up my own pack along with a lungful of sharp pre-dawn air. It feels much colder than yesterday, the sky looks blacker and my pack seems heavier too. As I trudge down the dark stone street I find myself wishing Colin back to my side, to slap my pack and lead the way into the night. But he isn't. I am alone out here now and until Burgos, in two days' time, this is how it will be.

I clamber up a rocky hill, beckoning a sunrise, see a solitary figure ahead slip into a thick morning mist and fade to black. At least there is someone to hear me scream. Across the valley, a pale building teeters upon a cliff's edge. It looks like a church but could be a monastery or a castle—it's hard to make out in the dark.

It's about now I'd usually ask Colin to check the guide-book, but remember again that I have left them both in Belorado. He's studied that thing like a bible every hour since we left Roncesvalles and told me I'd appreciate it some day. I'm almost glad he's not here to gloat.

Now there is nothing but the arrows to lead me to San Juan de Ortega. Suddenly, I love the arrows.

I continue to wonder about Col. The extent of his injury, the condition of his feet, whether the infection has spread, whether he'll be okay, whether he'll be there waiting for me in Burgos or if I'll have to track him down in a city hospital. What if there is more than one hospital?

He was like an excited schoolboy when delivering the news that he was staying on in Belorado. Maybe the break will be the time away from the Camino that he said he needed. Perhaps he was happy for an excuse to stop so he could work things through.

Personally, the chance to be alone could not have come at a better time. It's not Colin's company, it's just the Camino. It fills every space, corner, crack and crevice of your mind, constantly inundating you with feelings, thoughts, experiences, emotions, sights, sounds, people and a generous dose of pain to boot. Even the numb nothingness of hours alone can be overwhelming. After a while, you feel like a glass of water full to the brim. You need time alone to sort through the relevant and tip out the mundane before you can take in any more.

Already, a kind of filtering process has begun. Perspective shifts, focus changes, things that always seemed important just aren't anymore. These days, it all comes back to the same basic elements: food, water, health and shelter. What I used to refer to as 'the simple things' are now 'the *only* things'.

Nearing the top of the steady climb the mist thickens, limiting visibility to a few metres. The path disappears. It's eerie up here. The air is still, but ironically it's no longer cold. Through the dark a large crucifix suddenly appears upon me like an apparition, towering above the summit of the hill. *I've reached the peak.* It should be downhill from here.

The path winds through a trio of small towns, each with a smattering of cottages made of moss-covered bluestone. On the far side, the mountain goat trail expands into a broad bulldozed stretch of red soil. A pack of twelve young pilgrims covers the width of the trail ahead. It's a rare herd compared to the handful of soloists and couples typically encountered throughout the day. I'm not in the mood for talking so I hang back, keeping them in view. Safety in numbers.

The fog lifts to reveal a hazy day. The sun smoulders on a distant horizon and as the fear slips away, I become aware of other things. First to register is the knee. Until this point the pain was a dull ache, the kind of throbbing sensation you get following a firm massage. But now it's grown to a stabbing twinge that makes my back arch when it grabs every second or third step. I shake my foot about—hokey-pokey style—trying to loosen the joint and prod at the patella hoping to relieve some pressure but it swells further when I stop. As with many things today, I realise this is just the way it's going to be. I can focus on it or focus on something else.

I begin to riffle through memories, hoping to capture a thought—preferably something very painful—to contemplate that might serve as a distraction. But it doesn't work. Nothing from my past seems to hold as much relevance here as it once did.

It's a revelation that I hope is permanent. I'm told I think too much. Overanalyse everything. Find it hard—or near impossible—to let things go. These days, pondering anything I can no longer change feels like wasted energy. I've become far more pragmatic in thought. My only concern is with what lies ahead. My knee, Colin, and getting to Santiago.

Finally, it gets too much and I snap. I don't like it but have no other choice. Scouring the side of the path, I look for a stick. Yes, a pilgrims stick. I've caved. Colin's going to laugh. But if I'm to do this, my stick must have character. Also, I'm over six foot tall so it has to be at least five feet long and strong enough to hold my body weight to ease the pressure on the knee.

Testing a few possibles along the way, I finally find a branch poking through the mud on the side of the trail. It's a long and narrow staff, with a slight twist in the middle and a kink at the bottom end. It doesn't look very impressive on the outside but beneath the dirty bark the wood is bound to be beautiful and new. The twist reminds me of the scoliosis in my spine and the kink near the bottom is in exact proportion to where an unhealed stress fracture from past sporting days still lies in my lower back. Twiggy but strong; I decide it is the perfect companion to accompany me on my journey.

Unfortunately, when I attempt to remove the branch from the mud, I find it is in fact a root, attached to a freshly bulldozed tree. Unperturbed, I drop to my knees and begin digging the sucker out. I've made up my mind, this is my staff, my new buddy, the trusty 2IC that's going to see me through to Santiago. Determined, I yank and heave until, finally, I fall to my backside in the dirt and the stick is mine.

Inspired by my new toy, I overtake the group in front, proudly whittling the rod with the blade of my pocket knife as I pass. There are several sly Spanish remarks and no doubt there will be more to come. God only knows what Col will say when he finds out I got a root on the way to Burgos. But planting the stick on the ground, I realise Olga, the German woman, was right. It does help ease the pressure, and with new-found optimism I push on.

Entering an open field of pasture scattered with plots of high-stemmed maize, I look ahead along the trail and count eighteen fellow turtles lugging homes on their backs. The numbers on the Camino are growing every day. I want to be alone but it appears there's little hope of that today. I play a solitary game of cat and mouse to pass time: pick a pilgrim, catch a pilgrim, pass a pilgrim.

The trail leads on to a busy highway. The Way-marks cross the asphalt onto a narrow bike lane on the opposite side of the road. It's a wonder no one has been hit and killed by a passing car. At the base of a nearby tree there are a bunch of flowers with a scallop shell bound around them. *Someone has been!*

I pass a roadhouse at the edge of the next town. The majority of the crowd have gathered in Villafranca-Montes de Oca for an early lunch. Savouring an opportunity to escape, I fill my empty bottle at a nearby fountain and prepare to get ahead of them. Gathered on the stone wall is another small group, eating.

Something doesn't add up. I ask three pilgrims why so many people have stopped. The two French girls look stunned and point to the boy in the middle. The young boy removes his map from his back pocket and in perfect English tells me that there are no more towns until San Juan.

'How far is that?'

'Fifteen kilometres,' he says. 'Uphill.'

Looking at the terrain index on the map, I see that the mountain before me is a monster, a knife's edge that peaks and then drops on the far side. Straight up and over, through the Montes de Oca forest to San Juan de Ortega. This is it. My first solo challenge.

I call in to a *tienda* to buy food for the road, approach the sheer face of the mountain base, look down at my gammy knee ... *think happy thoughts*, take a deep breath and begin. It's just after 10.30 am. I have fifteen kilometres ahead. That's:

10 kilometres @ 4.5 km/hour = 2.22 hours

+

5 kilometres @ 3.5 km/hour = 1.43 hours

2.22 hours + 1.43 hours + 1 hour for accumulated rest stops along the way = 4.65 hours.

A total of 279 minutes. Therefore, I should arrive at the next town by around 3.09 pm. Give or take.

My high school maths average was C-minus, so by the time I figure that out I'm already through the worst of it.

Colin: Is Jesus a good thing?

The day off allows me to see the life of an *albergue* without pilgrims. Sylvie's husband is the retired director of a large Swiss bank. This morning I watch him sluicing out the bathrooms. Sylvie tells me this is how they are spending their holidays this year.

They are both extraordinarily kind to me. They show me more Christian charity than the nun in Chicken Town. What is it about the Camino that makes bank directors want to come back and voluntarily clean out toilets instead of sipping cocktails in the Caribbean?

Sylvie tries to explain it to me: 'It surprises me because when I do the Way, you know, it is nothing special to me. But then, in the next year, I have—what you call it?—flashbacks, of things I have seen on the Way, but I did not remember because I was so focused inside, on my thoughts, on my feet, you understand? And then every night I keep dreaming of the Way. My husband, too. And so this year we come back.'

I think I know what she means. I am not a religious man, as Mother Mary Goebbels will attest, but already there is something about the Camino I cannot explain. It is not a religious experience, for what has happened so far is that I have been repelled by the imagery here. The crucifixes in Navarran and Castilian churches are neither refined nor subtle: in anatomically precise detail they show the exact musculature and exquisite agony of a beautiful young man being slowly tortured to death.

These Spanish churches are a rich stew of imagery, scents, gods and bishops. Some of the statuary reminds me of the ride I used to go on at the amusement park in Southend when I was a kid: specifically, the ghost train. For example, in many churches you will find, in the gloom under the vaulted arches,

Mary depicted as a life-size kewpie doll in a black mantilla, weeping with a lace handkerchief to her face above a cross-section of a tomb, where Jesus lies in a glass coffin, face twisted from the pain of His death. It is a terrifying image: *Redemption Dogs* by Tarantino.

This is the Christ, the spiritual hero of much of the western world, doing this for us. Martyrdom and suffering are supposed to be the way to a good and holy life. But is Jesus really a good thing? Above anything He said or did, His ultimate legacy to us is sacrifice. Is this really the way to a fully realised life?

I don't want him, whoever He really was, to die for me, as the Catholics say he has. He cannot die for my sins anyway: I have watched my chickens come home to roost, with or without Him, as they surely must with us all if we are to learn anything from our lives. He can't change that.

Sylvie tells me what she has learned from the Camino: 'Everything you need is here, every day there are little gifts. If you think of what you need, you say it and you get it.'

You say it and you get it. Could that be true? Her words echo in my head for days, weeks, afterwards. *You say it and you get it.* Just not in the way you expect, perhaps.

I know what I need right now, though. A decent pair of hiking sandals.

Eli: A stone of my own

The path enters a lush forest. There is a canopy of leafy ferns and beams of light shoot through the greenery forming patterns on my skin. Spiders, bugs and giant slugs cling to the branches. The views are hidden but an occasional glimpse between the trees reveals a stunning panorama of hilltops and valleys. I've stepped off the highway into a tropical wonderland that reminds me of the rainforests of northern Queensland.

At the summit ridge, the landscape flattens out across a forested plain. I stumble upon a giant arrow, two metres in length, made of piled-high pebbles stacked in the middle of the path, a reminder of past pilgrims pointing the way to Santiago. It's encouraging and in keeping with tradition I stop for a moment to lay a stone for the pilgrims behind me.

Walking alone offers a different perspective; alone but never lonely, it's a different kind of freedom. Your own wants, needs, feelings and desires are all that matter. I see myself differently. It also changes the way other people perceive you in return. People I've only seen from afar make the effort to wander up to my side and start conversations. Those who I have spoken to previously open up in different ways.

I meet more people in the next two hours than I have in twelve days.

After hooking along like an athlete in the Olympic walk event, Canada approaches and slows down for a chat. He set out two hours after I did this morning. But there's a reason for his cracking pace. He's hoping to cover more than fifty

kilometres by the end of the day. I tell him he's mad, and
he agrees. Canada's running out of time before he needs to
return to start the school year and looks like having to bus
through some of the way. He's disappointed but his feet
aren't—they're down to their final weeping layers.

I wish him well before stopping for lunch at a clearing.
Squeezing canned tuna and warm cheese into a grain bread
roll, I sit briefly to enjoy the view.

Moving on, I catch up with a group of young German
boys, walking part of the Camino for a school excursion.
They speak fluent English because they are studying the
language intensively at school. The smallest in the group is
a cutie with loads of character. He tells me this section of
the Camino was dreaded in the Middle Ages as it was full
of bandits and wolves. Many pilgrims lost their way in the
forest. San Juan de Ortega was a twelfth-century monk who
constructed the monastery in the heart of the long, formerly
desolate stretch to offer protection and refuge to pilgrims.

I tell him his knowledge is welcome as I have no guidebook and no map. The other boys tease him and offer him
up as my very own personal guide, saying he has a crush and
admitting they've been watching me from a distance all day.

The trinity of church bells of San Juan de Ortega is a
welcome sight through the trees. Outside the attached
albergue lies a long line of backpacks, their owners hovering
outside a bar across the square. A backpack placed at the
door of an *albergue* generally assures its owner a bed inside.
In this case, most beds have already been reserved. The
doors have not even opened and already just three remain.

Sitting under one of only two umbrellas shading more
than a dozen weary pilgrims are Mercedes and Simon.

'*Hola, guapa!*' Mercedes shouts. '*Qué tal, qué tal?*'

'*Hola, chica, bien.*'

Relieved to see familiar faces, we kiss and hug before I join them at the table.

'How's the knee?' Simon asks.

'It's okay. How are you guys?'

'We're trying to decide whether or not to keep going. Will you have to stay?' Simon asks, pointing to my knee.

'Not sure yet. It's too hot to go much further but I think it's best to push on while my leg's still warm. What do you think?'

Just a few minutes sitting down and already fluid begins to flood the joint. Mercedes disappears inside the bar. Shaking his head, Simon drags another chair in front of me, lifting my foot onto it to try to minimise the swelling. Mercedes returns with a bag of ice. Packing it around the injury, she says she'd rather go on as well. She has also developed tendonitis in one of her knees and is keen to continue before she cools down.

Typically, Simon doesn't mind either way. His only concern is Mercedes, though it seems her only concern is my knee.

They're a rare couple, generous, honest and authentic. The kind of people you instantly warm to. The bond between pilgrims is one based on respect. It takes a certain personal quality to set yourself such a challenge and the nature of the people you meet generally reflects some aspect of the humility that the trail demands.

More pilgrims arrive as we talk, reserving the remaining beds, and the decision to stay or move on is made for us.

'*Vamos?*' Simon suggests. And together the three of us set off for Atapuerca.

By 5 pm, I've covered thirty-one kilometres, the longest distance I've walked so far in a single day.

Colin: Belorado—I spent a week there one afternoon

Here's the good news. Television in Spain is every bit as dire as it is everywhere else. I am sitting in a bar in Belorado watching a sitcom about a matrimonial agency. One of the actors is portraying toughness by continually hitting himself on the nose with his thumb.

The barmaid is sitting on a stool behind the bar, with the defeated look of someone who has found out her house has burned down and her car has been stolen. She is picking her nose and channel surfing.

Flick. A woman making love to a chair.

Flick. A woman wearing too much make-up making love to a microphone.

Flick. Spanish MTV, a clone of Enrique Iglesias singing about how much he'd be in love with his girlfriend if he wasn't already in love with his hair.

Flick. A *jai-alai* game, a Spanish version of squash, played in a casino where the spectators shout at each other and the players try to ignore them.

Flick. Back to the matrimonial agency where the truck driver is still punching himself on the nose and arguing with the proprietor for sending his girlfriend on a date with some poor bastard who in the next scene is in a full body cast and being fed through a tube.

A Spanish *bodega* consists of a wall-mounted television, a poker machine, and a row of bottles on glass shelves with every strong liquor known to man, all covered with two inches of dust—and, of course, lying under glass, three *bocadillos* as dry as a dead pharaoh. And always, but always, a man leaning on the bar drinking beer with hair in his ears thick enough to snare a moth.

And a coffee machine.

I spend a week in Belorado one afternoon drinking beer and eating chocolate croissants. A word here about croissants. Treat them like cocaine and blondes: they're so good you should stay away from them, or you'll get addicted and then you're fucked. Eli told me about a friend of hers, a young bloke sculpted out of testosterone and rock-hard protein, a living Adonis with a six-pack as hard as a hessian bag full of potatoes, who came to Spain for a short holiday, got hooked on chocolate croissants and put on twenty kilos in a month. Ended up looking like Homer Simpson. True story.

For some reason a gang of English tourists invade my bar halfway through the afternoon, all talking very loudly in Northern accents and then trying to impress the waitress with their knowledge of Spanish, which is actually negligible. But I can see how English people get the idea that if they shout loud enough at a foreigner and put an 'o' on the end of every other word they might be better understood. Spanish really is like that.

For example, to recharge your phone you *'recargar el móvil'*. Electrician is *electricista*. It's like one of those cheat languages that kids make up. *Información* is information. *Policía* is police. Tourist office is *oficina de turismo*. *Hotel* is hotel. The only difference is the way they pronounce the words and the only reason they all talk like Antonio Banderas is so they can pick up girls on holiday from Walthamstow.

My time in Belorado is well spent getting thoroughly drunk.

I am angry, at myself, at the world. And this hurts, it sits in the pit of my stomach like a cancer and it bleeds. I made myself everything to a woman, thinking she would need me and never ever leave. She thanked me for loving her, and for showing her the way out of the darkness is how I think she put it. Soon she will end it. But why complain? I have been the architect of my own misery. Outrage and disbelief compete. There is no one to blame but myself. I tried to control her, her life and her choices, and I've got what I deserved.

Then there is my wife. I made myself everything to her. She actually did need me, needed me so much that when I left life was not worth living to her anymore. It could be said that my insecurities cost my daughters their mother.

I buy another drink. And another, until the feelings of grief, abandonment and self-loathing go away. At least for tonight.

The next morning I grab my hiking boots, tip the blood out, and ditch them in a dump bin. I thank Sylvie for her kindness and promise to stay in touch, a promise that, as it turns out, I actually keep.

Then I hobble to the bus station and get the morning bus to Burgos to meet Eli. I feel strangely guilty. Somewhere out there in the hills Eli and Ireland and San Sebastian are still walking. I feel like I am letting the team down. Odd.

It takes me forty minutes to ride what has taken her and the rest of the *peregrinos* two days to walk.

Day 13
Atapuerca to Burgos

Eli: *Tonto and the dynamic duo*

A Frenchman sidles up beside me at the dinner table and says he knows of a secret way. A shortcut! My body struggles and my companion waits in a sizeable city with modern comforts.

But there are risks. The secret trail passes through industrial wasteland directly into the central business district of Burgos but the trail is narrow, unmarked and, at times, 'unpleasant'. There's a good chance of getting lost. The traditional route is safer. It's wide, dotted with Way-marks and ambles by a medieval monastery before dumping you on the city's outskirts. Less abrupt, more historically relevant. But there's one very important reason why the secret trail is more appealing than the traditional route. In fact, there are seven; it's seven kilometres shorter. That's one and a half walking hours.

What would you do?

I decide it is a no-brainer. I'm over medieval and sick of being passive and 'pilgrim-like'. My knee is buggered, and I need one night of normality to balance out all of this piety. I want to drink, smoke, yell, swear, dance, eat pizza and shower, goddamn it! Decision made, and knowing I would only have myself to blame should it all go horribly wrong, I say goodbye to Mercedes and Simon later that evening and catch an early night.

The next morning, I strap my knee, bandage my feet, take two aspirin, an anti-inflammatory and one of those fantastic little pink pills Mercedes's uncle prescribed, then set off for Burgos, eager for news of Colin.

Strolling through lush pasture, I see a figure in the distance. It's the Austrian girl who slept in the bunk next to me last night. Colin nicknamed her Forrest Gumpenberger. Unable to deal with the loss of her mother months before, she walked out of her house, gave her brother the keys to the company they'd inherited, and started walking. She walked through the alps of Switzerland, collecting a backpack and other necessities on the way, before picking up the Camino somewhere in France. Unlike the real Forrest Gump, she has no following, no entourage and only her stick for support. She's a stout, stocky girl, with more than twelve hundred kilometres in her legs. With only a couple of hundred in my own, the figure is astounding. More ludicrous than admirable.

She told me last night that she was born in a large city but, since the Camino, has developed a phobia of crowds. She is in no hurry to get to Burgos—she won't even stay there the night. She tells me she will, as always, walk the long way.

Crossing a motorway overpass, I realise I'm close to where the sneaky Frenchman indicated the alternative route would peel away from the main road. It should be up ahead, somewhere on the left. With the Austrian girl still in my sights my conscience begins to play on me and I reconsider my decision. This is, after all, a pilgrimage—I am *supposed* to suffer. Forrest is suffering. Isn't that the point?

On the other side of the bridge, Forrest stops, rises to her toes, prairie-dogging up the path, then checks for witnesses right and left. I duck below the wheat line before watching her dart off into the grassland through an open field, bounding across the paddock like a bunny on the run. Suddenly, I feel much better about my decision. I guess everyone has their price.

As the Frenchman warned, shortly into the detour the industrial wasteland turns vile with the stench of rotting garbage. Rats and crows forage through crap on either side. It never ceases to amaze me what a difference a day can make in Spain. Yesterday I was walking through a lush wonderland painted with brilliant life and colour, today I'm treading a purgatory of suffering and gloom.

The hours drag like no other day. Craving clean air, I pick up the pace and in doing so misjudge a rock and turn my ankle. *Ah—shit!* That hurt. I continue. Three steps later, the same happens again. *Ah—shit. Bugger!* That hurt more.

In the twenty-first century, your biggest fear on the Camino is not wild wolves or sword-wielding bandits, it's serious injury: a broken bone, torn hamstring or slipped disc. The kind of damage that can't be overcome with a day's rest, a pink pill or a bottle of bourbon. This is not one of those injuries, but it has the potential to be. I've struck the same outside bone in my right foot both times. Bones don't bend like backs or knees do.

Conscious of each step I push on, close my eyes for just a second to say a quiet prayer, and BANG! *Ah-bloodymother bugger—shit, shit, shit!* Another rock, the same foot, a stumble, a fall and a nosedive, face first into a wasteland of filth and crap.

Karma, kill me. Surely this is my punishment for taking a shortcut.

Along the bustling water's edge of outer Burgos, I find Forrest Gumpenberger and her good friend Xena, Warrior Princess, sitting on a wall beside the Arlanza River. Xena is from Germany, her real name is Monica and she looks a lot like Steffi Graf only she has darker hair and is twice as big below the waist. She too has been walking a long time.

In her fourth month, her legs are thick and strong like tree trunks.

I am both embarrassed and proud to have found the dynamic duo. The three of us certainly draw our fair share of attention as we walk the remaining distance into the city centre. Forrest is short and squat. Colin originally dubbed her Harry Potter until we realised she wasn't actually a young boy. But Xena is six foot tall, attractive, with long unkempt hair and olive skin. She has a staff—not a stick—that's taller than she is, with tribal carvings etched into the bark and feathers lashed to the tip. She has an intimidating presence for a pilgrim—she has forgotten how to smile—and she stands out even more than Forrest and me among the city daytrippers and suits out for a stroll on their lunch break. Stunned tourists stop and ask if they can take her photograph.

Xena confides that she's not fond of people; she's been travelling alone for too long. The trail has become her life and she likes it just the way it is. To even the score with the happy snappers, Xena has turned her looks into a lucrative little money spinner, charging a euro for each photo they take. By the time we reach the city, she has paid for her accommodation, along with the next three days' worth of meals.

Sitting in a cobbled square waiting for the *albergue* to open, a few familiar faces begin to stumble in. My fellow pilgrims are becoming like extended family now. We didn't choose each other—some you get on well with and others you barely know. You see each other regularly, share good times and tough times, and whether you like it or not, you're brought together and bound by a common connection, greater than each individual. The fact that several become friends as well as comrades is a precious gift.

Simon and Mercedes appear an hour later.

'Hey, you made it. Hab you found Colin?' Mercedes asks.

'No. He's here somewhere in the city. We said we'd meet at the *albergue* but I didn't realise there were two. This one's closer to the church. He'll find me if I wait. He always does.'

'So, you two are . . . you know?'

'No, we're not lovers.'

'Oh, I'm sorry.'

'Don't be. You're not the first to wonder.'

'He is a good-looking man, no?'

'You're not the first to say that either.'

'Hey, can I tell you somethink?'

''course.'

'I been watching him . . .'

'Yeah?'

'And . . . well, I notice he talks to himself.'

'You've noticed?'

'Like, all the time!'

'Yeah, I know.'

'Has he always done that?'

'Not that I know of.'

'Is he . . . okay?'

'Yeah, he'll be fine.' I smile.

She thinks it's funny, as I once did, but I'm not sure whether to be amused or concerned anymore. The truth is, I don't really know if Col is okay or not. He won't say. I know he's in more trouble than he's willing to admit.

We had talked about how challenging this would be for me. But neither of us expected how challenging it would be for him. I assumed he would be the backbone of the team. He assured me prior to our decision that he was fit and he would make sure we both made it to Santiago. He would be the rock that willed me on. But watching him wrestle with the ghosts that have sprung up in his path is even harder knowing I brought us both here.

Physical pain is one thing, but guilt is something else.

Colin: The good news and the bad news

Whenever Eli and I are separated, we never worry. I know I will always find her and she will always find me. It's like telepathy. Partly because I've got to know her pretty well already and I can predict her moves. But it is also something else, harder to explain.

Finding me isn't so difficult—she just goes around checking all the bars—but still, that we can find each other at all, even in a moderate-sized city within half an hour of looking, is remarkable.

We had arranged to meet in the *albergue* at Burgos. So when she is not there by three in the afternoon, I decide she is either dead or there is another *albergue* that's not in the guidebook. I walk into the city and find Clark Kent sprawled on his back outside the cathedral, presumably dead. His diminishing pack lies on the cobbles, but it's still as big as a refrigerator and twice as heavy. He is mumbling something about Lois Lane sucking his toes. When I rouse him he tells me he saw Eli the day before further up the track and that her knee had seized up and she is probably feeding the crows by now. Hope the crows have some other roadkill lined up, or they're going to need a snack before supper.

So that's it then. It's all over. Privately I think she's done well to get this far. Perhaps she has bussed the rest of the way here. I know I'll find her, there has to be another *albergue*. Eli's here somewhere. I can feel it.

I head on through the gates of the old town and down the cobbled main street and there she is, with Simon and

Mercedes, sitting on her cute little bottom as usual, drinking coffee and eating snacks. Outside an *albergue* that's not in the guidebook.

She flaps a languid hand in my direction. 'Hey, here he is! 'bout time you showed up!' You gotta love her.

Her knee has swollen to the size of a soccer ball. Simon and Mercedes have found ice and her leg is elevated on a chair. I think it's all over. I think wrong.

'How you going, Crusty Man?' she shouts cheerily. 'Ready to get walking again?'

After Superman's dire reports on her health, I'm pleased she's all right. I won't have to make that phone call after all: 'Mrs Best? I have some good news and some bad news. The good news? I have found a new pair of walking sandals in Burgos and they feel just great! What's that? The bad news? It's about your daughter. Were you very fond of her . . . ?'

And here's the thing. I have, in truth, become very fond of her, which is hard to explain because half the time we seem to piss each other off. The other half I love her to death. I wonder which way it's going to end. Because, you see, she doesn't really know me yet.

What can I tell you about Burgos? A good travel writer will describe the magnificent Gothic cathedral, the burial place of the eleventh-century El Cid, who some of you might remember better as Charlton Heston. Theroux might mention that Burgos has more ecclesiastical monuments than any other city in Spain, including the royal monastery, Monasterio de las Huelgas, and the Carthusian monastery of Miraflores with its alabaster mausoleum containing the bones of King John II and his wife Isabel. Bruce Chatwin might mention that Burgos was the headquarters of Franco's rebel Nationalist government during the Spanish Civil War.

All I can tell you is that Eli and I got wasted catching up in the *bodegas* and I bought a pair of sandals. I never thought it would happen, walking in sandals and socks. Until now I have always associated socks and sandals with sixty-year-old English blokes on the beach at Hastings or Brighton or Blackpool in some budget British comedy. But on the Camino, socks and sandals are more than a fashion statement: they mean you're serious. Not beach sandals, these are special hiking sandals, worn with very expensive anti-blister socks.

Next day, setting out from Burgos in my hi-tech $150 Chiruca hiking sandals, I feel like I am walking on rose petals. My feet are no longer my Achilles heel.

I have other Achilles heels, of course, but the Chirucas aren't going to fix those quite so easily.

Day 14
Burgos to Castrojeriz

Eli: *Tread carefully*

The team is back together again, fitter, stronger and far more fashionable than before. Colin's defence against blisters is a brand-new, state-of-the-art, ultralight pair of Jesus sandals—with socks! They keep me amused for the first hour of the day. They're fantastic!

After two days' rest, he's out of the gates like a racehorse. I'm not. Physically, I'm still not doing well.

An hour later, the sun is up, the wind is warm, the surrounding land consists of vacant fields of recently cropped wheat and there is nothing ahead but a burnt horizon. We have arrived in the Meseta.

The Meseta is a high band of featureless land, a plateau spanning the length of the country, north to south. It's two hundred kilometres across, and roughly stretches between Burgos and León. Due to the harsh conditions and flat terrain, the region is predominantly used for growing wheat and little else. The surrounding towns are few and far between, and are typically small, poor, working-class villages with limited facilities, if any at all.

We've been warned of the Meseta. Urban myths about its strange nature are rampant; stories of people entering sane and coming out crackers. Or venturing in and never being seen again. Many pilgrims choose to bus through and there's good reason to be concerned: Colin tells me this is where Shirley MacLaine lost the last of her marbles. He comforts me with the assurance that she had a head start on both of us. We'll be fine.

By afternoon, the punishing heat, shadeless land and uninviting vistas are taking their toll and our patience is wearing thin. This is the first day of this seven-day stretch and already it's become apparent that the key to keeping the peace will be silence.

Colin: *Cereal killer*

Today, for the first time since we started, it doesn't hurt to walk. These sandals have changed my life. They are the Anthony Robbins of footwear. And I have finally figured out how to work the straps on my pack so the ten kilos are sitting on my hips instead of my shoulders. I am walking without pain, as wild and crazy an idea as this seemed when we started.

Which is good. Because we are about to walk across the pilgrims' wild west, the notorious Meseta, a bleak wheat-infested tableland that occupies forty per cent of the country and most of Castilla y León. We follow a trail through a green valley, where sugar beet wilts in the sun. Then we reach a crest and from the brow of the hill we see an endless panorama of . . .

Wheat. Lots of it. Wheat. Wheat. More wheat. We have hardly taken a few strides into the Meseta and I am sick to death of wheat.

I soon realise that the Meseta is in itself like a meditation. Left with a flat horizon, silence and nothing to do but walk in the wheat-heat, I discover that my thoughts are endlessly repetitive and probably futile. If we are what we think, what does that make me?

'What are we doing here?' I ask Eli, and I can see she is not sure anymore either. But she is owned by the physical challenge of doing this: her knee wobbles and swells, a haematoma is growing on the back of her calf muscle like that thing that crawled out of John Hurt's stomach in *Alien*, and she has tendonitis in both feet, but still the damned girl keeps walking, except when she stops to pee, which is every seven minutes and forty-three seconds by my watch.

She is also having trouble with her nose and I feel I should share this with you as she is probably too shy. The heat has given Eli nosebleeds. It's close to forty degrees. She takes to walking with toilet paper stuffed up each nostril. It is a touching and poignant sight, and not at all confronting, though a Spaniard in a beret outside Castrojeriz saw her and fell off his bike, terrified. Some people just scare easily.

Her eyesight is something else.

'Look at that great castle,' she says, pointing to a hay bale on the crest of a hill.

'Look at that amazing monastery,' she says a few minutes later, pointing to a pig farm.

I hate to disillusion her sometimes. Okay, so what if the things she sees aren't really there? Does it matter? If she sees castles and monasteries and enjoys them, who cares? Her world is far more interesting than the real one.

My mind then leaps to another perspective: if the things we see are better than what is really there, are we wrong to cure crazy people? I'm sure their world is saner than my world, which is just full of fucking wheat. I am ready to murder someone if they piss me off. Will that make me a cereal killer? Or just as gluten intolerant as you can possibly get?

Eli: Hotfooting into Castrojeriz

Nineteen kilometres on, in Hontanas, Colin is set to explode and I am willing him to. Anything to stem the boredom.

We stagger into a bar. The cold hits my skin like a bucket of iced water. Colin orders a Coke and sits down. He has passed on a beer. It's worse than I thought!

I order a Coke Light and the woman behind the bar cracks a joke about my height to a guy stuck to a stool at the end of a bar. *Muy, muy* . . . something or other, she gestures with her hands.

The Spanish population is not a tall race of people. Vertically challenged, let's say. But Hontanas must be a town of particularly little people. Before handing across my change the woman calls her three children from the residence in the back. They come running out to marvel at the Fifty Foot Woman.

Soon, the lady's sister arrives at the bar and she too joins in. Better still, she's noticed my feet. Admittedly, my feet are uniquely large for a woman of my build. With cumbersome size twelve (men's) hiking boots strapped to the end of spaghetti legs, my feet look as large as a pair of oversized clown shoes.

It's fun for all but the fuss irks Crusty even more. He's over walking, and he's obviously over me for dragging him here. Today he blames me for the Camino but I'm surprised it's taken him this long. We move on.

Entering Castrojeriz, the skin on our arms and necks is burnt red from the ruthless heat. But the sun isn't the worst of it. The last ten kilometres we spend walking on asphalt so hot it's like a frypan radiating heat beneath our feet. My socks feel as though they've been dowsed in kerosene and set alight. It is by far the hottest, driest, hardest day we've walked. And the only day of the Camino that I actually stop mid stride and can't go on.

All I remember about the ancient town is that Col found me slumped on my side against a shadowed wall in a narrow cobbled street, and carried both my pack and me back to the *albergue*.

All I think about now when I recall that day is that was the day my left foot wore straight through all three layers of fabric and sponge padding on the back of my size twelve boot, fusing my sock to the plastic heel cup.

I lift the sock and my boot comes with it. Don't tell me I, too, need Jesus sandals!

Colin: *Suffocating in silence*

The *albergue* is cool and dark, an old stone building in a dry garden with a single gnarled olive tree. We both collapse on our bunks in the cell-like dormitory, to wonder privately what the hell we are doing here. We sleep.

It is evening when we wake up. The light has softened and swallows swoop and dive around the Romanesque bell-towers of the church and the harsh and unforgiving town looks friendlier, more like a picture postcard and less like a vision of hell. The yellow light from the *bodega* spills onto the cobbled square. A cool wind ushers the heat from the plaza.

The old people line up like bowling pins on a low wall next to the children's playground. The women are all in black with stockings as thick as hessian bags. The old men, their faces brown and gnarled as saddlebags, clutch walking sticks in arthritic fingers. They come here every sunset, waiting for the Grim Reaper to send one of them a curve ball they can't dodge. Twenty old people lined up on a wall. If One Grim Reaper should accidentally call . . .

I watch them, silhouetted against the yellow haze of the Meseta on the plains below the town. It is like a tableau of the cycle of life. Children laughing on swings, their grandparents looking on, wistful and proud. And there, in the distance, with the red dipping of the sun, is tomorrow. There is something poignant about the village square in Mediterranean life. The people are old but they are not lonely, not shut away at home. They see each other, perhaps as they have since schooldays, when their grandmothers and grandfathers watched them as they played in this same dusty plaza.

As I ponder them, in their companionable silence, I am hit by a wave of loneliness so intense, I almost double over as if kicked in the balls. This fucking pain is too much. What the fuck is going on? The ache sits here, right under the solar plexus, a furball of black regret and bewilderment. How could she say things like that to me and not mean it?

I have come to hate being me, out here in this barrel vault of haze and blistered sky, but I have nothing to do here except sit with myself. There is nowhere among all this wheat stubble to hide.

I am stalked by a dead wife and a lover who has tortured me with love passionately bestowed and then snatched away. I am furious and frustrated by my own helplessness in the face of it.

I didn't expect to discover that here. This walk was supposed to be a way to ease the ache, and help get Eli where she knows she needs to go, to fulfil her destiny. How do I play the role she expects of me in this splintered state? I am lost for words, mute with feelings I do not understand and so cannot explain. I can't trust what might come out of my mouth if I try.

Day 15
Castrojeriz to Frómista

Colin: *Post-Meseta tension*

Tomorrow starts for us with the low and slow murmurings of a Gregorian chant. Upstairs, the monk who runs our *refugio* has prepared *café con leche* and dry biscuits. We gobble them down and set off into the dawn.

A little German man with a pot belly and a bristled grey moustache whom we have christened Bavaria sets off ahead in his leather shorts and trident, strudel-thickened bum wobbling like a jelly on springs.

Ahead is an almost vertical climb up the cliffs where we watched the sun dip the previous night. It is like a shot of espresso: Eli and I walk it step by step, nonstop, to the very top, hearts thumping in our chests like balls being kicked around a gymnasium. We are at our best with each other here, urging each other on, even with our lungs burning and our thigh muscles screaming at us to stop.

The limestone path tracks through more . . . I don't know if I can bring myself to write the word again. Let's call it grain. And past a monastery that is now an *albergue* where the pilgrims are only just out of bed at 10.30 in the morning. They all have hangovers. No Gregorian chants for them. At this monastery they get wasted and sleep half the day: if only we'd walked another five kilometres we, too, could have woken up with hangovers and felt normal again.

More fields of . . . cereal . . . and then we follow a straight path through more fields full of the W-word for seven hours in the sun and I am hot and tired and hungry and Eli says something innocuous and this is my excuse to blame my mood, the heat, my feet, the wheat, my marriage, my affair and the state of world peace on her.

We hiss insults at each other and frighten a couple of ducks sitting in an irrigation ditch. By mid afternoon we can barely manage a civil word.

We have been walking for two weeks and Santiago is getting further away all the time.

Eli: *Beep beep*

Colin has the unique ability to both offend and befriend people while somehow remaining oblivious to it all. You have to know him to understand. He's complex in thought but simple by nature. Honest, genuine and direct. It's priceless to watch him and, for the most part, the result of his behaviour is completely unintentional.

Spotting three new pilgrims on a quiet and tranquil stretch of isolated trail, I prepare for the usual exchanges. This path attracts such a diverse mix of cultures. *Hola* and *Buen Camino* are the Camino's cross-cultural catchcries. Colin, however, refuses to attempt Spanish, preferring to maintain his direct approach with people despite our surroundings. We walk into bars and I go thirsty for ten minutes trying to work out the exact pronunciation of an order, while Colin yells, 'Beer thanks, mate, cheers,' toward the Spanish barman and takes a seat. He's on his third by the time I sit down. The barmen in this region don't understand English; there must just be a universal bond when it comes to men and beer. A secret language communicated with a wink and a nod.

As we approach from behind, the three new pilgrims don't hear us coming. Two steps back and *holas* at the ready, Colin beats me to it.

'BEEP-BEEP!'

The group jump, startled, and scatter as Colin marches straight through the pack. 'G'day, mate. How ya goin? Hot as a bastard, hey?'

No reply.

Instantly, the three scowl daggers at us from behind, and are left holding their hearts as we continue up the trail.

'Col, they hate us!'

'Hmm . . . what?' He starts to whistle a tune.

But as offensive as he can be, there's something endearing about the guy that reels you back in, time and time again. Sure enough, by 10.30 am he's won the group over and the three are laughing and drinking *vino* with us down the road, in the raucous monastery-cum-*albergue* St Nicholas. It turns out they are American. Crusty assures me that it's okay to be rude to Yanks: 'They're used to it!'

He's a proud ambassador for our country.

I vowed before I came away that I would not complain. Not a word, not once. This would be part of my challenge that no one else need know. On the outside, I'm winning. Inside, however, there's a storm brewing that's getting harder and harder to contain. Yesterday, while pacing uphill through a desolate stretch of rural desert toward the high plains of Hontanas, I snapped. I needed an answer, right then and there, an inkling, an insight, a purpose, a goal, something, *anything*, that would justify my presence here, inspire my next step or, at the very least, make it all seem less meaningless.

Hours and hours of dead wheat and heat and absolutely nothing to look forward to but hours and hours of more dead wheat and heat and wheat to come. What the hell was I doing? Would any of this even matter, to me or to anyone else? Would it make me a better mother some day? Did anyone really care what happened to me out here, in a wheat field in the middle of a foreign country, with a guy I fear may be slowly losing his mind? Hadn't my body been through enough? What was the point? I wondered what others had found on this path beneath the stars. Was there really something out here for me?

Suddenly I stopped, threw my head back and screamed toward a stark sky, '*WHERE'S MY STUUUUUFF?*'

Poor Col stopped dead in his tracks as if he'd been shot.

The Camino so far—the pilgrimage, the entire experience—has been nothing like I expected it would be. I expected to find distance, space, clarity and perspective. Peaceful thoughts, quiet contemplations, answers, insights and understanding. Future solutions among beautiful surroundings. But I look around and there is little beauty here. Camino commercialisation has raped what little there ever was. A once-sacred land has been brutalised by a five-metre-wide path torn through fields by modern machinery. The rubble remains piled high on either side. I know because I have to scramble up and over it every time I need to pee.

The elements are harsh, dry, lifeless and unsympathetic. The land is yellow. So very yellow. Through the lens of my sunglasses, it appears a varying spectrum of beige. Slightly more interesting but still, shades of yellow nonetheless. Can I not just have one glimpse of blue or green or something, to give me hope?

Colin: Walk softly and carry a big stick

Sit in a sauna. Close your eyes. Imagine wheat fields going on forever. In the distance is a church spire and a clump of houses. Behind you is another church spire and more little houses that look just the same. Have someone stamp on your feet until they're bruised and bleeding. Now you know what it's like to walk the Spanish Meseta.

Eli and I have an uneasy truce. She is a woman, a witness to the most vulnerable and shameful moment of my life, and she wants me around for all those reasons that I have manipulated before so many times in my life and come to regret so bitterly right now. I could kill her.

And yet I love her, her spirit, her determination, her unquenchable fire. Now she has walked two days without me, I am puzzled why she ever wanted me along at all.

'What do you think of guns?' Eli asks me.

'Don't like them. Always afraid they'll go off. Shot a rabbit once.'

'In a field?'

'No. It was in a cage in a pet shop. Couldn't miss, really. White fluffy thing.'

'I shot my aunt once.'

'Again?'

'I shot my aunt with a high-powered air rifle.'

'You shot her? Where?'

'At the back of our house.'

'I meant where in the body did you shoot her?'

'In the arse.'

'Why?'

'She was pissing me off. So I jammed a spit ball in the barrel and shot her while she was six feet up a ladder.'

'Jesus.'

'It left this awesome bruise like a big blue spider. She had to dig the spit ball out with tweezers. She wanted to kill me. Chased me down the street.'

'Remind me not to piss you off.'

'Too late. Lucky I don't have my rifle.'

I think she is just joking, but her crooked smile as she strides ahead tells me she is not joking at all.

The silences between us stretch. Finally, we stop talking altogether.

The towns on the Meseta have a sameness to them. There is always a plaza, and the plaza always has a church and a *rollo*, a pillar where they used to hang criminals. And there is always a *bodega*, or bar. Even the smallest crap-and-tractor town has at least three *bodegas* where the locals drink bulls-blood-coloured rocket fuel called *rioja*.

There is no more depressing experience on Earth than arriving in one of these towns in the middle of summer in the middle of the afternoon in the middle of a heat wave in the middle of the siesta.

Welcome to Frómista.

Eli: Riding the wave across Spain

It is all over the news: a heat wave in Spain. Weather warnings are posted in all the papers and, ever so slowly, Colin and I are edging our way across one of the country's hottest regions.

Nine hours after leaving Castrojeriz, we arrive in Frómista. We've not spoken since crossing the bridge after St Nicholas, the official entrance to the province of Palencia.

I'm excited about the ancient bridge. Not because of its historical relevance or the spectacular battles it has witnessed over hundreds of years, but because the province of Palencia borders the province of Castilla y León. The capital of Castilla y León is the city of León. The city of León rests at the foot of the Cantabrian mountains. On the other side of the Cantabrian mountains lies the province of Galicia. And at the end of Galicia sits Santiago. Believe it or not, I am genuinely ecstatic!

Col does not share my enthusiasm. He's still wishing he'd stayed at St Nicholas, the monastery where everyone gets pissed at breakfast and parties all night. I told him I didn't mind if he did. But he is caught between needing to be there, wanting to be alone and needing to be here with me. Though at this point, I'm wondering why. Perhaps, despite the circumstances, he is scared to leave another woman for fear she might break? Maybe I should've made it easier for him and insisted he stay. It may have been just what he needed. He's been particularly edgy since we left Burgos and his moods are becoming harder to deal with. I don't know how to treat him anymore. Being passive about it isn't working for either of us.

Until we separated in Belorado, Colin and I had made a good team. When one struggled the other would step in. Usually it was me struggling and Colin's company was a source of humour and assurance. But since then, we've both been fighting separate battles. I want to help, I want to do more, but the silence is killing me. We're like a pair of wounded dogs. One wrong move and somebody could lose a limb.

He talks a lot about religion lately. I've seen him walk into every church we've passed, stop at every chapel or roadside shrine, as if searching for a symbol or an image to exemplify his faith. Perhaps he thinks it will mean more if he can see it.

If the churches are open, he slips inside only to return more disappointed than before. I wonder what he expects from them, from the concept of a God or from ordered religion. What will it take for him to find peace? And why don't I feel compelled to enter any? Does that make me shallow or content?

In Logroño Colin asked where my faith comes from. And what inspires me to keep walking. I told him I've approached each mountain or hill we've climbed one step at a time. To stand at the bottom and look up to the top would mean certain failure. I'd talk myself out of it before I even got halfway. So instead, I pull the peak of my cap down over my eyes so I can only see each step ahead. And I draw inspiration from those in my life I've admired, stepping out the traits they had, qualities I hope to one day hold. Strength, courage, compassion, patience, persistence, love, loyalty, grace, honour and pride. This, to me, is a facet of faith. Believing in something greater than yourself that inspires you to do better.

Faith is never right or wrong. It is unique to each individual. And my own faith is broad, undefined. Like many, I believe in a universal force, a light, something stronger and far more powerful than myself, a source greater than this world. But I don't presume to know where it comes from or whether I am even capable of defining it. I have no name for my God. No title, label or official laws by which to abide. Just my own personal and very mortal moral values.

It's a far cry from my Roman Catholic upbringing; I was raised by a practising Catholic family, attended Catholic schools, but left the church behind long ago when I realised that according to the commandments, most of the people I loved wouldn't be accepted into the heaven I was taught to aspire to. They weren't bad people, they just weren't staunch Catholics. When I was seven, my second grade teacher told me they didn't drink beer in heaven either, so I decided then that even if they could get in, half my family wouldn't go.

Eventually I found that the church that told me not to judge was too judgmental for my rebellious teenaged liking. Either it was wrong, or everything I believed was. I couldn't change the Catholic Church but I could change myself and what I chose to stand for, so I did.

I spent years feeling guilty about religion, both in the church and away from it. Until one day, kneeling in the sand at Abu Simbel in Egypt, something inside me shifted. In the shadow of the massive 3500-year-old masterpiece and running a handful of desert sand through my fingers, I realised I was but a single grain in the entire desert around me; and that that desert was merely one among scores on Earth; and that the Earth was just one of hundreds of billions of planets in our universe. And so on. The world I was in was infinite. I had never felt so insignificant, and yet so profoundly inspired. For I knew then that although my life was essentially meaningless—a single grain of sand—it still meant a lot to a handful of other grains.

They say you can't change the world, but the truth is, you affect a number of lives within it just by being here. Suddenly religion didn't matter as much as faith did. And in letting go of one, the other grew. I don't question my faith anymore, I question myself. Faith is the only thing I'm ever sure of.

I don't know what a man does without it but it's something so personal, only Col can work that out for himself.

Naturally, I wish there were more I could do for him. Silence doesn't usually bother me but with Colin, it's excruciating. Hours of nothing interspersed with the occasional spat of self-chatter or a brooding sigh that can be heard from ten paces away—*Suck-HUUUUFF*—in and out, like sneezing dust from the lungs or, rather, clearing shadows from the depths of the soul.

I want to tell him to stop beating himself up but I'm afraid it'll set him off. Perhaps what I have to offer isn't what he needs. One thing is for sure, he needs to take this out on someone. I'm here, and whether it has anything to do with me or not is irrelevant. I'm the obvious target; it's a matter of time.

Suck—HUFFFFFFF!

'You right, mate?'

'Hmm . . . what? Yeah.'

Fine. Maybe I'm just being sensitive.

In Frómista, Colin finds the nearest bar while I find a bed. It's not a pretty town and my foot is in bad shape. It's not the blisters so much anymore, it's the bone in my right foot, thanks to the walk into Burgos. I'd not mentioned it until an hour out of town. It is slowing us down and that's frustrating Colin.

After dinner, four beers and a bottle of wine, Col finds me to ask about my foot, reminding me again of his twelve years' experience in the volunteer ambulance service in his home town of Perth. I lie back on the bed and lift up my leg to show him. He examines it, poking and prodding at the clump of swelling below the ankle. I grit my teeth and wonder why the first thing anyone does when examining an injury is poke it.

'Does this hurt?'

'Yes.'

'How much?'

'I could scream but I'd rather you take my word for it.'

By this stage, an interested young Russian cyclist has wandered over to watch. He sees the blisters and bruises and cringes.

'Just from walking?'

'Yes, just from walking.'

'Crazy!'

'Yes, crazy.'

Col informs me that he thinks the injury is serious.

'How serious?'

'Well,' he pauses, 'it's pitting.'

'What's pitting?' I scoff, amused by the term.

He removes his finger from the puffy mound leaving a perfect half-inch divot embedded in the side of my foot.

I heave with laughter. 'That's fantastic!'

The poor Russian boy just heaves, running for the door holding his stomach.

I take Colin's advice and agree to go to the medical infirmary in the next town, Carrión de los Condes, to get it checked. The divot is still there when the Russian boy returns with two friends who've come to see for themselves.

I can't blame them. It is hideous. But the smiley faces Col and I mould into it with our fingers are very funny.

They take photos.

Colin: The Tour de Santiago

Next morning the plaza is a kaleidoscope of colour: not birds or flowers, but cyclists in lycra. They pour out of the *albergue* in high spirits, as well they should; they have a support vehicle. All this particular band of happy pilgrims have to do is put gel in their hair, adjust their Raybans and look good. What's in the support vehicle? Spare bottles of hair conditioner, a blonde masseuse, a spa bath and all their luggage.

On the Meseta there is a continuous procession of cyclists; it has become the Tour de Santiago. There is something distinctly non-spiritual in this, it seems to me. These bastards just aren't suffering enough. They are outside the spirit of it.

I'm sure that in 1423 when St Peter the Po-faced passed this way, he didn't make his pilgrimage in a pair of red, blue, green and purple lycra leotards. But in 2004 no one cares. When they arrive in Santiago they will still get a certificate giving them remission of sins—the famed Compostela. There's something not quite right here.

Everyone tells me that I'm sure to go to heaven for doing this walk (they don't know about me and the nun), but if this is true I plan to use my new-found influence to right many of the wrongs of this world. One of these wrongs concerns pilgrims on ten-speed titanium mountain bikes. So when I'm sitting up there on God's right hand and a sweaty biker in crotch-hugging lycra stands before God's Holy Throne in his fingerless black gloves and holding his pilgrims passport, I'm going to lean over and whisper softly in His ear and God's going to take my advice and tell the Lance Armstrong wannabe to take his aerodynamically designed helmet and his fluoro-pink water bottle and fuck off.

Day 16
Frómista to Carrión de los Condes

Colin: *Buen Camino, you thieving bastards!*

There are two sounds distinctive to my memory of the Camino: one is the rhythmic *click-click-click* of a walking stick clipping on the cobblestones of a village street or a stone path as another pilgrim passes. Sooner or later every *peregrino*, of every age, finds themselves a walking stick. When you're heading down a steep hill with ten kilos on your back they are no longer a pose but a very practical accessory.

The other sound is a shouted *Buen Camino!* As the cyclists go past they shout *Buen Camino!* When another pilgrim sets off from the *albergue* everyone shouts *Buen Camino!*

Bon voyage. Safe trip. Have a good Way today, hey?

Leaving Frómista next morning we shout *Buen Camino!* to the usual suspects as well as others we will never see again; like Bill Candy, a Spaniard we think is from Barcelona, or who may be Barcelona itself. He is massive. A suburb on the move, at least. He looks as if he has a beanbag stuffed up his T-shirt. His wife helps him haul arse, sometimes literally, up the hills. He is the sort of man you cannot imagine walking

179

further than the kitchen to fetch another bag of Doritos. But like every good Catholic he has come this year to make a pilgrimage to St James and reserve his seat—and two other people's—in heaven. He only walks ten kilometres a day, on his doctor's advice.

On the other end of the fitness scale is Heidelberg, strong and blond, Hitler's Aryan dream, except he has a great sense of humour. He walks forty kilometres every day, blitzkriegs it. He has a smile and a nod for everyone. Except the French. We have noticed that the French keep pretty much to themselves on the Camino. Hard to thaw. I talked about this with Heidelberg the night before. 'Those bastards!' he scowled. 'If you can't speak French they don't want to know you. They think they're the speciality of Europe!'

The speciality of Europe.

He says this is why Germany keeps invading them. It has nothing to do with the Treaty of Versailles or *Lebensraum*, or any of the stuff my history teacher told me in school. Living next to these arrogant bastards, he says, is too much for anyone. In the end you just want to invade them to piss them off.

Buen Camino! Heidelberg shouts as he heads across the courtyard, smiling and waving at everyone as he leaves. Then he sees two French guys and gives them the bird.

A united Europe? One day. But not yet.

Austria—Forrest Gumpenberger—is last to leave and she is distraught. This morning she is not grieving for her mother but for her walking stick. It has been with her since Linz and this morning it disappeared. Someone has stolen it. *A pilgrim, looking for redemption from St James, has stolen another pilgrim's walking stick.* I find it hard to get my head around that one.

Already the atmosphere on the Camino has changed. Until now fellow *peregrinos* have been going out and leaving their mobile phones on charge, as pilgrims have been doing throughout the centuries; yesterday two went missing. The level of trust among pilgrims has been remarkable until now. The theft casts a pall on the day. Something more has been lost than Forrest's walking stick.

We pass a village with fall-down adobe cottages side by side newly built square houses that look like they were scooped up from a housing estate in Milton Keynes. They are built from ginger-coloured brick and all have window boxes with bright petunias. But there are no shops. A man comes around honking his horn, selling vegetables, washing powder and bread out of the back of his van. Meals on wheels.

In a dark *bodega* off the plaza the old men sit with their shots of black coffee staring at a TV above the bar where a primped Barbie doll in Madrid tells them the football scores.

Outside the village are other *bodegas*, caves cut into the hillsides with arched doorways and little air vents that stick out of the ground so that it looks from a distance like a Disney village of munchkins. This is where wine is made and stored. It would not be possible to live on the Meseta without alcohol.

Or soft drinks, apparently. There are bright blue Pepsi machines in the humblest of villages. They are built into the sides of thousand-year-old walls, chained like guard dogs in the middle of every deserted plaza. Another five years and my best guess is the Way will have a McCamino and a Starbucks Peregrino.

My feet are healing. It is fascinating to take the dressings off every night and watch my foot mend, see the little peninsulas of flesh pushing back into a lake of raw meat and start to join up again. The body is an amazing thing.

Eli's body is an amazing thing also. It keeps insisting she cannot do this and she keeps insisting it is wrong. Her knee looks like a bright red water balloon filled to near bursting. She has tendonitis, blisters and the haematoma on the back of her calf has turned black.

Finishing the Camino, getting to Santiago, means far more to her than to me; it seems to me that it means more to her than it does to even the most devout Catholic. I am in awe of this without fully understanding it. I really want her to get there now. In some strange way it will make it all seem worthwhile.

Eli: *Forget frosty Frómista*

Thankfully, the distance from Frómista to Carrión de los Condes is only twenty-three kilometres. That's twenty-two and a half kilometres longer than Colin's temper today. One look at his face this morning tells me we're in for another tough day. The harder this gets for him, the more he tries to hide it. But he was talking in his sleep again last night. It's becoming normal now.

All over Spain there are festivals, in every town, every city. (When the Spaniards say 'festival', they mean a chance to blame their hangovers on a saint.) Today is 25 July, the feast of Santiago. The shops are shut and the bars are open, full of men drinking *caraquillos*, coffee laced with a shot of very strong local brandy. The young are much more sensible about their drinking: they don't drink before noon, even on feast days, and when they do, it's just moderate amounts of *calimochos*, a cocktail of Coca-Cola and red wine, usually drunk out of a plastic glass the size of a saucepan, and never a drop more than twenty or thirty in a session.

We enter the wreckage of a village called Población de Campos. The whole *población* of Población de Campos is pissed. The streets are peppered thick with broken glass and plastic cups. There is nothing like a festival honouring a great saint for an excuse to go out and stay out. A dozen or so sixteen year olds stumble from a *bodega*. It is 7.30 in the morning and they have been there all night. It reminds me how far removed we are from the real world. Only a few weeks ago, saying good-bye to friends, I was one of them, stumbling home in daylight. Now I'm a worn smelly traveller in a strange land, smelling of cheese and carrying a big stick. How things change.

We stop in for breakfast and coffee. The pack of pasty-faced teenagers try to pour *calimocho* into us. At daybreak, they are still drunk and still drinking.

So is their mother, who's attempting to run the bar. It's a comedy of errors. Colin and I are sober and obviously not from round here so we become their novelty playthings. They reek and are as friendly as wet dogs. The boys gasp as we tell them we are from Australia. They cannot comprehend why we have come such a long way to walk across their country.

What can I say? It seemed like a good idea at the time.

They look at Colin and me the same way we looked at the bull-runners in the San Fermin news footage. That's twice I've been called crazy in less than twelve hours. And strangely, I feel an odd sense of pride about it.

Wheat plays somewhat of a cameo role today. So far, the morning has been spent on a quartz stone walking track running parallel to the roadside, which winds in and out of the odd town and village along the way. It's a pleasant change and seems to set the theme for the remainder of the day. Until we reach Revenga de Campos. Call me superstitious, but the name scares me.

Sure enough, the change of scenery was merely a bluff and before long, 'Return of the Fields' has earned its reputation and we are back among wheat. Yay!

Never is the tension between Colin and me more fierce than it is in the middle of a wheat field. The aspirin I'd taken with breakfast wore away early so I have the pleasure of pain to keep me occupied. His silence doesn't bother me as much as it did yesterday. Each step is growing more unbearable. To help matters, I'm still walking with a hole in the back of my boot and as the morning wears on, the sharp stab in my foot intensifies. It is obvious it is only going to get worse from here.

I tell Col a joke to take my mind off things as he studies his beloved guidebook. His feet are healing well and his new sandals have helped the tendonitis. He tells me he feels fantastic, great, strong as an ox, brilliant, but doesn't want to rub it in. For a brief moment we trade jokes. A splash of colourful humour to offset the bland wash of wheat. But pretty soon, the laughter subsides and silence returns.

Don't ask. Please, don't ask. Not today.

'What are we doing here, El?'

Cruel bastard! Without saying a word, I shoot Colin a threatening glare and shake my head. He knows as well as I do that I have no idea. What he doesn't know is how guilty and genuinely sorry I am about it. If only I had known. It's a subject better left. So I do.

One possible conclusion I've stumbled upon is that perhaps the Camino is like bungy jumping; a leap of faith that invokes a sensory overload so intense that it's only after the event—when your feet are healed or safely on the ground—that you can look back and realise what actually happened. Suddenly, why you did it in the first place isn't as important as the experience itself.

Life often only makes sense to me in retrospect. Typically, while the most profound events and lessons are unfolding, I'm flailing around disorientated and gasping for air like a hooked fish. You do your best to get through at the time. Then later, you look back and realise why it all happened, what it meant, and how the process changed you—for better or for worse. A sense of gratitude often eases the pain. I'm hanging on the hope that whatever is meant to happen out here for Col and me is already happening and that we will each figure it out once the Camino is long behind us. Until then, in the middle of the Meseta, there's nothing more to do but put one foot in front of the other, until you get somewhere. Else!

Because of the consistency in the direction we're travelling, I've started to resemble a block of Cadbury's Top-Deck chocolate turned on its side. Half brown, half white. The only time we're in direct sunlight is when walking; the rest of the day is spent in shade or, better still, indoors. As a result, the right side of my body is still winter-white, while the left side is a distinctive tone of bronzed mahogany. It's the summer Camino fashion. Two-tone is the new black and everybody's wearing it.

With Carrión de los Condes on the horizon, we pick up the pace for the last hour, marching double-time the remaining six kilometres into town. We pass the locked door of the *albergue* and head straight into a bar. Colin orders two beers and I order two bags of ice; one for the knee, one for the foot.

'So, how are you doing?' I ask Colin.

And this time, he replies. He tells me he can't find sense in the questions these past two weeks have brought with them. And the further we go, the more questions arise. We discuss this briefly over our beers.

After twenty minutes, he removes the ice from the side of my foot resting on the chair next to him.

'Jesus fucking Christ, El! You gotta get that looked at.'

He's right, but I'm not surprised. I've felt it every step of the way from Frómista. I hobble inside the bar, order two more beers and ask the barman for the nearest hospital.

'*Enfermería*,' he says, pointing across the street.

The feast day celebrations are in full flight. Colin wanders into the village centre to watch the street parade while I head to the medical infirmary.

His name is Tiba.

Tiba is a young, kind and gentle nurse with a beautiful smile and a great deal of empathy.

'*Muchas ampollas*,' he says, smiling as he scrapes the grains of dirt from my blistered feet and bathes them in Betadine.

Seven patches, one gauze wrap.

Noticing something I hadn't, he then happily digs out two ingrown toenails on both feet.

Seven patches and three gauze wraps.

Moving on, Tiba rubs Voltaren into my knee and renews my script for anti-inflammatory tablets, advising I also stock up on aspirin.

Seven patches, three gauze wraps and two prescriptions.

Finally, Tiba takes my right foot into his hands, pokes at the bulge, shakes his head and says something in Spanish that I ask him to repeat several times before we both give up.

'*Mañana. Las cuatro. Sí?*' he asks, settling for an alternative.

'*Sí*,' I reply, tomorrow at four o'clock. I got that much.

Then Tiba binds my right leg in a temporary plaster wrap from knee to toe.

'Hang on. What's this?'

'*Mañana. A las cuatro*,' he says again.

'*Sí*,' I reply, 'and . . . ?'

But my only answer is a soft smile.

The nurse then writes out a medical certificate for Colin and me to stay on the extra night in the *albergue* and orders, '*No ande*.'

'No walking?' But we're just days away from León. You can't be serious. Until when?

Tiba finally uses different words.

'*Fractura*,' he says.

'Fractured! Are you sure?'

'*Mañana. A las cuatro*.' He gestures to indicate a photograph.

'Oh,' I say. X-rays. That's not good.

Seven patches, three gauze wraps, two prescriptions, tendonitis, a swollen knee, a medical certificate, a day off and, possibly, a fractured foot.

Shit!

Colin: *Carrión up the crusader*

As the sun dips in the sky the town of Carrión de los Condes prepares for the Feast of Santiago. Everyone in town, except for children under the age of five, is going to get shit-faced. But first there will be a procession, and then a re-enactment of three battles fought in the Middle Ages against the Moors.

As I make my way towards the plaza the players emerge from their houses: the Queen of Navarre jumps in her car to drive to the church, the Prince of Aragon runs back into his house to fetch the camcorder. The procession has already started at the end of the street, where the massed bands of the Ponferrada Bridge Club are marching into the plaza dressed as Moors.

They are playing the theme tune from *Titanic*. From another street I hear the sound of bagpipes. It's the King of Castile's pipe and drum band, dressed exactly as they were in fourteenth-century Spain, in black kilts and Nike joggers. The king runs behind them while talking to his wife on his mobile phone, telling her he won't be late home. The King of Castile is a liar.

The action soon removes to the park by the river, where the battle of Centa is recreated for a crowd of Spanish tourists and wet kids who have run over from the local swimming pool to watch. There are horses, flags, and pretend knights with pretend swords flirting with pretend virgins. After the battle—which ends with the King of the Moors giving the King of Castile what looks like a large stuffed budgerigar—the bagpipes lead the procession out of the square playing a tune that sounds suspiciously like Britney Spears's 'Do It to Me One More Time'.

The whole shooting match moves back up to the plaza where another battle is re-enacted. A man dressed as Santiago appears in the nick of time to frighten away the Moors and save the day. In this instance, Santiago acts like the homeless nutbag who once shouted at me under Waterloo Bridge. He is dressed like him too, except he isn't holding a dog tied to a bit of old rope and his willy isn't hanging out of his trouser fly.

There is more talking and proselytising. The King of Castile starts reading from a script, holding the reins of his horse with one hand and droning on into a microphone held in the other. By this stage the crowd and some of the participants are getting antsy. It has all been going on a little too long and the adults need a drink and the kids want the ice-cream they were promised if they were good.

One of the Moors rushes over to the bar to get four more beers for the infidels. Two of the more youthful warriors— they are about four and dressed like they have just stepped off a *Star Wars* set in silver lamé and sequins—try to decapitate each other with swords. Mummy Moor has to step in and separate them.

It is then time for the Moors to attack the Christians again, and win, which is surprising, as two of them are pushing prams with small children. The two four-year-olds don't really care that they have vanquished an army of Christians, they're just happy that their side won. They run across the square with their swords, beat up a little girl in pigtails and steal her bag of lollies.

Meanwhile two of the women stand over a fallen Christian warrior and take this opportunity, while the bishop isn't looking, to stick their swords in his bits.

That's for sleeping with my sister!

That's for standing me up last week, you piece of shit!

The Moors are just Moors. They will invade you, murder your mother and enslave your children. *BUT YOU SHOULD NEVER, EVER, PISS OFF A WOMAN.*

We then all move on to the *Catedral* de Santa María while the Moorish band plays something suitably Moorish: 'Alice the Camel'.

Another battle. Some of the Moors fight with bottles of San Miguel tucked into their armour. Two youths pushing wheelbarrows with bulls' heads tied to them chase the Moors out of the churchyard. And that's it. The festival is over. It's time to head to the *bodega* for a beer and a smoke.

Eli: Questions and answers

I spend early evening watching the sunset from the lawn outside the church, across the road from the clinic. And wonder if it's over. The news has changed everything. After all we've been through to get this far, has it really come to this? I'll have to return to the clinic for X-rays tomorrow afternoon to find out. Until then, with my leg heavily bound, there is nothing more I can do.

As the sun slips slowly down the sky, the orange horizon smouldering low above the city reminds me of my grandmother, Mary. The most brilliant sunset I have ever seen set across the sky on the night she died. She was letting us know she was still close.

I had been holding her hand moments before, then remained by her side for some time after she'd passed. We all did. Eight of us stood around her hospital bed holding hands and cried together. She wouldn't let us cry while she was dying, she didn't want to see us sad, so we'd saved our tears for when we said goodbye.

My grandmother was a magnificent woman who taught me many things, both in life and in death. But none of them more valuable than self-belief.

'You'll be all right, love.'

That was one of the first and last things she ever said to me, a line I've heard many times since and can still hear today. Her soft sandy voice was so certain. It's funny, I believed her, despite my own doubts at the time, and those few simple words of assurance helped me through the years of uncertainty following her death.

I look down at my leg and wonder if her memory might help me through again. Then something in the grass reflects off the sun and catches my eye. I reach to pick it up and discover a pendant, the size of a silver coin. But when I lay it in my hand and look more closely, I find it is not just an ordinary pendant. It is in fact a Virgin Mary of Miraculous Medal. A symbol I'd seen many times as a child. A Christian sign of protection.

'You'll be all right, love.'

And with that, I know I will.

Day 17
Carrión de los Condes to wheat fields

Colin: *Carrión camping*

That last night in Carrión de los Condes, El and I did the only sensible thing: we got pissed with three Germans and decided to start walking at midnight. We also decided, again very sensibly, that the only way to deal with El's injury was to ignore it. Instead of waiting around for an X-ray, we took to her wrappings with a pair of sharp scissors and headed off into the night.

I'm a real pilgrim now. I have a stick that Eli found for me. I also have a scallop shell on my backpack—again a gift from Eli—and my feet are bandaged up. All the things I laughed at right at the beginning of the walk—the ski poles, the socks and sandals—no longer seem funny, but very practical.

A flat, dark horizon. The Meseta goes on forever. My sandals slide on the stones underfoot: the road out is straight, level, stony and treacherous. Behind us the fireworks—green, red and silver—blossom and fade over Carrión, followed several seconds later by the rebound of the explosion. We walk through the darkness towards the fading cheese-round blue moon.

After moon-set it is very, very dark, so dark that Eli finally agrees to put her battery torch on her head and wear it like a miner's lamp. I have been trying to manipulate her into doing this for days. It inspires my sense of the ridiculous but I keep my thoughts to myself because she has threatened to take it off if I laugh.

Our pace increases and she strides ahead like Arnold Schwarzenegger on coke. The Determinator. Earlier today the girl was encased in bandages from toe to knee and popping aspirin like M&M's, but tonight nothing will stop her.

What she does baulk at is sleeping in a wheat field. She's afraid of the mice. What is it with women and mice? They have no venom, they don't have teeth, they won't sleep with you and break your heart. What is there to be afraid of?

Eventually fatigue wins out. Exhausted, we throw our sleeping bags down in a field and collapse. We wake just before sunrise, shivering with cold. We prepare to start walking again just to get warm.

Day 18
Wheat fields to San Nicolás del Real Camino

Eli: A pair of pissed pilgrims passed out in a pasture

Though we lay there for over three hours, neither of us slept. Col sits up shivering with cold. I climb to my feet to stand and am reminded of my foot. I try to escape my sleeping bag, fall flat on my face and am reminded that I'm still drunk. Never mind.

We roll wet sleeping bags into wet backpacks, Col hoists my pack onto my shoulders—*doof!*—and, like true troopers, we march into a rising dawn knowing there will be no coffee until the stores open in another three hours.

Crunch-click crunch, crunch-click crunch . . .

'Hey, Col . . . what would you do for a coffee?'

'Fuck off.'

Crunch-click crunch, crunch-click . . .

'No, I mean it. What would you do right now for a hot coffee?'

'Fuck off!'

Twenty minutes later, an angel disguised as a smelly barman with sideburns is serving us coffee. I'm alive!

On the other side of Coffee de la Cueza, the trail divides into two routes. There are several options along the way. This accounts for the varying estimates of the total distance to Santiago. Every now and then there are two sets of arrows going off in different directions. Crusty's trusty guidebook indicates that the two routes link up a few kilometres down the trail. But typically, two trails will vary in distance, terrain and scenery, and access to facilities like shade, water, food and towns. Shorter is not necessarily better. I leave the decision to Col. He walks on. I follow.

It should be mentioned that my eyesight is not good at the best of times, however, due to the heat, enduring delirium and the last bottle of red wine I polished off just hours earlier, the next nine kilometres toward San Nicolás del Real Camino are a surreal experience as my Camino transforms into a series of Dali vistas:

- A single paddock of giant sunflowers *or* a scene from *Day of the Triffids*?
- A mud brick *mudéjar*-style church *or* another stack of hay bales?
- The miniature entrance to an underground *bodega or* the front door of a Hobbit house?
- A lone tree on a barren plain *or* a cyclist taking a leak in a wheat field?
- A desolate stretch of wheat-filled land *or* Colin's official motive for killing me?

Take me home!

Eli: *Love and other stuff*

The wheat fields give way to long straight highways and overpasses with no cars on them. We walk past a field of sunflowers standing to attention, eager, corn-yellow flowers like children's faces turned towards the sun.

Terradillos de los Templarios is an adobe village that was once a stronghold of the legendary Templars, a place of power and mystery. This morning it is grey and forlorn, and smells of cow manure.

Outside town we have to walk along the highway again. There is a road sign that indicates NO OVERTAKING, a red car beside a black car. A graffitist has been to work with a black pen—the guy in the red car now has a speech bubble: *Get out of the way you arsehole!*

The guy in the black car is shouting back: *Fuck off!*

And underneath: *Buen Camino!*

We've not seen anyone we know for days. The usual crew of familiar faces has dispersed, perhaps lost to the Meseta. Of those we have seen or met, conversations have been a combination of charades mixed with single-word sentences, to overcome the language barrier.

The last person I held a decent conversation with was Klaus, an Austrian who is walking the Camino for what he says is his fourth time. I don't actually know if I believe him. If he *is* telling the truth, I don't know if he's sane. What does he possibly think he will find this time round that he didn't fifteen years ago? Surely I've missed the point. Maybe I'm not trying hard enough. More pain perhaps?

If pain is what the Camino is about, then Col's obviously got the gist. He's suffered every day since Logroño. Whatever happened there has opened the door to a closet full of skeletons. He's a different man these days to the one

I knew before; so quiet and drawn. One look at his face shows that he is carrying a load greater than the weight in his pack. I've watched him ache, heard him question, seen his eyes fade and his body waste away. He's lost his famous passion for food and even his trademark sense of humour seems out of place in conversation. Now, we go about most days in silence and what few words he offers are generally thick with cynicism and contempt. When others are around, he hides behind the mask of the man he was; the sharp tongue, the quick wit. Some see straight through it, others laugh. Yet the longer this goes on, the worse his jokes become and the more layers drop away.

I've been sitting alone outside the *albergue* in San Nicolás del Real Camino for most of the afternoon, wrapped up in my own thoughts and enjoying the solitude. Col sits down at the table and asks if we can speak more about something we touched on earlier in the day, on the topic of love and women. Hearing him question his relationships and himself is a cold reminder of how cruel love can be.

'Have you ever been in love, El?'

'Yeah, unfortunately.'

'What happened?'

'Loved the wrong man.'

'Did he break your heart?'

'Eventually.'

But the truth was, he broke much more. And, in doing so, confirmed many fears as I secretly knew he would. I was young and naive, and although I knew I shouldn't have stayed, I did. From that point on, no thought could undo my feelings.

Like it or not, love is indiscriminate; a feeling, not a decision. It ignites a light inside and by the time it's burning, it's too late to try to put it out. You can stop feeding it with feelings so it doesn't grow, and it may even dim or fade with time, but it never really dies and knowing better doesn't simply switch it off. Regardless of what you want, need or think you know, somewhere beneath the veil of conscious thought the love remains.

Unlike Col, I felt no guilt when it was over, just crippling regret and devastation. I knew the only thing left to do was to move on and try to start again. But at the time, even that seemed impossible.

I think about Col, trying to start again. In a way, maybe that's what this trip has become for him. I know what it's like to be cast aside by someone you love; but I've not been a parent fighting for the life of a child, lost my life partner or my faith. Still, in a way, I share some part of his pain just by being here. It's cruel but, whether we like it or not, as we both battle along our own independent paths, we are each other's only source of strength and support. What affects one ultimately affects both and this is how it will be from here till Santiago.

The *albergue* owner's daughter appears, a pixie in pigtails with a smile as bright as a Spanish sun. She hands me a menu and offers to prepare me something. She is infectiously sweet and appears much younger than she is. She knows English, but she won't speak it. She says she's too shy. But she understands much more than she lets on. I watch her sitting in the background eavesdropping on conversations among other pilgrims. She has a spark in her eye that's too bright to be contained by this place, a desert town of eighty locals. The pilgrims are her way to the world.

She touches my arm with a look of encouragement and as she happily skips away I wonder, am I becoming the kind of pilgrim the Spanish cyclist spoke of, who doesn't talk much and wants to be left alone?

These days, I want nothing more.

Day 19
San Nicolás del Real Camino to Reliegos

Colin: Return to Senda

Postcard from the Meseta: *Endless flat horizon. With wheat.*

Wheat, wheat, wheat. I am so over wheat. I am never going to eat cereal again. Perhaps that will discourage the bastards from growing it.

We leave yet another fall-down village at dawn, to the lively gossip of songbirds in the trees and the crowing of a rooster, the overpowering smell of wheat reminding me of long-ago breakfasts in chilly London: Weetbix and hot milk, little cards inside the box with pictures of cowboys. Still only half awake and muscles aching from the previous day, we pass a sleeping dog curled up on a doorstep like a snake. We let it lie.

Out on the Meseta the sun rises from the horizon, stealthy as a mugger. It has lain in wait for us throughout the night. Today it will be thirty-eight on the plain in the shade and there is no shade. It takes its time to come after us. It has as much time as it wants.

We drag ourselves along the Senda, the name for the white stone path that follows the black and bubbling bitumen highway. We do this for twelve hours. Finally, at four in the afternoon, in the middle of this vast, flat, dry and airless plain, we stop for a break.

Eli is sitting on her haunches under a tree. She looks like she has been bullwhipped and then dragged here from Burgos chained to the back of a truck. She tells me how she tried to train for this walk before we came away but couldn't get past four kilometres. She confesses she usually takes supplements each day because of her blood sugar condition, but sent her stash home in the second week to try to lessen the weight of her pack.

If there is a point when I want to give up, it's right here, right now. Leave me here to die. I am physically exhausted. I ran out of water hours ago and I am dehydrated. I am hot. I am tired. There is, in my heart and soul, something like a toothache that has driven me slowly insane with relentless and nagging pain for weeks on end till my nerves are as raw as frayed lift cable. I am ready to drop. I collapse in the shade.

'Col, remind me again why we're here,' Eli says, poking at her knee and inspecting blisters.

I seem to remember taking this as my cue to tell El how to run her life. This is, you see, how I make things better. When things are fucked I think I have to find answers, have a solution for everyone's problems—except my own. If only the world and the people in it were different, everything would be fine.

There is a long and tense silence broken only by the fizzing of tar bubbling on the road as the earth around us fries in the heat.

Eli gets up, and for once she puts her pack back on herself and starts walking. Her attitude is incomprehensible to me.

I feel faint from thirst. I take a lick at the sweat on my arm. Not bad.

Eli: This far by faith

Ten past one: thirty-eight degrees. I sit at a filthy white plastic table, my legs resting on a white plastic chair, under a white plastic Coke umbrella outside a bar in a town named after a B-grade porn star, El Burgo Ranero, and wonder what my life has come to.

We have been walking since dawn, as we have done for seventeen days. Behind us are twenty-six kilometres of breathless heat and searing sun. Ahead lie thirteen kilometres more of pitiless drudgery; no scenery, hills or valleys, no shade, no food or water and no town between here and Reliegos. Three hours, no breaks. And I've been left with the decision whether or not we go on. At this hour of the day, in this heat, without access to water, shade or assistance, it's ludicrous to even think about it. But today, I don't care.

Seven hours in silence since San Nicolás and still I've failed to find my stride. Every step has been an effort. My mind is numb, my face like putty. My skin is no longer blistered, it's like the crusted flesh of roast chicken—the longer it bakes the darker and tougher it gets. I am not tired or hungry or thirsty or sore. I am nothing. I have nothing left.

A woman at the next table sits rudely staring from the corner of her eye. I light a cigarette. I don't care. Col lies in the shade of a tree outside the church across the road. I can see him from here. We can't even bear to sit together. But I don't care. My knee and foot are fucked as is my attitude, and today . . . I just don't care. Is this a new-found sense of surrender? Or is the Senda sending me mad? A Senda bender.

Not far back, we passed a monument to a German pilgrim called Manfred whose journey ended here, on the Senda, four

203

years ago. Not a bad place to die when you think about it, on the Camino. It's a place you travel to because you want to be here, to explore your spirituality, contemplate your life or to simply find peace. Seems almost perfect, really. Eternal peace. And breathless sleep.

I think about what it would mean to die on the Camino. The thought is neither frightening nor uncomfortable. Still, it's not something I particularly hope happens today. I'd be very disappointed. God knows, we've come so far and all of this has to be for something.

I don't know the circumstances of Manfred's death but I do hope his last moments were happy ones, filled with love, purpose and peace.

Col returns to hear the verdict. 'Let's go.' Lifts my pack and we push on.

Barren is barren. Hot is hot, no matter how you try to describe it.

Crunch-click crunch, crunch-click crunch . . .

A random thought: what if one of us runs out of water?

Crunch-click crunch, crunch-click—scrape.

Dropped my stick.

Crunch-click crunch, crunch-click crunch . . .

An hour down, two to go.

Crunch-click crunch . . .

We have run out of water.

Crunch-click crunch . . .

Some music maybe?

Crunch-click . . .

One hour and thirty minutes. Halfway there.

Crunch-click crunch . . .

More random thoughts. Will Marty get my email? Will my dog remember me? Do they have sushi in Spain? I wonder what Colin's thinking. I wonder what I'd be thinking if I wasn't thinking about what Colin's thinking.

Crunch-click crunch, crunch . . .

There isn't another pilgrim on the trail. Not one. They all have better sense. And when we finally arrive, the *albergue* in Reliegos is almost empty. There are a handful who arrived earlier in the day, and two of them are sick in bed, vomiting with heatstroke.

Later that night, I take a meal I prepare in the communal kitchen to a cool patch of grass in the centre of the village and think about what we've just done.

Surprisingly, I feel good, inside and out. The last stretch of the day instilled in me a renewed level of faith and confidence, not only in my physical ability but in Colin and me as a team again. At any given point throughout the day you could have cut the air with a blunt knife. Yet despite the fact that it gets difficult between us, we are bound now by a common cause and when it comes to the trail, any time we need each other, we are there, side by side. Neither of us would have made it without the other. And from that moment, Santiago never felt closer.

I remember the advice a wise man gave me the week before I left. He said, 'Don't get so caught up in climbing the mountain that when you get to the top, you realise you've forgotten to appreciate the views along the way.' I knew at the time his words would come to mean more than they did. And never have they meant so much as they do as I sit here on the grass with a soggy plate of chickpeas and stewed vegetables.

There is no fear of failing now. With seventeen walking days behind us and sixteen ahead, we've overcome the worst of it. No one day here on the trail could possibly be as challenging, as difficult, as hot and desolate, as today. Nothing the

Camino can throw our way will stop us. I feel a certainty and confidence I've been missing before now. In sixteen days we will arrive in Santiago. The time has come to stop focusing on our destination and start appreciating the journey. Soon this experience will be over and I will never have it back. It is time now to slow down, take a breath and take in the view.

Day 20
Reliegos to León

Colin: *Almost there, what could possibly go wrong now?*

The next day, at a place called Mansilla de las Mulas, we find ourselves in the middle of green fields of corn, gravity-fed with concrete irrigation channels. We are almost out of the desert. We stop and gape at a service station like a couple of hillbillies. *Gosh, Pops, looks like them petrol pumps we done seen on television!*

Hills rise from the plains and beyond are the shadows of mountains painted on a mauve dawn. Mountains! After the Meseta I'd slaughter a mountain right now.

In the *bodega* there is another pilgrim. He is wearing yellow and blue lycra and his jersey has LANCE ARMSTRONG written on the back. His crotch bulges like he has a bag of potatoes down there. His bike is parked in the doorway, blocking the entrance. Another fellow traveller on the spiritual journey. I mark his name down in my little black book for when I'm with God on Judgment Day.

Later that day we reach León, one of the largest and most ancient cities on the Camino. The outskirts remind me of the suburbs of Perth, where I live. There are car dealerships and agricultural machinery, chain-link fences, baying guard dogs, a market garden.

The Senda wilts to a narrow strip of unprotected bitumen that parallels the main highway to Burgos. Once the danger for pilgrims was being attacked by bandits; today you risk finishing your pilgrimage being hosed off the radiator grill of a twenty-wheel Volvo Globetrotter at the main roundabout at Puerto Centro.

Eli: A city at last

Col stops me at the summit of Portillo Hill on the outskirts of León. Still three kilometres away, a stunning panorama of city sprawl engulfs the horizon. Home to around 185 000 people, León, as a city, eclipses any we've seen so far in Spain. As we stand side by side, Colin points across the rooftops toward the distant cathedral spires.

The infamous Meseta lived up to its name and surpassed all expectations. But we won. With the final day of the barren stretch behind us, we walk the remainder of the way through the busy streets of León, silent and triumphant.

The next big city will be Santiago.

It is the Europe I know from guidebooks and travel programs, the Europe I've seen and imagined myself in. Apart from landing in Paris, my experience of Europe has consisted mostly of the modest villages and rural hamlets found along the Camino. But in León, I find more: ancient architecture, stunning stone work, classic cobblestone causeways and alleys, grand plazas, fashion boutiques, coffee houses and a towering cathedral that simply defies description. A city, at last! I never thought I'd be so happy to see a traffic jam.

Leaving the crowded *albergues*, *menus del día* and military-style sleeping quarters behind, Colin and I check into an affordable hotel, rewarding ourselves with a touch of comfort: clean, crisp bed linen, private ensuite and late checkout. We are back in a big city, spoiled with a selection of food and wine, history and culture, shopping, sights and sounds. León feels as close and as far from the Meseta as it could possibly be. Among the hum of city traffic, the buzz of crowded streets

209

and the endless parades of people, I am home again. But better still, I am at home in Europe.

On arriving at the hotel, I shower, hand wash some clothes in the bathtub with the remainder of the shampoo from the miniature complimentary bottle, shower again, then hang my clothes out to dry over the handrail of the terrace balcony. Hair is washed and dried, teeth cleaned. Wearing a fresh set of clothes, I slip my raw-meat feet into Birkenstock sandals and do what any woman would do when faced with spare time in Europe . . . go shopping.

For the next twenty-four hours Colin and I don't see each other. I spend most of the time café loitering, journaling, people-watching from the outdoor wine bars, catching up on emails and exploring the many side streets and laneways of the central district. Eventually, I manage to get the local scoop on the city's largest shopping complex and department store, El Corte Inglés—along with a nice young Spanish escort who walks me six blocks to the door. I hope the store might be my best opportunity to find a pair of Teva hiking sandals. I need to replace my boots after wearing through them in Castrojeriz and Tevas are *apparently* what all pro pilgrims wear.

My hopes are dashed when the attendant tells me the store only stocks the brand to size ten. Due to the enormity of my feet, I am forced to settle for something else, something plain and beige but very comfortable.

With new hiking attire, I head toward the *correo* to post home the boots that have all but crippled me, with full intentions of cashing in on the warranty when I return. The salesman assured me they'd last fifteen to twenty years. He'd obviously never walked the Spanish Meseta in a heat wave. I'd be lying if I said I was sorry to see them go.

Day 21
León, rest day

Colin: Pietà with a fishbone

León wakes later than my city. Eight-thirty and the streets are deserted; no joggers, cyclists or people rushing to work, just an old man shuffling along and a police car slowly patrolling the cobblestones. Church bells toll the quarter-hours.

I find a bar that is open. Inside a solitary businessman nurses an espresso and watches the news reports of bushfires in the west of the province on the TV over the bar. It's a typical Spanish bar; dusty bottles of J&B, Cutty Sark, Frangelico are lined up on shelves. Some of them look like they have sat there since Columbus was in short pants.

After breakfast it is time for a little sightseeing. I take a stroll around the Pantheon. I have heard it compared to the Sistine Chapel; having seen it, I have to tell you that is like comparing my passport photograph to the Mona Lisa. All I see here are some very touching images of soldiers disembowelling and beheading small children, and even these look like they were painted by my ten-year-old nephew.

If the Pantheon is a disappointment, the cathedral is breathtaking, one of the most awesome works of art you will ever see. It is too beautiful for heaven, let alone León. I gaze open-mouthed like a country boy at a vault of golden stone and stained glass that could have been cut from sapphire. I may not be in the presence of God but I know I am in the presence of great religious art. It is not like a church; it is a museum with no cloakroom.

A sign says no photographs but everyone ignores it. Kodachrome has usurped humility. In one of the chapels another sign says 'for pray only', but people just lollop on in, gawp and roll the videotape anyway. *Hey, Martha, get a shot of that woman praying over there. No, not her. That one crying and praying for her sick baby, you moron!*

There is even a *pietà* that looks like Mary with Jesus over her knee trying to dislodge a fishbone from his throat.

I wander the streets. Nothing works, nothing dislodges my own fishbone. I don't know what to do with myself. This is more than suicide, heartbreak, estrangement. There is an aloneness at the heart of this. Is it an occupational hazard? A lot of writers are weird, even the famous ones. Look at Greene, O'Neill, Hemingway: a litany of depression, alcoholism and self-destructive behaviours. After they shot Hemingway full of juice and made him normal he blew his own brains out because he couldn't write anymore.

At home I can distract myself. Here it's not possible, and I can't stand this, trying to live with my strangeness, trying to justify it, explain it, to myself and other people. I am raw as an open wound.

I do not know if it's me or the world. For years I did not connect, could not understand why my wife sometimes described me as distant and aloof. When I did feel this spark, this connection, I could not detach from an engagement with the world I had kept so long at a comfortable distance. Is this normal? I have no idea. I have talked to guys who claim they have never been in love in their lives, and one of them had been married for twenty years, as I had. To follow my heart I had to break someone else's.

Am I going crazy or finally going sane? I feel like I should be in a dark room with a case of bourbon, not out here in the sunlight where everyone can watch the pieces drop away. When Eli sees what a mess I am, she'll lose respect for me. If she hasn't already. I'd rather she hate me than feel sorry for me. And getting her to hate me . . . well, I know how to do that. When it comes to women, it's a reflex I learned at my mother's knee.

Eli: A good thing gone bad

There's good and there's bad. In life. And in people. We all have it within us, and it's the way of the world around us. Pleasure and pain, love and hate, the light and the dark, right and wrong. Some say the way to happiness is learning to find the good *in* the bad, to turn tragedies into triumphs, problems into opportunities. To accept and appreciate that all experiences hold value, despite the circumstances. That way, regardless of the outcome, if a lesson is learned then no experience is ever lost. It's essentially about acceptance.

As far as I know, the theory works well in relation to most things. But on a practical level, it's another story. When it comes to human nature, the rules aren't so simple. Sometimes good people do bad things. Other times, bad people surprise with good deeds. And acceptance of all is not always rewarded. Search too hard for the good and you can overlook the bad. Passive can be perceived as powerless. Make allowances, and people tend to take advantage. Demonstrate too much patience, and they lose respect for you. Compromise too often and eventually you lose respect for yourself.

Every situation we face brings with it a choice about how we act or react. You can search for the good, practise patience, make allowances and compromise. Or you can choose not to. But despite your decision, or how rationally you appear to handle a situation, some things just hurt. And you have to let them.

Unfortunately, León is not all fun and fashion. Time spent in the city is both good and bad. In many ways it is both the breaking and the making of Colin and me.

214

We meet mid afternoon outside a café. He's obviously got a few beers under his belt and is wearing the same bitter expression I've seen every day since the morning he woke in Frómista. The moment we sit down together, the clock begins ticking. A few shots of sarcasm to kick-start the conversation pre-empts what's ahead. I order a glass of wine and settle in. *Here it comes.* 'So what now, Eli, after this book, what then?'

I tell Col that I hope to keep writing, but that I first need to prove to myself I can. It's part of what this trip has come to mean to me. A physical challenge, an emotional test and a professional endeavour.

My reply infuriates him and as my drink arrives, there is an explosion. Across the table, his eyes grow wide, his face twists like a wrung-out rag, he arcs in his seat, his voice changes tone. Suddenly, I no longer know the man.

My lack of confidence angers him to the point of rage. The storm sets in. This is the big one I've been dreading. And as it begins, I turn away. I've seen that look before. Hard to describe but even harder to look at.

I sit stunned, listening to harsh, spiteful words spill across the table. For a moment, I switch off. The sound cuts out, my body goes numb and I'm afraid to move. Time slips and melts away; seconds and minutes pass.

Then, from the corner of my eye, I see him launch in his seat. The sound of the table rocking on the cobblestones snaps me back to attention. We sit staring at each other, both aware of the disruption we have caused, each waiting for the other to move. In the street, passers-by have stopped mid stride; a small boy stands before us looking up in fear.

Turning back to Colin, I suddenly realise I have just lost all respect for the man I had, until then, admired. Not even like or dislike remain. He's no longer right or wrong anymore, he is just there. And yet, there I sit at the same table, a world away, refusing to move.

Over the past three weeks I've witnessed guilt eat away at the man like acid in his stomach. Given things we've discussed, the last thing I want to do is leave now and become another dose. Nor do I want to let him push me away, like he has so many women before me who've gotten too close. And I refuse to fade at the hands of another man as I have done in the past. I will not crumble or crack, break or take the easy way out and walk away.

Colin is not a hurtful man. But he does hurt. That doesn't make him wrong, it makes him human.

Yet things like that don't just disappear.

Colin: *See it my way or die*

I meet Eli for lunch in a tapas bar. The tapas bars give you little plates of food with every drink you buy: potatoes in cream cheese sauce, slices of Spanish omelette dried to the texture of foam rubber, cheese croquettes or, if you're unlucky, the local Spanish delicacy—bits of gristle in pig fat. But mostly it's good and filling snack food. Eli has the excellent idea that it would be possible to live in the bars and never have to pay for anything to eat. The more you drink the more nutrition you get. Drink your way to good health! I like the idea of the Latin life.

But this is not a good lunch, and I'd love to say that it was Eli's fault, but that would not be true.

'What do you think, Col, can I do this? Will I make it as a writer?'

A pretty innocent seeking of reassurance from someone who has, on his CV, quite a few books, so it's reasonable that she should ask it of me. Done it many times myself in the early days. What she gets back is unadulterated fury. She blinks at me in disbelief. A shoeshine boy sitting nearby runs home to his mother. Couples at the surrounding tables drop their forks and stare.

And did I just call her Helen?

Me? I sort of levitate and watch myself slip out of Jekyll and into Hyde and wonder, from a distance, why I am doing this. But it has only been a matter of time. The volcano has been rumbling away ever since we started walking.

Because, you see, this is the trouble with me. I set myself up as the mentor: Big Brother, Guru and Yoda all rolled into one. But guess what? It's lonely on a pedestal, and the pigeons shit on your head. No one asked me to be there but me. I think this is the only way anyone will ever love me, and

I resent it so much it makes my teeth ache. They either thank me for showing them out of the darkness and leave, as my lover has famously done; or they buy the act and I am left trapped, lonely and needed.

And you know what? It's a game, a manipulation. It's all about control. And it has rebounded on me in unimaginable ways, as it does in every life, if you live long enough. My lover left me; my wife took pills; my daughters probably still love me but one of them cannot stand to be in the same room as me. Grief, loss and self-hatred spill out of me in the main square in León and Eli—you remember her, the poor girl with the knee and the fucked-up feet—is the recipient of three years of pent-up rage and frustration.

I could not articulate any of these feelings, of course. It takes a geologist to explain lava; the volcano just blows. Even if I could have told her, I was caught in a double bind. People love me for being the strong, silent type, not for being me, whoever the hell that is. So halfway through our pickled pig's foreskin soaked in olive oil and our second beers, we stamp away from each other in opposite directions.

Poor Eli has no idea where this huge overreaction has come from. Mr Control is losing control. Of himself, primarily. Thanks to a week looking at nothing but wheat fields, drinking too much and, apparently, talking in my sleep to my dead wife, my anguished daughters and a lover who bewilders me at every turn, the fault line is shifting under pressure.

After Eli has gone I drink another couple of beers and my considered and rational solution to our problems is then to go looking for her to tell her it is all off. Finish the fucking book yourself. I'm going home. Fuck this, fuck that and fuck you. Which is just about my answer for everything these days. León has an airport and I am going to book a flight back to Australia.

Until now, whenever I needed to find Eli, whether we were separated in a village or a large city, I always knew where she would be. We have always found each other. But tonight I don't find her, thank God. For the first time I can't find her anywhere. When I finally get back to our hotel room late at night, she is asleep. And by the morning I have sobered up and calmed down.

I decide to keep walking, see this out. And for some reason that is entirely beyond me, considering my erratic and abusive behaviour, so does she.

Day 22
León to Hospital de Órbigo

Eli: *Stations of the Camino*

By the time we leave the city, León has become a signpost along the Camino. One of those places or events so significant, you know that in time it will become a point of reference, like a family Christmas that went horribly wrong. From that day on, there would be pre- or post-León.

Colin needed me to stay there at the table, I needed to be alone, so after waiting for the air to—somewhat—clear between us, I excused myself, assured him I would return, then escaped to a dark cave in the doorway of a quiet street, curled into a ball and privately fell apart.

I had known moments like these but such cruel words had never been delivered with such sincerity. I wanted to hate him. But I couldn't. Nor could I blame him. 'I want to be a better man,' he said. One look at his face told me that he did.

Perhaps it had all become too much. Perhaps I had expected more of him than he could give. Either way, Col and I have a commitment to each other that has grown beyond the path ahead and, despite what happens between now and Santiago, it's one I need to know I have done my best to keep.

Nevertheless, I wake angry the next morning, seething from the event. Thinking about it makes me physically sick. I skip breakfast and stick with coffee instead. We were both doing our best under the circumstances and although I held no animosity towards him for what had happened, damage had been done and his words were now sitting in the pit of my stomach like rancid deli ham.

I spend most of the time walking at a distance. I don't want Colin to bear the brunt of how I feel, even though I know my silence suggests I am trying to punish him. I'm not. I am ready to snap and am dreading something that might set me off. It won't take much.

The Way passes through the suburbs and industrial estates of León before we veer off along an alternative route that offers distance and reprieve from the noise of traffic roaring along the N-120. Still not a word has been spoken between us. And this time, we take the long way. It is flat, hot, stark and endless. The wheat of the Meseta is replaced by dry, open fields and shrubbery. Tumbleweed races across the path before us. Later corn and maize fields appear with an irrigation channel running parallel to the sealed strip, sections of barren expanse followed by hours along a desolate road.

It's along this sealed road that I spot up ahead a German girl I met in a café in León the day before. Her name is Daniela and she has a sore foot. She got her first blister yesterday. I'm not sure where she started walking, I didn't want to know. But she is a school teacher and has limited time so began just three days ago. We've met many school teachers along the Camino. It's approaching school holiday time in Europe and it appears many have taken the previous week off to walk. I can think of better ways to spend a vacation.

We're gaining on her at a rate and as she comes into view, it appears quite obvious that she's struggling. She's alone. She stumbles, with cross-steps and looks like I did on our second day. I stop and wait for Colin.

'What do you think?' I ask, breaking the silence for the first time all day.

'Yep, she's in trouble all right. Oops . . .' He pauses as Daniela stops on cue and leans forward without bending at the waist, then sways back as if gauging her centre of gravity. 'There you go!' She staggers off.

'I'm going to see if she's okay.'

I jog up behind her on the trail.

'*Hola*, Daniela.'

'Hi,' she says, squeezing out a pathetic try-smile.

'It's good to see you. How are you feeling?'

'Oh, is hot,' she says, 'so hot and I'm not going too good, just got to get together with the legs and the head. Is all going to be a good day. Pretty!'

Her English was much better yesterday but today she's slurring words like a seasoned drunk.

'Hey, I'm thinking of stopping for a break up ahead. Do you want to join me?'

'No, I think just to . . .'

'Just to . . .?'

Nothing.

'All right, are you sure?'

'Yes, just to get the legs together.'

Well that would be a good start.

'Okay. Hey, do you have enough water?'

'Yes, I have a Platypus, like Australia!' she states happily.

Huh?

'Well, you take care and, remember, Colin and I are not far behind if you need anything.'

No reply.

I jog back to Colin.

'She's buggered!'

'Yeah?'

'I think it's the heat.'

'El, it's forty degrees, we're walking on hot asphalt—do you realise how fit we've become? I used to envy those European bastards in Roncesvalles as they marched past us up those fucking hills, but look at them now. They're melting! Being Aussie, the heat is about the only advantage we have.'

He's right. The heat is not even a factor anymore. And for a moment, we're laughing again.

We walk on. Rippling heat. Geography. Time.

A year ago, I was speaking at a conference in Western Australia and hadn't been back to Perth since meeting Colin at a literary festival the previous year. We had kept email contact throughout that time. I called him the following day to let him know I was in town and see if he was free to meet.

That afternoon he picked me up at my hotel and we drove along the coast to Indiana's, a teahouse in Cottesloe overlooking the ocean. It was there, over a pot of tea with milk and honey, that Colin and I first talked about his wife, Helen.

Today, the conversation continues.

Colin begins to tell me a story about his wife.

Crunch-click, crunch . . .

'Hey, El, can I get your opinion on something?'

'Of course.' But hearing him mention Helen and my opinion in the same breath makes my stomach grip and turn worse than before. Though it's not bothered me before, I realise how significant these issues have become for him in recent weeks and, equally, how important my reply will be.

Colin speaks of his wife's death like a riddle, with an answer he knows is there but just can't find. We spend time sharing thoughts about her, their lives together, the good times, the hard times, their daughters, her suicide, the affair, the guilt, and the funeral.

He seems happy we spoke and finishes by telling me that I help him understand women in a way no one can. He says it's my 'honesty'. But we both know it's because I am so similar to most of the other women in his life.

I am complex in thought, overanalyse everything, vacillate hourly between confident and self-conscious, and generally confuse the hell out of everyone. Including *myself*! I can only imagine how frustrating it is for men to try to understand. But while many don't, Col has always found sense in the things I say.

Suddenly I am walking alone. I turn to see Colin stooped by the side of the road, his head in his hands, and I wander tentatively back along the trail. He tells me that the conversation has sparked a flashback. He's remembered a dream he had last night. I draw a long and sorry breath. *God, what have I done?* I drop my pack, crouch down beside him in the dirt and reach across to comfort him. 'So, mate, where do we start today?'

Trying to make sense of the mess has become a daily exercise for Col. But despite how long it takes or how much progress he seems to make, establishing some kind of peace by nightfall doesn't guarantee it will still be there by morning. Typically, it starts all over again each day.

Day by day, step by step. Welcome to the Camino.

In Hospital de Órbigo that night, I lie awake, with Colin screaming in his sleep and tossing in the bunk beneath me. I think back to the sight of him fallen to his haunches, head in hands, a shattered man. *What constitutes a breakdown? When is enough too much? Who would I call if I needed to? What would I tell his girls?*

I lie awake that night and cry; for Colin, for the daughters he constantly compares me to, and for his dead wife, whom I never even knew.

It has been a long day.

Day 23
Hospital de Órbigo to Astorga

Colin: El Castillo Erróneo

In front of her adobe house a bent woman dressed in black is brushing dust from her doorstep with a witch's broom. In the middle of the square is a red brick mansion with an Italianate fountain, bright with azaleas. It sits like a ruby in a cow pat.

Someone shouts *Buen Camino!* to us from an upstairs window.

The residents on the Way don't take much notice of *peregrinos* anymore—after a thousand years the novelty has started to pall. Yet it's still hard to get lost on the Camino. If you lose sight of the little yellow arrows, a local will stop and point the way. You think they're not watching, but they are. Hesitate for a moment, to look at a map or scratch your crotch—I do this, not Eli—and a Spaniard is at my side in moments, grabbing me by the arm and pointing me back to the Camino.

We are on our way to Astorga, see it sitting there in the distance, an old Roman town built on top of a hill that lies on the plain like a sleeping cat.

The previous day's events sit heavy with me. She has seen what I have been trying so hard to hide: that I hurt, and that I am vulnerable. That's when I am most dangerous. Like the Phantom of the Opera, see me without my mask and I know you will never love me, and I can never love you. So instead I will try to drive you out. Behind this charming exterior there is a monster, at least that's what I think. Did I bait Eli a little yesterday, before the fight started? May have done. Perhaps. And she fell for it, didn't she?

I wonder if Eli thinks this is just about my wife. God knows, she has few enough clues to work on, and the loss of a wife is something people can relate to. But what has confronted me here is the guilt of having loved another woman more, the regret of not knowing that I could feel that way about anyone, and the grief of not having that love returned. The self-loathing at having betrayed someone I had shared my life and history with for so long. I did love her, but not passionately. How can I ever explain that to my daughters? I believe now it was that knowledge, never expressed, that broke my wife, not the leaving of her.

The morning is hot, the plain yellow with sun and dust. We stop in a little village for Cokes, see a French guy with a donkey heading in the opposite direction. He has wild curly hair and a beard, and an interesting face. At first I think he's a local. He stops for a coffee and talks to Dan, the Canadian— also known as Clark Kent—who can speak French at least as well as he can English. Dan, gentleman that he is, listens intently and translates for us.

He is, he says, from Le Puy. Four years ago an eighteen-year-old drunk driver hit him in his car and left him in a coma for a month. They told him he would never walk again. He did.

Two years later his wife died of cancer. Before she died he promised he would walk the Camino for her, go to Santiago and say a prayer for her in the cathedral in Santiago. And this is what he has done. Now, he is making his way home to France the way he came.

He says she has been walking with him; he saw her, he says, in Santiago. Just for a moment.

'Don't you feel angry, don't you feel sad?' I ask him. 'For all that has happened to you, to your wife? Angry at God, angry at the drunk driver?'

He shakes his head. 'To be angry you must think you understand how the world works, what is real and what isn't. How can we know? Life is a mystery—how we came to be here, where we are going. Nobody really knows, not the Pope, not the Dalai Lama, they're all just guessing. So how can I presume to know how life should be? Why should I be angry at myself? At you? At anyone?'

He gives us a soft smile. He knows we think he's crazy. But there is an aura of serenity about him. I like him. I wish my French was better. His name is Robert Bonami. It is the first and last time I ever meet him.

Astorga is the last time I will see Francesca also. Francesca is the woman in the wheelchair who has come from Rome to make her final pilgrimage.

Until these last three years I've never known pain before, not like this. I did not have a lover with MS, was never hit by a drunk driver or beaten anorexia days from death like Eli, had my wife die slowly of cancer. I wrote about some of these things in fiction, perhaps imagined them in my own head, but never understood then what black, soul-destroying pain was. I think I have a much better idea now. Yet I cannot imagine the inner lives of Francesca or Robert Bonami. I shy away from these people a little; I don't want to imagine their pain, and so I take a step back.

We do not go to the *albergue* in Astorga; my publishers have organised an interview with a newspaper from home about my latest novel—written under yet another name, no wonder I'm schizophrenic—so I check us into a hotel in Astorga because it has a phone in the room. It seems all too easy.

Only it's not. The call comes through at six the next morning but the receptionist is unable to feed the call up to my room. So what's the point of having one there? She screams at me very slowly and very loudly in her own language in the hope that I will understand her problems. To me, her main problem appears to be her hair, a Marge Simpson beehive. She looks like a female version of Sybil from *Fawlty Towers*. *El Castillo Erróneo*. Manuel could have done better.

I run down the stairs shouting at her that I have a journalist on my mobile from ten thousand kilometres away telling me they are on the hotel's landline, and I would like to talk to them. La Sybil shrugs her shoulders, looks at the switchboard and pulls out the plug. I give up.

Just after dawn, as rain bounces off the cobblestones and a thunderstorm shakes Astorga, I stand in a phone box in the middle of the plaza shouting my ideas about marriage, relationships and love to a journalist in Sydney. Does anyone really care about the life I am still running from, and trying to reconcile, here on a remote path in northern Spain?

My life has become surreal.

Eli: A cool change

Yes, it is selfish. And after leaving Belorado, I never thought I'd be setting out alone by choice. But following another fight in Astorga, I make a decision.

Colin's slipping downhill so fast, he frightens me. He's become completely irrational, unpredictable, and at times downright mean. Watching him reminds me of a time when I too lost my way and, possibly, my mind. Even now, six years on, I continue to marvel at those who managed to remain by my side. I wonder how? But I'm afraid there is nothing more I can do for Col. Not like this.

He has started indulging in his own self-destruction. He's grown gaunt, eating less, drinking more. Days ago he told me that food has become a game. He's enjoying the challenge of seeing how little he can get by on each day. He says this to someone who once took up the same challenge and wound up losing so much more than weight. If he wasn't drunk at the time, I'd have told him he should have known better. But he's barely sober after lunchtime anymore.

The fact is, I'm not doing well—personally—with any of this. As much as I wish it weren't true, I feel like I've given all I have and now it's taking too much away. It's not my patience wearing thin, it's me. My own journey has been overshadowed. Our pilgrimage has become Colin's tread of penance, and the Camino his act of contrition. It's overwhelming. I've lost sight of myself in it all.

I wish I knew what it is that Colin needs. I wish I could give it to him. But Santiago is still over a week away. And neither of us stands a chance if we continue the way we are. Something has to change and at least this way, it's being done amicably, with all the right intentions.

I spend hours sitting before the Bishops Palace in Astorga thinking about the decision and choose my words very carefully later that night: two days apart to get perspective, refocus, gain strength and confidence, may well be best for us both. Perhaps then I can offer Colin more than I can now. And perhaps, by Villafranca, he might have managed to find some peace or progress of his own.

Yes, it is selfish. But I'm determined not to feel any guilt or shame. It's a decision I need to make.

Day 24
Leaving Astorga apart . . .

Eli: Where the heavens meet the Earth

Today I set off alone, without a map or guidebook, and again without Colin. There are two nights, three days and seventy-five kilometres ahead before we are both scheduled to arrive in Villafranca. Though he's agreed to meet me there, I would not be surprised if he doesn't.

I am approaching Cruz de Ferro, the highest point of the Camino. It is the iron cross icon that the beautiful Swedish pixie, Petra, had shown me in her guidebook the night before we set out from Roncesvalles. That night twenty-five days ago, I imagined myself standing at the foot of it—the highest peak—and knew that if I made it there, I would have won. Santiago from Cruz de Ferro would be a formality and nothing more.

We've not seen or heard of Petra since. I look back now and wonder if she may've been an angel sent to Roncesvalles to give me hope; tiny, frail-framed, softly spoken, gentle-natured Petra, who along with a dreadlocked Yoshki had walked all the way from Sweden and would one day walk all the way home again. She had come so far and fallen in love with the world she'd discovered on the way. She had no injuries and no blisters—she wore Tevas! Her little legs and beautifully spoken simplicity had demonstrated a strength I'd not considered. She was content and had found peace, with herself and her place here. So passively happy.

I knew then that I wanted what she had. And that perhaps I would need to walk to find it.

Colin: Heaven on a stick

At sunrise I am at a place called El Ganso, stone houses crowding in, a dog barking, alarmed at my scent. *I'm* alarmed at my scent. It's a very hot morning. I'm sweating like a cheese.

The trail winds to dun and green hills, then narrows through a grove of chestnut. Not one stalk of wheat in sight. Heaven on a stick.

I am walking alone. Eli has said she needs some time alone. In Astorga we fought again. She wants to prove to herself she can do things alone. And me? For the first time in my life I am frightened to be alone. I don't like my own company. I cannot understand what is happening to me. The Meseta with its space and heat and ghosts and lovers has made me a little crazy.

I feel guilty and ashamed of my outbursts with Eli. I see no way back. I have lost her respect, I am sure, as well as her friendship. This whole journey has gone to shit, in my opinion. My life is a bad joke. I keep walking now out of habit. Instinct. And despite what has happened, there is in me a perverse desire to see her finish this damned thing.

I have become what they call a scary guy. And let me tell you something, in case you get too complacent out there. It's not that far from there to here. Not that far at all.

Eli: A new view

Near El Ganso the red sand pilgrim path runs parallel with the secluded local road, made of loose grey gravel. I'm not sure where I will walk to today but I want to get as far as possible. Colin and I left Astorga just hours apart and it would defeat the purpose if we were to meet earlier than expected. I couldn't walk away a second time.

The trail enters a town which appears as deserted as the road leading to it. The houses are uninhabited and there's no sign of life. I haven't stopped since daybreak and wonder how long it will be before I find a place to rest. My foot is awkward, clumsy and weak, and my knee has again swollen with the heat. With that, I round a bend to find the perfect paradox: amidst the old stone walls, deserted streets and abandoned cottages stands the colourful edifice of Cowboys Bar. I step through the door to find a shrine to all things kitsch and Western: whips, lassoes, horseshoes and six-shooters. 'Wanted' posters and movie memorabilia adorn the walls. The sound of Johnny Cash belts out from behind the bar. The barman himself is a cowboy wannabe with matching dress sense; leather boots over denim jeans and a flannelette shirt with a sheriff's badge pinned on the front.

All this in a dilapidated ghost town that takes just four minutes to walk through. I've learned to stop being surprised by the Camino. Instead I order iced coffee.

Further down the track I meet Jonas, a well-presented German who lectures at a university in Madrid. Jonas speaks five languages, has detailed knowledge of the Camino and is walking the Way for the fourth time. I ask Jonas what first inspired him. He tells me he first walked in honour of a sick friend, 'but now I walk not for my friend but for me,' he says, explaining that his friend has long recovered. He tells me he made the hike from Madrid last year and that the stretch we're crossing took nearly a week to pass due to waist-deep snow. I tell him it's hard to imagine it in this heat.

Jonas explains that he has become addicted. A self-confessed 'masochist', he says he likes the pain, comparing it to the same buzz that marathon runners get hooked on. 'Endorphins!'

His English impresses me. I tell him so. We walk together while he offers a running commentary on the scenery around us. The history, the culture, the nearby mines and the Templars of medieval times.

The Order, as well as being rather mysterious warrior monks founded originally to protect pilgrims from marauders in the Holy Land, were also fabulously wealthy. Jonas tells me they established what was essentially the first international banking system that allowed travellers to cash in their belongings at the beginning of their journey and reclaim them at the end, so as to make them less appealing to bandits who would otherwise thieve from them. Although dedicated to a life of chastity and poverty, they had access to enough funds to later bankroll the Crusades and operate lines of credit for kings and princes. Their legacy, in churches, castles and preceptories, is seen all over Spain. I compliment Jonas on his knowledge and he tells me it has become his passion. When he's not walking the Camino, he's studying it and when he's not studying it, he is training for it. For the past four years he has lived the Camino all year round. Jonas tells me he will continue to walk every year until . . .

'I hope to die on the Camino.'

I turn to him, surprised. 'Why?'

'Have you seen the monuments along the way of those who have died?'

I tell him I have seen them and that I said a prayer for each fallen pilgrim and their families as I passed.

'You see? They build a stone, mark your name, put you in the guidebooks and people pray for you forever. You are famous!'

It seems a morbid view but he speaks with a gentle smile and I can see his point. To some people, the concept of death is not as frightening as the prospect of being forgotten. He wants to live forever.

'I will not have children,' he says. This is his way of achieving immortality.

Jonas and I enter Rabanal del Camino, where he will spend the night. The sun is at its hottest and Jonas asks if he can buy me lunch inside until the heat passes. I explain that I have something to eat in my pack and must keep moving if I am to get over the mountain ridge before nightfall. But Jonas insists.

Not wanting to offend him, I wait in the lobby of his—very plush—hotel while he showers and changes his clothes. Jonas did the hard yards the first time round. These days his Camino is walked in comfort and style. It's not endured, it's enjoyed.

After a delicious lunch with fine wine and silverware, I thank Jonas for his generosity and his company, wishing him the best and promising to keep in touch. It is mid afternoon and I still have a mountain to climb.

On the edge of town the land drops away to reveal an open valley pre-empting a monstrous mountain pass. It is like standing before an endless ocean. The landscape has changed again. The bleak vistas of stark tablelands have become lush, fertile terrain and for a moment I am back among the purple-hazed mountains of the Pyrenees. Preparing to enter the valley I hear a voice call from behind and turn to find three middle-aged Spanish men propped against a stone wall in the cool of the shade, waiting for the heat to pass.

'*No vayas, tontita, es demasiado peligroso, hace muchísimo calor!*' they warn—it's too hot and too dangerous. The three tut-tut as I thank them for their advice but go on regardless. Here we go with the *poco loco* again. *Yes, it's hot and I might well be mad but I'm fit now and . . . I'm Australian!*

Leaving Rabanal del Camino is exciting. The narrow trail ahead is empty and I am happily alone, the summit in the distance. Winding up and down the path through fields of green towards the sheer ascent, I note the energy throughout the hills is thick and unsettling in a way. Passing the remains of ancient Templar ruins, I am reminded that this had been considered sacred land to many denominations throughout the ages who inhabited the region and still is to the dissident hippy communities who live off the land of nearby valleys.

The mist thickens as I edge further on. On the other side of the bleak ruins of Foncebadón, a harsh summer's day turns grey and a brooding cloud hangs on the summit. Staring up at an eagle, I see flashes of lightning directly above. I am walking into a storm.

I think about my family at home, my friends, my life. I think about where I have been and wonder where I will go from here, what the years ahead will hold. What will I wish for when I look up toward the pinnacle of the iron cross and know I have achieved that which, only weeks ago, seemed impossible? Whether I have stopped to acknowledge it or not, a lot has changed. I have changed. I would not be here alone if I hadn't. I would not still be here at all. This task is no longer daunting, it's fun and, as crazy as it seems, alone out here amidst the heavens and the earth I am having the time of my life.

Colin: A walk in the park

At Rabanal del Camino there is a church attached to the monastery. I go inside and find two solitary pilgrims in silent contemplation. The church is small. There is no high altar, just a single crucifix, Christ hanging on the cross, simply lit from below by a small lamp.

I cannot sit here. I do not want my contemplations to be of a man suffering and slowly dying. Get enough of that at home. Got enough of that now.

I look around the narthex but there is no Madonna here, just a dark church with agony central, illuminated and revered. I walk out into the misty cobbled yard, hoist on my backpack and keep walking.

From Rabanal del Camino the path ascends into the clouds through the ruins of Foncebadón. It is sad and mistily beautiful in the fog, most of the stone houses in ruins, overgrown with brambles. I could have taken a prize-winning photograph that would have been reproduced in every Thomas Cook brochure around the world if not for the big green council garbage bins and the bright blue Pepsi Cola dispensing machine that ruined the frame wherever I stood.

A Spanish *peregrina* sits on a crumbling stone wall performing running repairs on her feet. Every single one of her toes is encased in gauze and plaster, as is her heel. I suddenly realise how far I have come in three weeks. She began her pilgrimage in León and now she suffers as I did, as Eli did, with *ampollas*—blisters. León! I raise my eyes to heaven. A walk in the park! Three hundred kilometres. I could do that in a day!

My own feet now resemble a pair of well-worn leather sandals; hard bits peeling off, encrusted with dirt and small insects, no feeling whatever. They may not be beautiful but these buggers will get me to Santiago now. I take off my socks, showing her how ugly my feet are, like a seasoned knife fighter showing his scars to a kid. Look at these, *chica*. They didn't get this ugly, this smelly and this mould encrusted sitting on my arse in an *albergue* in León.

The whole tone of the Camino has changed since León. It's the start of the school holidays and for some devout Spaniards walking the Camino is a vacation. They are noisy, exuberant and travel in packs. They are as well-meaning, disruptive and chaotic as a litter of puppies. The Camino is a different experience for them. They haven't been pushed from Rome in a wheelchair, they don't walk in memory of a dead wife. This is just their summer holidays, not the trip of a lifetime. Reverence is replaced with hilarity. Why not? It's their country.

They hobble along beside me with blistered feet, getting no sympathy, only disdain, from the small contingent of foreigners who started in the Pyrenees and who are in turn treated with tender contempt by those who started in Saint Jean Pied-de-Port and spent the first day climbing mountains.

Outside Foncebadón I am lost in the clouds. It is a silent planet where I am the only inhabitant in a world of gorse and loose shale. There are shrines everywhere beside the road, piles of stone laid neatly at the base of stone crosses.

These are days I wouldn't mind curling up under one of them.

Day 25
Walking apart

Eli: *Got a problem with that?*

By afternoon I have conquered the summit, all one thousand, five hundred and four metres of it, the highest peak of the Camino. I reach the iron cross, take time to sit alone on the mound of stones left by centuries of pilgrims before me, give thanks, say a prayer, make a wish and toss a small pebble onto the top, adding my own piece of history to the Camino.

My stone resting at the peak, I blow a kiss skyward, send *Them* all a smile and continue on to Manjarin, and then a further seven kilometres to the small village of El Acebo. I'd heard there was a quaint refuge there that few people know about.

Unfortunately, having trudged for two hours through rain and gathering darkness, I find my quaint ten-bed refuge is, in fact, a forty-bed dormitory above a bar chock-full of bodies, both upstairs and down. There is no room at the inn, and it is still raining outside.

In the downstairs bar I meet a fellow Aussie chick, from Bondi, who teaches me my favourite Spanish saying to date: *no pasa nada*. One thing Australians and Spaniards share is a fabulous, lax, 'no worries, she'll be right, mate' attitude.

No room left? *No pasa nada.*

Nowhere to sleep? *No pasa nada.*

No shower or food? *No pasa nada.* Have another drink!

Jodie is homeless too and appears far less concerned about it than I am. So I follow her lead and order another *vino.* Eventually, after many *vinos* and an impromptu rendition of the Spanish national anthem that gets the entire bar jumpin', someone takes pity on us and tosses us a flea-bitten mattress to lay on the floor.

Bung knee. Blisters. Sore foot. Tendonitis. Crazy travelling companion. Sleeping on the floor of a dodgy bar . . . *No pasa nada!*

Next morning when I wake, an elderly man hears me get up and appears in the bar. He smiles and says good morning, then offers me coffee. I opt for herbal tea. My liver has a headache.

Knowing we can't communicate much further, the precious fellow takes a seat beside me, watching on intrigued as I sit on a bar stool, popping fresh blisters and tidying my feet for the day ahead. A needle, a cigarette lighter to sterilise the tip, a tube of Betadine, a roll of gauze, a pair of scissors, some Bandaids, plaster strips, sponge padding and outer dressing to hold it all in place. I'm good at it now.

He nods approvingly. '*Bueno!*'

He has a gentle face and reminds me of my grandfather.

I set off into the thick mountain air. It was dark when I arrived last night but the new day reveals a stunning landscape of mushroom mountain tops breaching thick strokes of sweeping cloud. I breathe in the views in every direction, like perusing the timeless works of the Louvre. Today, I will make my way through Molinaseca and on to Ponferrada. The old man tells me it will be one of the prettiest days of the Camino.

Already, it is.

Colin: *More Tomás and less Coca-Cola*

I reach the Cruz de Ferro, the emblem of the Camino, a simple iron cross that runs out of a long wooden post and is surrounded by *milladoiro*—a huge mound of stones. Many pilgrims throw stones onto the pile, symbolic of casting their sins aside. Some have been carried all the way from home.

Hordes of Spaniards crowd around the base having their photographs taken, whooping and swapping high-fives as if they have just climbed Everest. Tourist buses pile up, a stop-off on the way to Santiago.

Coming down off the hill I hear a bell tolling in the fog. I have reached Manjarin, the ruins of a town deserted for years until it was revived by one Tomás Martínez le Paz, who camped here with a sleeping bag and lantern on his way to Santiago twelve years ago and decided to become a modern-day Templar knight and dedicate his life to the service of pilgrims, as the Templars did. (Or as they were supposed to have done.)

On the edge of the town there is a cross bearing the name Eva in memory of a seventeen-year-old Dutch girl who was planning to walk the Camino with her cousin in 1996. She was murdered in her bed by an intruder a few months before she was due to leave. Her cousin walked the Way in her memory and erected the cross here.

A hundred yards further on is the *albergue*, built out of one of the ruins by Tomás himself. Pilgrims once slept on the floor but now there is a refurbished barn with thick mattresses. There's no running water; it has to be fetched each day from a well three kilometres away. But this at least is authentic; the Templars never washed either. Apparently they looked great and stank.

There are dogs, children and geese on the loose every-where. It is basically a hippy commune—Woodstock with chain mail.

When I arrive Tomás is conducting a service, and a huddle of pilgrims are standing in a circle around him and one of his 'knights'. They are dressed in white robes with the red cross pattee, and Tomás is holding a Templar sword and saying a prayer in Spanish. An aria lilts softly on the cassette player.

The walls of the *albergue* are decorated with newspaper articles, some about the refuge, others from *The Messianic Times*, a right wing Christian lunatic fringe newspaper. The coffee is cold but the biscuits are still pretty good.

Tomás's past is murky. He left behind a wife, two teenage daughters and a comfortable middle-class life in Madrid to take up the call. He is obviously eccentric, possibly cracked, but does not appear to be dangerous. There aren't enough eccentrics in the world, so God bless him and keep him. I leave some money in the tin that says *Donativos*. More Tomás and less Coca-Cola: my prescription for a more interesting world.

After Manjarin, I climb through trails of chestnuts, encrusted with moss. Like my socks. The maw of the crouch-ing hills forms the arms of a sphinx. These hills are known as the Maragatería. The path has been bulldozed through shale, over hills thick with purple and orange gorse. The houses are stone and wood, with slate roofs.

I have a late lunch, the *menu del día*, in a dodgy bar in El Acebo. Green beans and bacon, a whole trout with soft pink flesh, and fruit. All for eight euros. I am wasting away to nothing but Christ I'm getting my vitamins doing it. I have the most perfectly balanced diet of any skeleton I ever saw. As I whack down the complimentary bottle of local red wine, I realise I have just walked for eight hours with barely a break and I am not even tired. When did I get this fit? What happened between Roncesvalles and here? Screw the SAS. I'm trying out for the next Everest expedition. Hold the oxygen— just give me an extra pair of socks.

The guidebook says that leaving El Acebo I should look out for an iron bicycle that commemorates the death of a German pilgrim killed here en route to Santiago. The miracle is that the body count isn't a lot higher. The Senda often meanders close to the road and a lot of drivers, early in the morning and on weekends, are pissed out of their minds. And that's just the police.

On the way out of town it starts to rain. Let's pause here a moment and watch one half-pissed Australian trying to shrug his poncho over himself and his backpack while crying for his dead wife. The weight of my backpack and the effect of a litre of wine with lunch overwhelm me and I fall on my back, in a ditch. I lie there, looking up at an indifferent heaven, the rain stinging my face.

Clearly, I am not holding it together. I am coming undone; slowly, delicately, painfully, silently. This walk, this strange and haunted landscape, the heat, the terrible aloneness, are eating at my sanity like sharks feeding off a sick whale. There is still more than a week to go, and I don't know that I can take another step. This is what grief does. It's like a mugger. It lies in wait in the bushes and jumps out at you and grabs your wallet while you're looking the other way, thinking of something else. Or someone else. I've got a litre of wine in me and I'm defenceless. *Bang.*

Her face the first time I saw her. *Knee in the groin.*

That same face in her coffin. *Elbow in the teeth. Poncho smothering me in a gust of wind.*

Oh fuck this poncho. Get me off this mountain!

I try to stand and fall backwards into the bushes, on top of my backpack, and lie there kicking like an upended turtle.

What am I doing here? Where's Eli? Why are my wife's fingernails raking my heart? Why now?

I get my shit together and roll down the hill to the next village. This will end one day, I hope. But that's what I want to go to Finisterre to talk to God about.

That night in yet another village, yet another bar, I see a picture on the front page of the local newspaper: a donkey standing forlorn by the side of a major highway while paramedics work to resuscitate a man in the background. I recognise the donkey before I recognise the name. It is Robert Bonami, the Frenchman we met on the road outside Astorga, the man from Le Puy who had walked to Santiago for his dead wife. Walking by the highway at Valverde de la Virgen he suffered a heart attack and died. He was fifty-six. He had kept faith with his promise to her, and it seemed to me then that whatever God is out there had kept faith with him. He had not asked more of him in this life without her. He made his pilgrimage and then He took him home. What a nice thing to do. Both of them, man and God.

Reading on, I realise that the moment Robert was dying was the same moment I found, in the dirt by the side of the road, a small silver miracle medallion, sold cheap in any church souvenir shop. I had picked it up on impulse, and now retrieve it from my pack. On it there is an engraving of the Madonna, the goddess. Robert has his miracle; this romantic, this head case, still hopes to find his own. And however it comes, in happy endings or with paramedics and donkeys, perhaps we are not to know.

It seems to me right then that there are harsher things in life than death.

Eli: *Eggs and endings*

In Ponferrada, I have a conversation with a man and his two daughters in the *supermercado*. It starts when I ask for two eggs.

Where are you from?

Australia.

You came all the way to Spain *just* for the Camino?

Yes, just for the Camino.

Incredible. Where did you begin?

Roncesvalles.

Roncesvalles! You must have caught a bus through the Meseta?

No.

No bus? Incredible!

The three are amazed—they didn't call me crazy—but what's more amazing is that I have so far understood every word of their Spanish! They have obviously dumbed it down for me but, broken or not, it is a conversation nonetheless.

The man takes my hand to focus my attention. With his arms stretched out wide, like a fisherman boasting about 'the one that got away', he tells me that Roncesvalles to Ponferrada is a very long way. Then with his fingers side by side, he indicates that Ponferrada and Santiago are very, very close. Not far at all.

I look at the two-inch gap between his fingers and it hits me. The majority of the Camino is behind us now, nearly six hundred kilometres. With only two hundred to go, we are actually close to Santiago.

'*Si?*' I ask.

'*Si!*' the beautiful sisters confirm in unison.

Their reply brings a gentle sense of achievement that only now I feel safe enough to enjoy. The end is in sight. We're on the home stretch!

247

The next day, I leave the tent city in Ponferrada and head back toward the bridge to pick up the trail on the other side of town. Temporary campgrounds have been established from Castilla y León all the way to Galicia, to take up the overflow from the *albergues*.

It is the Jacobean, the Holy Year, and compounding this, the Spanish school holidays have just begun. There are thousands more on the trail now than when Colin and I began, more than were here this time last year and more than will be here this time next. The Holy Year is awaited and celebrated years in advance. The next is not until 2010. With so many new people around, most of whom have only been walking since León or Astorga, or who may even be setting out right now beside me, the atmosphere has completely changed. I opted for the alternative accommodation while standing among a hundred other pilgrims lined up in a fight for beds outside the *albergue*. The tents are much quieter and less intrusive. At best the newcomers are loud, obnoxious, inconsiderate, rude and unfriendly. Like a raucous football crowd all cheering for opposing teams. I feel out of place among them. This will be the next challenge. To hold on to what we've known of the Camino so far: the peace, silence, acceptance, generosity, space and surrender, amidst an unaccommodating environment.

And to *find* the good in the bad once more.

Colin: *The House of Holy Horrors*

A long descent to Molinaseca in the darkness, orange lights burning in the spire of the church, slipping on loose shale underfoot, the barking of dogs welcoming the entrance of pilgrims who have made the pre-dawn trek before me. The smell of charcoal from a recent forest fire hangs in the air like a pall.

The town looks like an alpine ski village: something Disney would build if he were making a cartoon about the Camino. I would have stayed longer, but the Camino is like watching the world from a very slow moving train. I huff and puff on through: *Miles to go before I sleep, miles to go before I sleep.*

Picture postcard is not a description you would apply to the next big town, Ponferrada. Unless you like sending people postcards from places like Birmingham or Pittsburgh. Ponferrada is not pretty. It may have been once, when the Templars built their castle high on the hill, but now there are just rows of cranes crouched over apartment blocks like wading birds over a polluted pond. There is a disused coal station, straight out of Dickens, and acres of coal yards fallen into disrepair. On the outskirts there are allotments where old men in track pants and rubber boots toil over root vegetables.

I try to slow my pace; I know Eli is struggling with her knee and foot, and I don't want to catch her up just yet. I figure she needs time on her own. For one thing she needs time away from me; and the other thing she needs, because she said so, and it occurs to me she's absolutely right, is that she needs to prove to herself she's not dependent on anyone else's encouragement or strength to do this. In fact, I suspect she never was. But I'm one of those guys who have just one pace;

walk hand in hand along a beach with the most beautiful girl in the world and I break into a jog.

Market gardens and two-storey square brick houses flash past. The scenery reminds me of old Yugoslavia but without the ethnic cleansing.

I climb past vineyards. There is in my breast the burgeoning hope that I have seen the last, at least in this lifetime, of wheat.

There is a church in Cacabelos town square. Or is it a church? For a moment I believe I have stumbled into the Cacabelos Catholic Schoolboys Under 15 trophy room. There are cups everywhere—what are they for? Fairest and Best Guilt Passer, 1999? Most Choirboys Buggered Behind the Confessional, 1905–1941?

The place is terrifying. Along the walls there are more life-size Barbie dolls in black mantillas, and these are, I assume, representations of the grieving Virgin Mary. And here is the son she is grieving for: on the cross, blood everywhere—Christ, bring in the forensics team and a fire hose. I feel physically sick. It reminds me of a waxworks torture chamber they built on Southend Pier when I was a kid. There were moving waxworks of racks, thumbscrews, branding irons and the Spanish Boot, which you could enjoy for sixpence while you licked your candy floss. This is just like that. The House of Holy Horrors.

I turn around and bump into a martyr with a knife sticking through his torso, like a scene from *Aliens*. He looks so real, I say: 'Excuse me.' For fuck's sake.

I go across the street to a bar and order a *café con leche*. To take my mind off the House of Holy Horrors I start a conversation in pig Spanish with the bar lady. She tells me she'd like to fuck Roberto Carlos, the Real Madrid left back. Of course she would. Doesn't everyone in this weird country?

Eli: Sidesteps and detours

It is a perfect walking day.

The morning passes rather uneventfully as I tramp through three small villages: Columbrianos, Fuentes Nuevas and Camponaraya. Then further on, I stumble across Jodie sitting on a tree stump by the side of the path, grinning from ear to ear and smoking a . . . let's say, a cigarette.

She screams, 'Me Aussie mate, how are ya, 'ey?'

I jump, startled. We hug and laugh.

Jodie plans to stop further on but for now, we wander together through fields of vineyard grapes and olives while she tells me about how she came to be on the Camino.

Jodie was an elite athlete, a national soccer player. She was in training for the Olympics when a knee injury ended her career. In a cruel twist, the injury occurred during a celebrity charity match when she was taken out by a federal politician. She would never play again.

She took off travelling once she had recovered. Her limbs are adorned with homemade jewellery and gifts from people she's met along the way. She carries postcards of Australian animals to give in return: koalas, wombats and the international favourite, kangaroos. She has a natural energy, a kind of spark; whether it's for five minutes or five hours, being near her makes my day a little brighter.

We pass an open shed with two old men sitting inside, whistling as they bottle a new batch of regional wine. Jodie gets a gleam in her eye. 'Up for a glass of red?'

'We weren't offered a glass of red.'

'Not yet we weren't,' she says mischievously, and we turn around.

Sure enough the old fellas are more than happy to see

us and we spend a large portion of the remaining afternoon sampling every type of wine produced from their vineyard, as well as corking a few bottles of our own.

From sumptuous red blends to pinots, whites and sticky desserts, one by one the men proudly present a never-ending procession of cleanskins. Before long, all my major organs are buoyed, floating freely in a concoction of rocket fuel and I'm glowing like a neon sign in Kings Cross.

The old guys offer to drive us into the next town. I like the idea but Jodie won't let me accept.

'C'mon,' she says, throwing her arm around me, 'we'll be right. *No pasa nada.*'

Of course! *No pasa nada.* What was I thinking?

We thank the men for their hospitality. They kiss us on both cheeks, one slaps me on the arse with a wink and off we stagger toward Cacabelos.

Day 26
To Pereje together

Colin: And there she is

I stumble out of the bar where the ancient barmaid is still shouting what she'd like to do to Roberto Carlos if she had a couple of balloons, a packet of maraschino cherries and some whipped cream.

'Hey, Crusty!'

It's my sidekick, Tonto. She looks ten pounds lighter since Astorga and it's good to see her. I missed her; I missed her constant snacking and her goofy grin and Birkenstock sandals and dodgy knee and determination. I miss the company and our conversations over coffee. I missed her obsession with getting to Santiago. I just can't find the words to say so.

Eli: Stuck somewhere between here and there

Finding Crusty's familiar face in a street full of strangers is an unexpected surprise that brings with it a warm and very welcome sense of relief. It may be the buzz of wine vaporising brain cells but it feels like weeks have passed. And one look at Col's face tells me he has done it tough throughout our time apart. White lines across his forehead suggest he's spent the last two days frowning in the sun. His T-shirt has not been washed; by the strong scent, neither has he. And the end of his prized pilgrim stick is beaten down to a frayed daisy. The tip of it is two inches shorter than it was in Astorga and turns out 360 degrees like the face of a flower. He barely says a word but it's still nice to see him. Following hugs and a few smiles, it is straight back to business and, half tanked, I follow on to Villafranca, hoping we'll spend time catching up over dinner.

The rest of that day we wander along scenic mountain trails. A church floats on distant clouds, an elaborate old house hangs on a far-off cliff edge. Hills lush with greenery tumble down on top of each other into the horizon. Arriving in Villafranca, however, is not the end of our day. Rather than stopping for the night as planned, we are turned away at the front door of another full *albergue*. In a cruel blow, even the tent city across the road is full up. With no other choice but to walk on, Col buys us both ice-cream and we set off out of town.

The distance doesn't bother either of us anymore. We both feel we could walk all day and night if we had to, until we reach Santiago. From here it would only take three full days. But we are back in the mountains and suddenly it is cold again. I cross my fingers and hope it doesn't rain. Nothing dries in damp air and a pack is just too heavy to lug when it's wet. As are your legs. Dry, my cargo pants already weigh over a kilo. Pockets full of snacks double that, and when they're wet, I can barely keep them up.

The next town is Pereje, an unappealing hamlet set in the deepest part of the Valle de Valcárcel, seven kilometres through the mountains. It's getting dark. We have no choice but to stay here. After finding the *albergue* there also overflowing with weary bodies, we stop at the town's only bar—which supposedly has some limited accommodation. I don't get a chance to find out, however, as my attempt to ask the female owner 'How much for a room?' goes horribly wrong. And I really thought my Spanish was improving.

It appears we are homeless for the night and as darkness descends on the valley, I stand outside, looking up towards the fortune of stars suspended in the night sky and count each of them as times I have wanted to give in. Not just along the Camino, but in life. I wonder why it's easier now to keep going than to quit. I suspect Colin is asking himself the same question. He had every reason to throw in the towel weeks ago. He thinks he stayed for me, but the truth is he's stronger and more stubborn than he knows.

Perhaps that's why I feel so much for him. And why we relate. Beneath all of his sarcasm and cynicism, his strengths and weaknesses, his decisions or regrets, lies a simple man with simple needs; to love and be loved, by others or just by himself. Isn't that at the heart of every human being?

Colin: The Albergue Torquemada

In the days apart we have both noted how the whole atmosphere of the Camino has changed. It's just a race for beds in the *albergues* now, which open early, eleven o'clock, and are already full half an hour later. So when we arrive late that afternoon, in the rain, at a place that sounds like Purgatory, it is no surprise that we are turned away from the only *albergue* in town.

At Purgatory I look through the register in reception: the pilgrims sleeping here tonight have walked from Astorga, Ponferrada, León. Most of these bastards have only been walking two days! I feel a growing sense of outrage. Suddenly Eli and I are part of an elite group; hardened veterans who have been walking nearly a month and now we can't get beds because of a bunch of sissies who haven't even worn their boots in yet.

We try to book into the local bar. I leave Eli alone with the owner for two minutes and by the time I get back, the woman is shouting at her from the door: *Get out! Get out!*

'What did you say to her, El?'

'I don't know.'

'You must have said something.'

'I didn't, honest!'

I am later told, by an English-speaking local who witnessed the incident, that rather than asking the female bar owner 'How much for a room?' Eli had inadvertently asked, 'How much for your body?'

Nothing like calling a Spanish woman a lesbian whore to help get a room in a crowded village.

So we go back to the *albergue* and throw ourselves at the mercy of the *hostelero*. He doesn't have any. He's a Catholic. His forefathers used to heat irons for the Spanish Inquisition.

But finally one of the Spanish pilgrims intervenes and pleads for us to be allowed to sleep in the garden. It looks like it will rain again soon but at least the barbecue pit is under cover. Hostelero Torquemada relents, providing we pay him just as much as we would have done for a bed inside.

Included in his Christian charity is a cold shower, which the next day spreads a raging infection to a blistered welt on Eli's foot, and bad drinking water that gives me the squirts. All for three euros. God bless them.

I opt for the cement floor of the barbecue pit. It has a roof and I have an air bed. El takes her chances with the rain and a kindly donated blanket—tossed in pity out a window by a fellow pilgrim when the *hostelero* isn't watching—on a flat patch of garden grass.

Interestingly, not one of the 'outsiders' is Spanish. I wonder if it's like this in heaven. Are all angels swarthy and excitable?

We're so close now, if Pereje isn't purgatory it is, at least, the beginning of the end.

Day 27
Pereje to Alto do Poío

Colin: *Getting the hell out of Purgatory*

I don't want to do this anymore. I could have happily quit on the second day. This journey has not been what I had antici-pated. But I made a promise to El, and for reasons of her own, my presence seems to be important to her. We're the Two Musketeers, all for one and one for both. The one thing that I am sure of is my physical endurance; I can do this now that my feet are healing. If not for anything else but for Eli.

My tenderness for her grows; this long, complicated, blis-tered, feisty bugger of a woman. I want her to go all the way and I want to be there to see that she does. It has stunned and amazed me that we still have a relationship after my behaviour these last few weeks, my outburst in León. She has seen the very worst of me, and seen me broken. Yet still she seems to see something worthwhile in me, without the mask and the control games. What that is I cannot begin to understand. It is the first time in my life I have let any woman see me defence-less and her acceptance of my failings has changed my view of the world somehow.

We leave Purgatory along the highway, walking cold and stiff like zombies. And here's a sight first thing in the morning: a man wearing a Petzl headlamp, two ski poles, Raybans, knee-high hiking socks folded twice, fluoro cycle shorts and a backpack the size of a baby's fist. The Obsessive Compulsive on pilgrimage. I feel shabby and overdone groping along in the dark with my homemade walking stick and a backpack that looks like I have Brazil in it.

The silhouette of the mountains looms from the fog like the interlocking paws of a giant cat. Eli lopes ahead; she has a new walking stick, and she is twisting it from side to side and over her head. She thinks I can't see her in the dark, but now she stands revealed: Elizabeth Best, at heart, is a frustrated cheerleader.

At first light she stops to lean against a wall and rips off her sock. Three viruses as yet unknown to medical science spill all over the stone wall.

'Doesn't look good, El.'

She pops one of her blisters and we are greeted by my mother's favourite dessert when I was a kid—custard with raspberry jelly.

'Think you got a real problem there, Eli.'

'Fuuuuuck,' she murmurs, which just about sums it up.

Privately, I still don't think she'll make it. Especially now. The closer we get, the more her body protests. The psychological blow may be terminal. It looks so wretched and wrong, I don't even crack a joke to try to cheer her up. After so many physical setbacks already, I wonder if this might be the last straw.

'She'll be right,' Eli says, splashing on a ridiculous amount of both Betadine and Mercurochrome.

Some pilgrims overtaking us think the Mercurochrome is running blood and pass out on the road. Eli puts her sock back on, flicks the real excess blood on the stone wall until her socks are dryish, and straightens her backpack.

'Ready Freddy?' she says with a brave if unconvincing grin.

And we take off back up the mountain.

We start to climb the cobblestoned lanes that look like green tunnels. They have roofs of green branches, moss green and dew heavy. The walls are made of pieces of slate placed end to end like piled gravestones.

Herrerías is a typical Galician village; it looks and smells like shit. Cabbages the size of small trees spill over slate walls, international flags hang above a street redolent with cow dung. A woodshed leans drunkenly against a wall, wooden balconies, minutes from collapsing into the street, sag from stone houses. The rush of a stream drowns out every sound. You can smell river peat and mould and cold. It looks as I imagine it did five hundred years ago, except for the white plastic chairs and the San Miguel umbrella that sits outside a hovel not unlike Shrek's outhouse.

The houses are like farmers' houses all over the world: crap everywhere, rustic charm juxtaposed with the pragmatic things of farming life—rusty machinery, bright mandarin fertiliser bags, black plastic. The chimneys leak white smoke. The houses themselves are built of grey shale and mossed grey tiles, stones perched on the apexes of the roofs to keep the loose slate tiles in place in a storm and break up the snow in winter. The walls are overgrown with wild blackberry.

Around a corner we stumble on an ivy-covered cottage with bright pink stucco and brand new aluminium windows. Next door their neighbours live in a barn that almost fell down a hundred years ago.

'You could make a mint here,' Eli says, sounding like Bill Hunter in *Muriel's Wedding*. 'Rich Spaniards are buying these places up for weekenders, they're right on the Camino, and the Camino's been here a thousand years, it's not going anywhere, and if a pilgrim dies on your doorstep the value goes through the roof! I reckon you and me should invest in one, Crusty.'

As we walk we see no one but pilgrims. It is like a Disney movie set. Except for the detritus of modern pilgrimage which now starts to litter the route: Aquarius orange fizz cans and Fontesneder cookies.

All the villages smell of manure and shit drips through the streets. We are crowded and shepherded by stone walls, howled at by dogs. Strangers in a ripe land. A woman steps out from behind a pile of cow shit and offers us a steaming pancake, throwing the towel aside from the plate like a conjurer producing a rabbit. A man on a donkey squeezes us against a wall. He has a battery sitting on his lap to power the cattle prod in his right hand. Clouds billow up from the valley to meet us.

We know we're in Galicia because of the rolling green hills—and the rain. It starts raining almost the moment we step across the border. Wherever you look, there is green, every shade of green: jade green, pea green, dark green, light green, greeny green. Just green. And not a stalk of the W-word in sight.

And we hear cowbells; we have not heard the sound of cowbells since the Pyrenees. I see a cow licking another cow's head while she munches contentedly on the grass. I feel a pang of loneliness. This is what I miss about being single again: not just having my head licked, but feeling such affection from someone else that I'd want to lick theirs back.

'Eli, will you lick my head?'

'What?'

'Lick my head. Will you?'

'Col, you're scaring me again.'

'I'll lick yours.'

We come out of a leafy green tunnel at the foot of the mountain, loping up the ascent like mountain goats. It is again a shock to realise how fit we are. We have been walking nearly a month now, and most of these people have been walking just two days.

Halfway up the hill we stumble across 1970. Two guys with dreadlocks and thousand-yard stares are making hash pipes on the steps of a fall-down cottage. They have a cloth laid out on a trestle table selling everything a pilgrim needs: *tao* necklaces, crucifixes—and hash pipes. They are doing a good trade from the invading army behind us. This is no longer a pilgrimage, this is a frontal assault on Galicia by packs of Spanish kids with baseball caps and blister plasters. A pillage of pilgrims. D-Day of the Devout.

Suddenly there are signs for Santiago by the side of the road every five hundred metres. Just two hundred and five kilometres left. A long way now from the wooded dales of Roncesvalles. The pilgrims who started in Ponferrada seem to think just getting here is a long way. We lope past them like Ethiopian long distance runners lapping the wild card entry from Papua New Guinea in the Olympics.

At the peak we follow the line of chestnuts and oaks along the ridge to Cebreiro. The town is going off. We find ourselves in Man of La Mancha Land, a toy stone village with souvenir shops, piped medieval music, and a funky little downstairs bar that plays music videos. We stop for a quick beer in the bar. There is a Spanish soap on the television, and it looks every bit as bad as they do at home. The actors are all impossibly beautiful and as self-absorbed as models in a hair gel commercial. They give each other long looks that seem to say: *I farted but now I'm going to pretend it was you.* The music is from *Invasion of the Monster Bananas.*

There's a mural of Santiago on a wall: he's dressed in traditional style, Captain Pugwash hat with a scallop shell insignia, brown robes, staff with a gourd tied to it, sandals. He looks like Father Christmas back in his whoring days.

We decide not to stay in el Cebreiro—too much adrenalin and the overflow accommodation for the *albergue* looks like the latrines at a biker heavy-metal rock festival. It's an hour's walk to the next *albergue*, which appears to be a pig farm, and it's full. Even the pigs pay to stay there in high season. This is a long way from the homely little *albergues* out in the middle of the Meseta. We look back on our welcomes there with a kind of nostalgia. Here they wouldn't even urinate in your ear if your head was on fire.

The pilgrims are a whole different breed also. They are predominantly Spaniards who know the local terrain and have back-up. Some families even hire a bus to take them from village to village so they can get a stamp from the local *albergue* for their Compostela. They bus most of it. So much for struggle and self-reflection.

.The guidebook told us before we left that you could not be thrown out of an *albergue*, that no one would ever turn away a pilgrim. 'They' were wrong! *Hosteleros* will dismiss you like you are a homeless derro walking up to reception at Fox News and asking for small change. Their lips curl, their noses twitch. You're not Spanish. So you walked six hundred and fifty-odd kilometres to get here? Tell someone who gives a *merda*.

By the time we leave the pig farm, we are exhausted. I have the squirts from the water at Purgatory and we can barely stand by the time we get to the top of the next mountain. The *albergue* is full there as well. Full of fucking cyclists, which really rubs salt into the wound. We do what every self-respecting Australian would do in an emergency: we go to the bar in the local hotel.

Eli: *Countdown or meltdown*

Once again, the lessons of patience, acceptance and surrender have returned, as we expected they might. Any sense of control or advantage we thought we'd earned—or by this stage, deserved—has been taken away.

Whether we are fit now or not doesn't matter anymore. Neither does the fact that it's much cooler and easier to walk longer hours. We've been slowed by the influx of numbers and the race for beds and we no longer have the luxury of picking our place, marking distance or dotting our day's destination. Just when we thought we were nearing the end, the Camino reminds us that nothing here is yours to claim until it's granted. The rules have changed and again we are back at the mercy of the Way.

By five o'clock that afternoon, another four *albergues*, hostels and hotels in three different villages have turned us away in a period of two hours. Having spent a major part of the day hiking the peaks of Cebreiro, I've arrived at the end of my tether. Tears and all. I throw myself across the bar in shame. The barman takes pity and makes a call to a local woman who runs a B&B a few kilometres out of town.

The mother figure who saves us at the summit is a godsend, just when all hope seemed lost. We are rescued, cooked for, hugged and even laughed at adoringly. To someone accustomed to showered guests, I imagine the sight of us desperate and forlorn would be hilarious. It's fair to say Colin and I now look exactly how we feel: dishevelled and tragic. If only the Man Booker Prize judges could see us now, we'd be nominated out of sympathy. After twenty-four hours of rejection, it is so nice to feel welcomed, wanted and loved. Albeit by a complete stranger who charges us for the luxury.

Poor Col picked up a stomach bug in Purgatory that has well and truly set in throughout the day. He's as white as a bed sheet and as steady on his feet as a toddler taking its first steps. Like a toddler's, his stomach and bowel have been just as unpredictable. I spent the day walking upwind. The minute we arrive he sheepishly locks himself away in the bathroom.

I wander through the house and can't help but feel we have been plucked from a crowded Camino and dumped in a nature resort. It's like somewhere you'd go for a cosy weekend away. Not another pilgrim in sight.

In the cottage, I watch fascinated from the first floor bedroom window as our host does the rounds of neighbouring houses collecting fresh produce for our dinner: sliced *jamón* from the lady next door with piglets, *queso* from the family across the road with cows, half a dozen *huevos* from the hen-pen two doors down and *tomates* from her own garden on the way back to the house. The clustered hamlet is an organic supermarket.

From my first-floor bedroom window in Melbourne, I used to watch a succession of men slipping discreetly in and out the front door of the brothel across the street. That too was interesting to watch, but in a different kind of way.

Colin has only just ventured out of our room as Maria, our surrogate mother, and I begin preparing dinner. Almost on cue, he turns a flattering shade of olive green and about-faces. She makes him a cup of manzanilla tea and orders him straight to bed. In spite of the circumstances, he is the happiest he's been in weeks. Sheepishly grinning, cracking jokes again and laughing at his own expense. The frown on his face has eased. After the mess of mixed emotions we've endured in the last thirty days, it's as if the squirts are the final straw. If you don't laugh, you cry. And on the Camino, you do both.

We've climbed the final peak and what's more, we did it easily. The Meseta feels like a year ago now, and Roncesvalles another lifetime. Colin and I have come a long way, in a physical sense and in other ways as well. And with it, our friendship has grown beyond the hardships. The time apart has served a worthy purpose for us both. Maybe it is the thought of being so close to the end, but Colin seems almost relieved.

Day 28
Alto do Poío to Triacastela

Eli: Holy Camino, Rainman!

No matter the distance—short, long or in between—if we find a bed, we've found our home.

At seven the next morning, the beautiful Maria drives us back in her Land Cruiser to where she picked us up the night before. And not a step further.

'How's your tummy?'

'Rrrr . . . bit better.' *Shuffle, shuffle . . .*

'How's your foot?'

'. . . not sure yet. We'll see.' *Shuffle, shuffle . . .*

I spend most of the day listening to music to try to block out the noise of the Camino cartel. Within an hour we are part of a convoy. I try to stay positive by focusing on the scenery. It is awe inspiring and, at times, completely humbling. I've never been the 'outdoorsy' type and could never quite understand it before but nature is like a drug: the more time you spend with it, the more alluring it becomes and the harder it is to be away from. I wonder if it will last back in the 'real' world. However, despite the beauty of the views, it's impossible not to notice the hordes of people. It feels like there are new pilgrims arriving on the trail every hour—either that or they're multiplying like amoebas. We try speeding up to break away but the crowd is evenly spread, both ahead and behind.

You only need walk the last one hundred kilometres of the Camino to receive a Compostela and in a Holy Year, a Compostela is your one-way ticket to heaven. Even so, instead of walking, some are bus hopping from town to town collecting stamps from bars and *albergues* for evidence. Is this what Led Zeppelin meant about buying a stairway to heaven? Everybody is racing to have their sins forgiven and they don't care how many they have to commit in the process. There is nothing we can do to make the situation any more bearable so Col and I decide to stop at a roadside bar.

Colin skipped dinner last night but this morning he has found his appetite again. We sit at an outside table and watch the procession pass like kids watching a parade.

'Oh, look at that one with the fluoro-pink Nikes and portable beat box.'

It is just fourteen kilometres to Triacastela, the nearest substantial town. Barely a morning's walk, but we have decided to try to stop there for the night. I need to get to a pharmacy and a doctor as soon as possible. I have developed an infection in a blister on the left foot and it has already spread and blown up my ankle. If we leave it much later in the day, we are likely to miss out on a bed again.

At 11.30 we stumble out of an old wood forest, checking into the first *albergue* on the outskirts of town. We are the first to arrive for the day.

It's siesta by the time we make it into the town itself, so nothing but a bar is open. Col takes a seat outside. His face is still the colour of putty. I join him, lifting my foot to rest on the chair beside me, hoping to ease the swelling. But taking the weight off sparks a bolt of pain that shoots up the back of my leg like an electric cattle prod and makes me jump in my seat. I quickly put it down again.

Moments later, a group of Spaniards at the table next to us catch sight of it, raging red like a beacon.

'Oh, *Dios mío! Mira, mira* . . . *está horrible!*' The woman points as her three friends, too, express their disgust.

I humour them with a closer look. My feet do look hideous, but their hideousness is also a source of great pride. My feet have become a metaphor for the journey we've taken. They have carried me through a lot and the state of them is evidence that we have suffered to get where we are. They won't stop me reaching Santiago. The sight of these ugly things only serves to inspire me, even if it discourages others.

I see a flash of elegance against the backdrop of slate rooftops and mountain peaks.

'Who's that sexy Spanish princess?' I call out.

Mercedes stops and turns.

'*Hola, guapa, hola!* Oh, I'm so happy to see the boat ob you.' She runs toward us with open arms.

It has been two weeks and I was wondering if we would see them again. Mercedes tells us that Simon is very sick. She is not sure he can walk tomorrow. She left him in bed to try to find medicine, but everything is closed. I explain our situation and she joins us for a drink while we wait for the pharmacy to open.

Mercedes doesn't drink. Ever. But something is very different now than when we last saw her. She appears more laidback, relaxed, content.

With Simon sick and Colin weak, the wheels have fallen off the fun bus. The crew is looking the worse for wear. It is like the first half of our Camino played back in reverse; in the beginning, I was ill with gastro; we met Simon and Mercedes; Simon was fit and strong while Mercedes was struggling. Together, they helped me through the next day. Then Colin's blistered feet became infected. Now, nearing the end, Colin is ill with gastro, we have met Simon and Mercedes again, Mercedes is fighting fit while Simon's in bad shape. And now I have the infection in my blistered feet. The wheel turns.

Colin and I decide that we will stay close and walk with them until Santiago. It is time to repay the favour and, as we began, so we will all finish what we started together.

That afternoon I head to the infirmary alone. Sure enough, my blisters are infected and the infection has spread. The doctor also notes the clump of swelling on the side of my right foot and I use the only Spanish I have to explain that it is the least of my concerns, *No pasa nada*. He orders two days' rest to wait for the antibiotics to take effect. For the first time, I am genuinely concerned, as is Col. He knows the consequences all too well. This time last year he spent ten days on an IV drip in a Thai hospital with an infection that turned systemic. I thank him for telling me this now. But neither of us has any intentions of taking days off so close to Santiago. From now on, we will plan our stops around medical facilities. The injury is bearable but the infection is visibly spreading fast and will continue to do so until we stop moving. Colin and I agree that if the rash of swelling passes my knee, heading north to Kidneytown, we will stop.

The race is on to Santiago.

Day 29
Triacastela to Sarria

Eli: Rise on

Next morning, we pack up and set out. All four of us are back on the trail again, leaving Triacastela in the cool morning dawn, among thick misted mountains. It's a stunning way to start the day. The end feels near. This is the Camino in all of its unpredictable splendour but—surely?—nothing can stop us now.

Metres apart and in single file, we wind along canopied paths, surrounded by ferns and freshwater streams. It reminds me of the Pyrenean foothills we walked through during the first days, leaving Roncesvalles. Only this time, we're fit enough to appreciate the views, experienced enough to know what we are doing and are actually comfortable in our surroundings. Among the newcomers, we have all the advantages I once admired.

In a clearing with cattle grazing the pasture, I watch the sun rise over the belltower ruins of an ancient church, knowing it will be one of the last. Rain begins to dance across the surface of my skin. It is almost apt amidst the lush scenery.

At the next tiny roadside township, we call into a *cantina*. It reminds me of the roadhouses from Hollywood road films set in the Midwest: lino floors, odd-coloured bar stools, laminated benchtops and booths. There are forty pilgrims crammed

271

inside, riffling through their packs for waterproof ponchos and raincoats. They look more concerned than we do, but they are mostly Spaniards, so they know the reputation of the region: *the potty of Spain*. Mercedes reminds us that we're in Galicia now and once the rain starts it doesn't stop for days.

We do our best to cover up. Colin has a huge hole in the front of his poncho and I sent mine home a week ago to try to lessen weight. I remove my damp, muddy socks and we move out amidst a pack of shivering pilgrims. It's like walking to the famous MCG to watch the weekend's sell-out footy match on one of Melbourne's notoriously wet and windy winter days. Only the loyal fans truly committed to their cause would dare venture out.

It's a melancholy kind of day and I'm in a contemplative mood. I walk with memories of weeks and days gone by. People, places, familiar faces, other sunrises, sunsets and burnt horizons, conversations and unspoken moments Colin and I have either shared, or experienced alone. I wonder what they will one day come to mean.

I no longer believe this journey will end in Santiago, or in Finisterre. I'm not sure it will ever really end at all. Santiago, the city, has lost relevance. The fact that I now feel comfortable and we have earned our place here is reward enough. I get the feeling it will be sometime after I return that the magic of these experiences will be realised.

I look back at the others, everyone lost in their own thoughts. It's pouring rain, we're sludging along a muddy path lined with log fences. It's the same path locals use to transport cattle to pasture and market each day. I remind myself it is August, I will return from Spain to the start of an Australian spring. Sunny days, backyard barbecues and hot summer nights spent with friends on St Kilda beach. The rain has washed away the dressings on my feet. I look down and watch the stew of mud and dung ooze through the open wounds of blistered toes.

The Spaniards are right, I must be crazy. But I'm in good company.

Day 30
Sarria to Gonzar

Colin: A bocadillo and a dead dog

Apparently I have been snoring again, a combination of all the red wine I drink with dinner and a sinus problem that I refuse to have fixed because I am scared of ENT surgeons. Eli tells me that during the night the other pilgrims have been sighing, grumbling, shaking the bed, calling the police, that sort of crap, and when she finally woke me and shouted: 'Colin, you're snoring!' people clapped and cheered. Well I didn't hear a damned thing. I suspect she is making it all up.

The Spaniards wake at three o'clock, stretch as if they are warming up for the Olympics, then race on to the next *albergue* so they will have a bed. This is what the Camino has become: Petzl headlamps and alarm clocks that go off at 3 am and sound like an electric rooster on speed.

We leave in the dark and follow a steep stone path through crowding chestnuts. There are splashes of cow shit everywhere, and every hundred metres we have to jump out of the way of bovines driven from one field to another by Spanish farmers with three-day stubble.

Eli has overcome her blisters, swollen knee and foot injury, and she's facing her final challenge. Her Achilles tendon is so sore she can barely walk. The infection has got hold of it, just as it got to mine in Belorado. She should stop, for her health, for her sanity. But we're so close. I think maybe it has crossed her mind that if she stops now she might never get going again.

She is limping and shuffling, and she doesn't want to get her feet wet so she has wrapped them in colourful plastic bags. What a sight. But she won't quit. We joke about it. If the tendon snaps it won't hurt anymore, I tell her. 'It will just fire up behind your kneecap and we'll strap your bad leg to the good one and you can hop the last two days.'

We come out of the woods and lose the little yellow arrows in the dark. So we navigate via the litter of plastic bottles by the side of the trail. We must be on the Senda again. It works for a while but then the four of us get lost anyway and end up on a freeway flyover looking for yellow arrows on passing juggernaut trucks. We retrace our footsteps and go back into the woods. In minutes the juggernauts are a memory and we are walking through overhung lanes staring at corn and cows, passing hamlets of stone cottages with russet red roofs. There are eucalypts and pine.

The flies are driving us crazy. There are more flies than in India. Flies live on cow shit and Galicia is built on cow shit. There are little stone huts made of bricks. They look like houses for very thin tall people, but it's just where they dry corn so the mice can't get to it. Every house we pass has one.

The walk is like a school camp now, a procession of boy scouts and religious Spaniards, some so devout they are wearing monk's cowls. Many of them are my kids' ages. Why aren't they off doing drugs and getting laid? I guess when you're that young, being wet and uncomfortable and over-crowded is not a problem. This is just a rock concert only the songs are different.

We reach the hundred-kilometre Santiago marker, which is devoutly splattered with orange paint and graffiti. Eli stops a passing German pilgrim and asks him to take a photograph of the four of us—Simon, Mercedes, myself and her—standing beside it. It means more to her than it does to me. I just want to get off this bloody trail, except I've now realised I don't want to go back to my life.

Later that morning we reach the bridge at Portomarín. The skeletal ruins of the old town, sacrificed to make way for the damming of the river, are visible below. We're just about there.

'Well, that wasn't so bad,' I say to Eli with a grin. 'This bit's easy.'

Like life, the Camino takes you down when you feel the most confident, the most in control. As we climb out of the town it starts to rain again and it gets colder, fast. We are soon cold, hungry, tired and very, very wet. We take shelter in a brick factory. This is depressing.

'We can't stay here,' Eli mutters. 'It's freezing.'

It's also summer. In Spain. So we trudge on through pine and corn, socks soaked, blisters wet and chafing. We are looking for warmth, shelter, good food and somewhere comfortable to sleep. Instead we find Gonzar.

Gonzar has one *albergue*, a two-storey brick house with twenty beds, one bathroom and a hundred pilgrims queued up outside waiting to get in. It is like lining up to sleep in a concentration camp.

We wander downtown—not that Gonzar has an uptown, it's just a figure of speech—and find a guesthouse with a private bathroom for twenty-five euros and almost force the banknotes into the woman's trembling hand. A wise decision. Two hours later the guesthouse is packed, and by late afternoon there are pilgrims offering our benefactor ten euros to sleep in the dog basket in the kitchen. By nightfall the dog is paying her to sleep under her car.

There is one bar, and pilgrims who have been put on the waiting list to sleep on the floor in the *albergue* are living there. The menu consists of beer and *bocadillos*. So we order a beer and a *bocadillo*. The barman is totally uninterested. Why should he be pleasant? He doesn't have to be nice to anyone. If you don't eat at his place, you don't eat.

Outside, a priest is sitting under a stone crucifix surrounded by piles of sand and cement, playing 'House of the Rising Sun' on a nylon string guitar. Later he holds an impromptu mass. He doesn't have an altar so he's using a day old *bocadillo* balanced on a dead dog.

We watch while we eat our *bocadillos*, which smell vaguely of manure. Eli picks a fly from hers but eats it anyway. Rain drips off the canvas awning. A dog raises its leg to pee against a five-gallon drum full of beer bottles.

People actually live here.

Eli: Ten things I've learned so far

1. People who complain about snorers are often the worst snorers of all.

2. It's not always good to rope others into your idealistic misadventures.

3. Stainless steel vats used to produce Coca-Cola are exchanged every three years due to corrosion. Based on this theory, if you happen to contract a stomach bug or virus while travelling abroad, drinking copious amounts of the premium grade, artificially coloured and preserved, caffeine-infused, sweetened soft drink is guaranteed to kill all living organisms (including the bad ones), promptly returning you to a robust state of health with vitality.

4. Never shower in the mornings before setting out to cover long distances. Hot water softens the skin on your feet, guaranteeing fresh blisters by the end of the day.

5. Taking aspirin daily thins the blood, thereby reducing the risk of swelling while relieving pain without the effects of drowsiness.

6. Using sunscreen as moisturiser helps to rehydrate aching muscles.

7. Double doses of prescription painkillers generally make a day more pleasurable.

8. Eating deli chicken that has been in your pack for five hours while you walked through a Spanish desert can have hallucinogenic effects.

9. Hay bales are not always churches.

10. Massaging your feet with methylated spirits for two weeks prior to walking a pilgrimage (just like my eighty-three-year-old chemist told me to) in fact mercilessly

dehydrates the skin, reducing its elasticity and therefore greatly *increasing* the chances of cracks, peels and blisters, along with considerably compromising the body's ability to heal affected areas.

Day 31
Gonzar to Melide

Colin: *Gotta getoutta Gonzar*

Next morning we set off at 4.30, stumbling out into the cobbled street. Only it is not empty. Everyone wants to get out of Gonzar. And if you ever go there, you will too.

The Camino has now degenerated into a race between *albergues*: a pilgrimathon. They travel in packs. Boy scout leaders ferry backpacks from *albergue* to *albergue* in vans and book ahead. This is not a pilgrimage: it's a battle of wits.

I talk to a Spaniard who has travelled all the way from Roncesvalles as we have, and is now turning back in disgust. Some may call him a purist but he has a point. In Castañeda they told us the twelfth-century lime ovens were once used to make the cement for Santiago's cathedral, and medieval pilgrims each carried a heavy stone all the way from Triacastela for use in these kilns. These days they don't even carry their own packs.

Cyclists zip past shouting *Buen Camino* to pilgrims they have just knocked arse over tit into a hedge. Armies of scouts tramp along like the SS invading Poland. Some sport toy crosses made of pine, and little boys with plastic gourds on sticks and funny hats jump out of cars that have ferried them the whole distance to an *albergue* so they can walk the last two hundred metres.

Shops now sell brown felt St James hats, four-euro ponchos, and Camino T-shirts. All these souvenirs remind me of the English seaside town where I was raised; daytrippers would come down from London and buy Kiss Me Quick hats and sticks of rock.

We stop for the night in Melide. The Spaniards sit around complaining about how sore their feet are, competing with each other for the biggest blisters, the worst tendonitis. Just as we did back in Pamplona. Long before they get hardened to it, it will all be over for them.

Eli meets a Swiss guy she tells me is cute and falls in love with him for about ten minutes until he tells her she has the ugliest feet on the Camino. What a smooth talker. (But he's right, she does.) Eli is shattered. She is proud of her feet. They are mangled, bloody, blistered, lumpy and swollen but they have become icons, symbolic. Possibly worth framing.

Eli: *Well, well, well ...*

I wake in the middle of the night in a stairwell. The last twenty-four hours are a daze and we've now become homeless in every sense of the word: cold, wet, tired, hungry and sleeping on the landing of a warehouse lined with plastic gym mats that someone's decided to call an '*albergue*'. Clutching my stomach I realise things are not quite kosher. *Must be the ham.* I look left to see Simon, Mercedes and Colin huddled in a tight row beside me. I sit up. *Oh, not good.* Suddenly I'm scampering across dormant bodies in the dark toward the bathroom ... *I'm not gonna make it! I'm not gonna make it!* I reach for the door, the light, the toilet seat, my knees—*made it. Yuk!* Then repeat the mad dash another four times before first light.

For hours I heave and cough so hard that I wake several other pilgrims in the next room. By morning, my ribs ache. I feel like I did when I was fourteen and threw up after a bottle of cheap Spumante. (The illustrious two-buck chuck—they don't call it Spew-mante for nothing!)

Finally I drop off to sleep, exhausted, for all of fifteen minutes, only to wake to Colin's hand on my shoulder. He is oblivious to what has happened. It is time to go. I look up at him, shake my head and beg.

'Not today?'

He just smiles reassuringly. 'You'll be right, Tonto!'

We pack up and set off in silence through the bitter morning chill. Neither of us is having fun anymore.

Colin: The lightweight championship of the world

It is the second last day: the *albergue* in Melide is so crowded we have to sleep in a stairwell. Eli is stricken with another virus. In the last month she has battled with a swollen knee—she has no cartilage in it, she told me a week into the journey, the result of a teenage sports injury—a haematoma on her calf, tendonitis, blisters, infections, a virus, fever, dehydration, vomiting and is possibly still walking with a stress fracture in her foot.

It is fascinating to watch the two sides of her battle it out; the side that believes in herself and the side that never has and seems intent on finding new ways of doing her in. It's a heavyweight prize fight between two featherweights both determined to win.

It's not the best night's sleep I've ever had, and when we wake just before dawn—you don't sleep in on a stairwell—Eli is not looking good. I know she is battling with herself because her voice is barely audible. It ensures she is either misheard, misunderstood or completely ignored.

In Zubiri I would have put her on the plane and sent her back to Melbourne. But right now I don't care if she has Ebola virus. She is going to get to Santiago tomorrow. I'll fucking piggyback her if I have to.

Eli: The Eli belly blues

The rain falls heavy from above, the day breaks to a dull grey. The four of us walk single file in silence along a muddy trail, as we did for nine hours straight the day before.

Simon and Mercedes lead the way as they did when I was sick on the second day leaving Zubiri. But this time, I can't see them. The rain is falling so hard against my face it is difficult to see more than a few metres ahead.

Beneath the plastic cape of my new poncho my body shakes with cold and fever. The rain sporadically turns to sleet, then hail, then rain again. The thick scent of the eucalyptus reminds me of home, frosty mornings and childhood winters in rural Victoria. How I wish I were there now, curled beneath the covers of my bed with a bottle of flat lemonade and the wafting scent of my grandmother's chicken noodle soup.

Suddenly, memories of all the years since begin to flash through my mind in single frame images, like a slide show. And in a blink, my entire life is reduced to nothing more than a fleeting thought. *What does it all really mean?*

The good times, the hard times, poor decisions, doubt and achievements, sorrow, success, love, loss, family and friendships, even joy. Out here retching every few steps with the weight of my pack strapped tight around a tender tummy, shivering with cold and cringing with the thought of cow crap grating against the raw flesh of blistered skin, trudging through shit and crying in the rain, does any of it really matter? To me or to anyone else?

Does my life matter?

Over the last month I've learned to trust and believe and even depend on myself, daily. I've learned to stand before a mountain and to know that it's mine to climb, to fight when I've felt defeated and to trust that, somehow, I will always get to where I'm going. There have been other experiences in life that have taught me these things too. So why then, at times like these, do I forget, doubt, question and feel so weak, so small, so insignificant? Why am I so forgiving of others, yet not of myself? How many times will I learn to stand so strong before forgetting it at times like these? Why do I think so much? Do other people think like this? Is it normal? Am I normal? What's the point?

I sob quietly beneath the hood of my poncho, caught somewhere in the maelstrom of exhaustion, delirium, dehydration, viral infection, pain and pre-menstrual tension, feeling weak, weary, sick, sad and sorry for myself.

Yes, in hindsight it will be hilariously pathetic I'm sure. But here, so close and yet still so far from the end, it is hideous and suddenly it hits me—after thirty-two days on the trail, with all its blood, sweat, tears, isolation, deprivation, injury, revelation, fear, faith and sufferance, my pilgrimage comes back to this. As it has done time and time again, throughout my life.

Self-doubt.

I am back on the bus in Roncesvalles! Full circle. Have I learned nothing?

I remember the line I wrote in the monastery outside Pamplona—*Each and every step makes me stronger, without and within*—and decide to stop thinking and keep moving. Colin walks two steps behind as I shuffle on, hitching my pants every second step, his elastic camping clothes line tied through the belt loops to hold them up.

For the rest of that afternoon, every time I stop, wondering if I can go on, Col places a steady hand beneath my pack, takes the weight from my shoulders and, together, we walk a few steps more.

Colin has stopped carrying his stick—instead, today, he carries me.

Day 32
Melide to Santa Irene

Colin: *Counting the beats*

I had planned to take my walking stick to Finisterre and toss it in the ocean, as is the tradition. Instead it starts to rain and I need a spare hand to hold my ripped poncho together. Suddenly the walking stick is a burden. Like regrets, like old habits. How many times have I walked through my life with baggage I didn't need? I drag it with me as I have every damned thing I no longer need in my life but have kept with me as part of my perfect picture.

Suddenly it hits me. The damned thing is useless. Why didn't I see it before? It no longer fits me, or me it. It is time to stop before I smash it in fury against a tree. If I leave it by the track some other pilgrim may have use of it. I have pounded out the beat of the Meseta with this stick. There are no more beats. I have counted them all. Me and the stick are over.

We walk on endless trails through pine woods and eucalyptus. The rain hasn't let up. There are tall stands of blue gum dripping with rain and the scent of eucalyptus hangs in the air like mist. It reminds me of the forests of Australia in winter.

There are dairy farms and prosperous villages, all sodden with rain. The day passes like delirium. Every *albergue* is full of Spanish boy scouts and it is close to dark when we finally reach an *albergue* where the *hostelero* has given up trying to maintain any semblance of order and just lets everyone in. He tells us we can sleep wherever we can find room. The only place we can find room is in the kitchen, so we sleep there.

Next morning I wake with a headache and fever; my eyeballs feel twice their normal size. A German student with thighs like sides of pork is standing over me making porridge on the kitchen range. Eli is asleep on the kitchen table, there is someone sleeping underneath it and the German guy is about to eat his breakfast off her stomach.

I've had enough.

I get up, throw a hissy-fit at the German student, curse her unborn children and her cat, and sit on the stairs waiting for the others to hurry up so we can just fucking leave. I feel like death.

Yes, the Camino has finally taught me patience, humility and forbearance. I knew I was here to learn something.

Day 33
Santa Irene to Monte do Gozo

Eli: *The lesser of evils*

Yesterday a stairwell, today a kitchen table. But before I even open my eyes, I realise how close we are to Santiago and that this will be the last serious day's walk for a very long time. Already, I feel better. The vomiting and nausea have passed. I open my eyes to find Colin shivering and holding his head—he looks like I felt yesterday.

Why am I in a kitchen? Who's lying underneath me? Why is this cold wooden table so wonderfully comfortable? And what's that guy doing with his porridge?

We pack up and move out. Mercedes wraps her arms around my waist, tucking her little Spanish self under my wing on the way out the door, reminding me the end is in sight. But the moment we step out onto the road it becomes painfully apparent that the Camino is going to make us work for every wet, heavy, cold, muddy and miserable last step.

The ground sinks underfoot. We are walking in torrential rain and gale-force winds. An hour through a forest of pine, oak and eucalyptus, the packs on our backs are acting as sails, tossing us across the path from one side to the other. Towering gum trees sway ominously above.

Today's destination is Monte do Gozo, the Hill of Joy. But there will be little joy in getting there. What would typically take three hours will take us twice as long now. It's hard to believe the breathless heat of the Meseta is just one week distant. I never thought I'd wish it back.

Colin: Hill of Joy

We set off in a howling gale. Weak and feverish I keep my head down, follow Eli's feet. She has one foot wrapped in a blue plastic bag, the other in a green. She may look weird, but this is not a fashion parade and if you don't stop the water getting through your socks you get blisters, and blisters are still the arch enemy, even at this late stage.

We are part of a procession now, an invading army. Once I look back in the rain and it is like the *Attack of the Killer Condoms*, people wrapped in blue and green and red waterproofs as far down the muddy hill as I can see.

We reach a ridge, next to Santiago airport. A jet reaches tentatively for the tarmac as a gust of wind picks up this particular coloured condom and nearly sends him freewheeling into the turbines. Thunder cracks overhead like an artillery salvo and rain stings my face like a handful of sand. This is not part of my perfect picture. I once imagined us entering the cathedral plaza in bright sunshine to the cheering of an ecstatic grandstand full of fervent and awed Spanish Catholics, there to have a medal hung around my neck by the Pope himself. Like the World Cup final.

Instead, here in the middle of a European summer, the toilet of Spain is bleak and grey and windswept. I realise that tomorrow we will pile into Santiago with thousands of other coloured killer condoms, line up for days to get our passports stamped so we can get a discount on our train fare, then hurry off to find somewhere to sleep that's better than a kitchen table, a stairwell or a barbecue pit.

Today I keep walking because the only other choice is to lie down and die, and that is not on my agenda until tomorrow, or perhaps the day after. And also, I want to see Eli walk into the square in Santiago. Even if the Pope isn't there to put a medal around her neck, after all this, I know I'm going to enjoy seeing her do it.

After the airport we enter Lavacolla—its name apparently means 'to wash one's loins' so, roughly translated, it's Soapthegenitalsville. What a nice address to have if you're from these parts, so to speak. It is so named because this was the place where medieval pilgrims finally, after months of walking, sweating and whoring, splashed some fresh water onto their groin area to cleanse themselves before entering the holy city.

Soon after we get to Monte do Gozo, the Hill of Joy, where these same genitally fragrant pilgrims got their first glimpse of the cathedral spire. Monte do Gozo does not have such an inspirational view now. A TV station dominates the hill and all you can see are busy highways and unattractive suburbs. Today we can't even see those—in fact I can barely see a hand in front of my face, the rain is so dense.

There is no *albergue*, just a vast holiday camp, row upon row of barrack dormitories, shops, cafés and restaurants. Pilgrim City. From here it is just a stroll down the hill to Santiago. An hour or so. Our journey is done.

We walk into our appointed dorm. All I can smell is socks. And the showers are overflowing. Good-oh.

I don't give a shit about Santiago. I'm not sure I ever did. I don't care about the cathedral or about Jimmy the Fish. But I do give a shit about not having to walk anymore. I want to see Eli win, and I want to deliver a prayer, as I promised myself I would. I have carried it into every church, repeated it until I knew every damned word by heart. The woman who wrote it never asked for me to do it, but a prayer's a prayer, and I said it anyway, and whatever anyone else thinks of that doesn't matter.

When this is done, I'll leave it up to those gods on the other side of the ocean to pick up the pieces and make up their minds what it all means.

Eli: Leper in lace

At last, finally, the sprawl of Santiago appears in the distance. The cloud cover is thick and barely broken. But, as if scripted in a B-grade film, a single ray of sunlight suddenly bursts through a tear in the clouds to light the city centre.

I turn to Colin. He looks worn and weary—worse than he did two days ago in Alto do Poío—a man on his final legs. We both laugh. We have become pitiable in appearance. I am a patchwork mélange of plastic bags and Bandaids. He's huddled beneath his poncho shivering with cold. His teeth chatter and the hair on his bare legs stands erect. But still, through his tight grimace he manages a grin. Not of joy but of relief.

The fact that he is so sick doesn't matter to him now. Nor does my foot matter to me. The swell of infection is hovering just below the knee, which is also swollen with tendonitis. The bottom half of my left leg looks like an oversized German salami, puffed up and stained pink. But the rain, the hail, the mud, the fact we have not worn dry clothes or eaten a decent meal in four days, none of it matters with Santiago in sight. We are nearly there. From Monte do Gozo, there are just four and a half kilometres remaining until our journey is complete. And despite the circumstance or how long it takes for us to get there, I'm determined to enjoy every bitter step of what is left.

When you are already this wet, sore and miserable, what do you possibly have left to lose?

We'd heard it pegged as a 'holiday resort', a type of utopia. In the Middle Ages, perhaps it was. This is where the real pilgrims in their capes and worn leather sandals toasted port wine around a campfire overlooking the brilliant spires of the Compostela. But a lot changes in a thousand years and today Monte do Gozo feels like stepping into the athletes' village of a past Olympics. Set on a hillside, a paved walkway joins rows of dormitories on either side, a food hall, bar, laundromat, gift shops, internet café, medical facility, adjoining function rooms and hotel. Six hundred and fifty thousand square metres of commercial cash generators—not so much a hill of joy as a hill of hefty price tags and vending machines.

It feels strange, manufactured. Not particularly bad, just different than expected and, as a result, a tad disappointing. I suppose that in itself has been a strong theme for me here. No aspect of the experience has been as expected. Time and time again along the Way, the Camino has taught me to abandon expectations, not to value them. Why should the end be any different?

Still, I had hoped that Monte do Gozo would at least serve as a meeting point for many of the friends we had met along the Way. The old crew from the trail—Jodie, Petra, Jonas. They had all planned to spend their final night here celebrating before heading in to Santiago. Instead, arriving at Monte do Gozo feels bizarre. We are strangers among the newcomers. Without a word, Colin disappears, Simon and Mercedes have an argument and go their separate ways, and I, predictably, wander off to find the medical clinic.

Walking alone down the paved open corridor toward the clinic, not one of the new pilgrims I pass returns my *holas*. Not one familiar or friendly face among the bunch. Instead, they glance at me and shy away as I have while passing bag ladies in city streets.

In the clinic I greet the woman behind the counter and rather than battling through in Spanish, I lift my leg to show her the problem. No translation needed. Immediately she jumps up and rushes to get a doctor, bypassing two other pilgrims already waiting, and sends me straight through to one of the cubicles. Seconds later a female doctor arrives in a rush, looks at my feet, grabs my arm and marches me across the hall to a ground-level wash trough and basin. I showered just minutes before but it is as if I've shown up with leprosy. She leaves, ordering me to wash my feet. When I'm done two young nurses appear and take an arm each to escort me back to the cubicle. I'm surprised by the fuss.

The three stand looking grief-stricken and shake their heads in resignation, patch me up and send me off with antibiotics and strict instructions to attend the clinic the following day in Santiago. They offer me crutches on the way out.

Two weeks ago, during the feast day of St James' celebrations when Colin and I walked through the desert night, Lou Reed, Massive Attack, Bob Dylan, Iggy Pop, The Cure, The Corrs and Red Hot Chili Peppers played here to thousands across a three-day festival. How different the night would've been if we'd left a little sooner, walked a little faster, been a little less . . . disabled along the way. But that evening, Colin and I meet for a quiet drink in a corner of a smoky bar. It's a modest and low-key event between friends. In a way, appropriate for the journey we've all but completed together.

After a few rounds and laughs, I leave Colin and return to my room. I sit up on the end of my bunk bed, still trying to comprehend the occasion. I can see Santiago in the distance less than five kilometres away but despite the view, my mind will not accept the fact that we have arrived. Day after day for more than a month it has been a distant goal, a dream. Though it is now so close, it still sits far in my mind, and will remain that way until I can see, in a single view, my own feet before the front doors of the cathedral. Then and only then will it be real.

I look down at my gammy feet and marvel at the distance they've carried me so far—eight hundred kilometres across an entire country, the second largest in Europe. I remember the day when walking just a few metres down our driveway to collect the mail was an occasion worth celebrating. And we did. I was supposed to have died less than a week before.

I had been rushed to hospital late at night suffering hypothermia, massive internal damage and threatening cardiac arrest. An ECG showed I'd already gone into heart failure while sleeping through the night, two days before. My mother stood helpless by my bedside, watching the nurses' futile attempts to insert a drip into my collapsing veins. It was, they said, a final attempt to keep me alive. I was twenty-one.

As the medical staff raced around frantically trying to save me, I lay on a gurney, completely unperturbed by the commotion. By then, I'd lost almost half my body weight. With it, too, much of my hair, hearing and cognitive function. I'd disconnected from the world. I couldn't speak, I could barely think or breathe. Though I could see, I couldn't hear or feel anything anymore and at that point, I didn't care. I'd been so sick for so long, I didn't want to live. I'd forgotten how. Tired of the struggle, I was just relieved by the prospect that, once and for all, it might soon be over.

That's what anorexia does to a person. People think it's about weight, but it's not. I didn't want to be thin. I was so sad I wanted to die. Losing weight was just one of many symptoms that followed.

My mother broke down on hearing the doctor's final diagnosis. Too much damage had occurred. There was nothing more they could do to save me.

I am not the same person now who once lay defeated, wishing for death, six years ago. It feels like another world—and in many ways, another lifetime. It's hard to even relate to that lost little soul lying on a hospital bed preparing to die.

But I do still remember how it felt to be trapped in a body riddled with such pain. I promised I would not forget.

I can't tell you what it was that turned it around. It happened in a single night. The doctors can't explain it and neither can I. They say life turns on a dime. And so, it seems, does death. An epiphany perhaps. A miracle? Whatever it was, it was a gift, sent from somewhere that, until then, I never knew existed.

Suddenly, as my mother had assured me all along—regardless of what I had become—I believed that there was still something left inside worth fighting for. I knew I could live. But not in the state or mind frame I was in and that was something no one else could possibly change but me. Once I had made that decision, made up my mind and chosen life, as difficult as the years of treatment and physical rehabilitation promised to be, the rest would be—as Santiago is now—a formality.

It's no surprise that physical health has played such a prominent role throughout the past thirty-three days. After all, that is the nature of the Way. The very point. And possibly the reason I was called here. A reflection of life, to repeat and review. Perhaps Colin and I both came here needing to shed our shadows to make peace with the past and move on? I know I did. You can leave a history behind but to write a new future for yourself is a different story.

However you have lived you will walk and in your time here, all will be returned. The Camino is your life. No doubt. Laid out before you to pace and repeat. Your tools here are your lessons, the things you've learned throughout your life. And your challenge, to trust and believe that you have all you need to make it to your destination. Of course, a pair of Jesus sandals and a good stick help too.

Six years ago, when faced with the challenge of starting over, I promised myself that despite how overwhelming or impossible the years ahead appeared, each and every step along the way would somehow make me stronger. Every day I chanted, wrote and reminded myself of that until I believed it. There were days when the thought alone was the only thing that got me through. But eventually, in time, it did.

It may take a while for Colin and me to fully comprehend or understand the significance of our journey here or exactly what to conclude from the experiences of the Camino, but I at least know that—as before—each and every step I have taken along the Way has made me stronger and contributed, somehow, to who I am.

The city lights out my window shine brightly on a distant horizon against the backdrop of night. I take a small bottle from my backpack and, hanging my feet over the edge of the bed, spend time painting my toenails (dodging wads of gauze tape and dressing). Then I pull the lace underwear I washed and kept safe for the occasion from the plastic seal in a front pocket and lay it out on the bed before me.

This journey has become far more significant than a city. But Santiago is still the end of our trek across Spain and arriving tomorrow will mark the realisation of an achievement I will hold dear for a very long time. I may look a little worn around the edges, a tad shabby and slightly the worse for wear. But with bright red toenails and black lace beneath my tattered clothes and bandaged feet I will, at the very least, arrive in style.

Day 34
Santiago

Eli: *Follow your feet*

It is a morning I'll never forget.

The first day it hasn't rained in almost a week. The hour spent walking in to Santiago passes in complete silence. Colin and I walk only a few paces apart yet we're in our own private worlds and not a single word, from either of us, is spoken.

I walk the whole way without lifting my head. Instead, I follow my feet and time the rhythm of every step with the beat of my stick, trying as best I can to remember every detail: the sound—*clip-click*—the sight of cargos rolled up above swollen feet, the cool breeze across the surface of my skin and even the pain, savouring the moment in the hope I will never forget.

Tears of joy come and go as I recall the last thirty-three days and feel each of them as if experiencing them for the very first time.

Then there, along the roadside, Colin's voice gently calls my attention: 'There you go, girl!'

I stop and look up along the corridor of shopfronts and buildings lining the street and there they are, the spires I have admired in photographs for too long, there in all their glory, before my eyes.

Col and I break into a sprint. I hold my breath in expectation as we race toward the cathedral along cobbled laneways, underneath a stone footbridge and past a busker playing 'Amazing Grace' on bagpipes. The notes echo off the stonework and as we slow to a pace, Colin reaches back to take my hand.

We round the west wall of the Compostela and enter the historical Praza do Obradoiro. *We're here.* Heads down, we march with the church behind us, to the very centre of the square then stop, share a smile and, side by side, we turn to face our prize.

There she is, all eight centuries of wondrous glory. And at last I am here.

I drop Colin's hand and step forward, resting my chin on top of my stick, breathing in a victory so sweet, a flood of frantic butterflies fills my stomach. Finally free. Tears spill down my cheeks.

I don't speak, I don't smile and, for a moment, I don't move. I just stand weeping before the steps of the Compostela. *We made it!* Then, without breaking my view, I turn to Col and smile. 'It's a lovely prize.'

'It is indeed,' he laughs.

With the final steps taken, we drop, legs folded, and collapse beside each other in the centre of the square. A car alarm sounds from the left. The sun shines from above the right spire of the church. Colin and I sit in the middle of the plaza, unperturbed by the noise or crowds of people passing by. We've earned our place here and, despite the bustle, we take a moment to appreciate it.

Over a thousand pilgrims are arriving in Santiago each day now. On top of the countless tourists, one of whom steps over me in an attempt to take a snapshot. Yet in the time Colin and I are seated there in the Praza do Obradoiro, I don't spot another pilgrim. Instead, the bulk of admirers wandering the square are daytrippers and holiday-makers who've driven, trained or bussed in from surrounding Spanish and European cities. Though I am a foreigner here, visiting for the first time, I feel a sense of belonging. Having walked each step from Roncesvalles, Col and I have become a part of the place. A modest fraction of its revered history. A tiny clump of moss clinging to the Compostela's ancient wall.

Tour groups—with city guides delivering bilingual commentaries—continue to come and go. Several of them stop a few feet away and point us out. The tourists stare wide-eyed and gooey-faced, the kind of face you pull when admiring a newborn baby. One of them even takes our picture. 'Real pilgrims!' he declares to the others, while pointing to the view-finder of his Olympus.

Col still has his pack strapped to his back. As the group passes, he reclines against it and folds his arms across his chest in satisfaction. *A job well done!* I sit with my legs outstretched, toes before the door of the cathedral—my gift granted, my goal achieved and my partner by my side. Real pilgrims indeed.

Colin's smile that day in Santiago is real as well. Genuine. I know it won't last. Santiago to him is a bit like Eurovision—a novelty. He knows he shouldn't laugh but we both know he will. For now, though, his smile is soft and free of sarcasm. The spark in his eyes has returned and, in recent days, so too has his appetite. He's even managed to kick his addiction to the guidebook—albeit grudgingly. The look on his face comes from somewhere honest and sincere. It's so precious, I take a picture of it as he sits gazing toward the cathedral, then toss him the camera as he, in turn, snaps me where we sit.

Then the clouds open up, the sun disappears and, again as if scripted, a steady rain starts to fall across the square.

'Time to go?' I ask.

'Looks like it,' Col replies. 'And I think we've earned a drink, 'ey, Tonto. Waddaya say?'

Colin: *Collagen-free cathedral*

A thousand pilgrims a day are descending on Santiago. The ancient walls echo to the sound of drums and bagpipes for there is a strong *simpatía* between Ireland and this part of Spain. The roots are deeply entwined, twisted around Catholicism and the pagan goddess cults.

Walking in I see a tiny dumpling figure with blonde hair and headband: Forrest Gumpenburger walking out, already heading back to Austria. For the next week she will have to battle the hordes coming the other way. I hope that when she finally reaches her front door in Linz, the door she walked out of five months ago, this will finally be enough.

We tramp on cobblestones through the ancient and narrow streets of the old town. We get lost a hundred yards short of the cathedral—we can see the spire but we just can't find a way through the maze of old streets. Bagpipes are playing 'Amazing Grace'. Yes, really.

And then we walk through a medieval arch and there it is.

The square in front of the cathedral is crowded with scouts and tour groups. A silver Jaguar parked outside the Hotel Rey de Católica has its security alarm blaring: BLAH-BLAH-BLAH-BLAH. On the cathedral spire Jimmy the Fish looks displeased.

I am so very proud of Eli; I did not think she could do it. This is a girl who could barely walk four kilometres at a time just weeks before this and she has now walked eight hundred kilometres in thirty-three days, just to prove to herself that she could. This was her Everest and I am proud to stand at the top with her to admire the view.

She has seen me at my worst and still chosen to walk beside me; she has conquered her dark angel and yet continues to set her sights on the next mountain. I love and admire the girl. I wish, in a way, I felt like I had earned the respect and love she has returned to me.

Tour groups block out the sun as we sit on our packs in the square. They stare at the cathedral without getting it at all. A cathedral is just a cathedral: what we are admiring is a journey. I know this cathedral before I step inside it, because I have understood it through the eyes of a thousand years of pilgrims who have held it in their minds for hundreds of miles of bad food, sore feet and cold sleep.

Though the place itself means nothing to me, staring up at it now it seems more significant than I had ever imagined it would be and evokes both humility and deep satisfaction. Seagulls screech and wheel over the spires of the cathedral, which are grease green with age. What I already love about this cathedral is that no one has thought to clean it. For all its Gothic grandeur, León looks sanitised; Santiago looks every one of its eight hundred years. There has been no nip and tuck, no boob job, no collagen implants. It is old and it looks it.

A sign outside the door urges visitors: *Visit the Tomb! Hug the Apostle!* It's like Disney advertising a new ride. Ride the Apostletron!

Inside, the cathedral is a seething mass of the faithful. Flashbulbs pop, and pilgrims with video cameras jockey for position. The incense of body odour is intense. So many pilgrims, so few showers. But the bulk of this heaving mass of devotion consists of tourists, bus groups from Bilbao and Madrid and Alicante with toy walking sticks decorated with false gourds and plastic scallop shells, their kids wearing brown felt Santiago hats.

Pilgrims touch the central pillar of the Portico de la Gloria in which St James is portrayed welcoming the tired pilgrim.

Innumerable hands have left deep finger marks in the pillar, like a kid's hand in the icing on a cake.

The queue to hug the Romanesque statue of St James stretches out of the great double doors. There he is at last, Jimmy the Fish, standing up there on the high altar, looking unbearably cheerful, like he has just scored a line of coke. Everyone wants to touch him. Tourists and pilgrims together shuffle up the staircase next to the altar, wanting their brief moment to embrace the cold metal of the gilded bust.

Now I have to break this to you gently because I know you'd rather hear it first from a friend: the cathedral is one of the least holy places I have ever been, with the possible exception of the Pussy Ping Pong Club in Phat Pong Road, Bangkok, about twenty years ago. The cuddle huddle for Santiago stretches all the way to the Praza de Immaculada. Santiago maintains a benign grin through it all: group hug, group hug! It looks to me as spiritual as a kid going up to sit on Father Christmas's lap in the Grotto of a department store.

There was a tradition once that pilgrims would put their hats on Santiago while they hugged him: sadly this has been discontinued. Otherwise I could have brought my stubby-holder hat at the cricket or the baseball cap that says: *I'm with Stupid*. I turn away, disgusted but amused.

In the nave there is a statue of Santiago Matamoros, Moor-slayer, Jimmy the Fish, waving a sword and trampling bleeding Moors under the hooves of his horse. Call me a sentimentalist but I prefer him as Santiago, Group Hugger.

The three-ring circus that is Santiago cathedral in the summer is not a modern blight, nor is the pushing and shoving. They hadn't even completed this cathedral before there was trouble inside. In 1207 some pilgrims were jostling for best position in front of the altar and things got so out of hand that next day the priests had to mop the floors to remove the blood pools and one section of the cathedral had to be reconstructed.

Today, after the pilgrims have seen the reliquary and attended a special pilgrims' mass, they get a framed certificate to hang on the wall of their hovel. Called the Compostela, it is supposed to count as a remission of sins. You get these certificates at the Dean's Residence on the Rúa de Villar but the queue snakes halfway through the old city and it takes some people three or four hours to get one. I decide they can stick their Compostela.

I don't deserve to have my sins remitted. Besides, even if I do get to heaven, looks like I'll only have to queue up for months to get in.

Day 35
Santiago

Eli: With light and love

Next morning, I wake at daybreak to a view across distant mountains from our first-floor window. I get up and dress, and slip outside before Colin is awake.

Stepping out into the empty streets of Santiago and wandering the laneways toward the church, I can't help but grin a wry smile of content; there will be no lugging a load, binding feet or climbing mountains today. No more yellow arrows to abide by, curfews or early morning alarms. No lining up for a place to stay only to be turned away. No mud to trudge through or cold showers waiting at the end of a long day's walk—in fact, there will be very little walking done at all today. Or tomorrow. And for many days after that.

The roof of the cathedral is shrouded in low-level cloud. I shelter from the rain under an archway on the far side of the plaza.

The fact that Christians have labelled this a place of spiritual significance means little to me. But I do have a prayer to deliver for many people whom I have carried in my heart and would like to wish good things. The way I see it, anywhere that humbles you to a place of gratitude—whether it be in the waiting room of a hospital or here, at the end of a long

305

journey—makes a prayer worthy of being received. It is something I need to do. And as with faith, I will do it in my own private way.

Taking a eucalyptus branch, an Australian native collected three days ago from the forest and strapped to the outside of my pack, I tear a page from my notepad filled with the names of those I wish to pray for. I have been keeping a list since boarding the plane in Melbourne.

One by one I carefully write a name on the front of each leaf with a felt-tip pen, until the branch is full. Almost one hundred names of loved ones, family members and friends. Some I've known all my life and others I have met recently along the Camino: Mercedes, Simon, Jodie, Jonas, Manfred, Forrest, Yoshki and Petra; Francesca, the woman in the wheelchair, and her lover; Robert Bonami and his donkey; and Colin, his daughters and his wife.

It takes almost an hour but when it's complete, I wander across the empty square through light rain to the church. Climbing the stone steps of the cathedral to the bolted double doors waiting at the top, I lay my branch beneath the architrave. On one knee, I bless myself and bow my head, holding my heart, I send a prayer for each of them to the heavens, with light and love.

Colin: A day in a not so holy city

The next morning at 7.30 the queue for the Compostela already snakes right through the city to, ironically, the Rúa da Conga. Scout bands sing songs while they wait. The man I saw get out of his car and run into one of the *albergues* to get a stamp is right there at the front. It just proves what I always suspected: it is possible to lie and cheat your way into heaven.

Inside the cathedral folk have started hugging Santiago already. He looks resigned to another day of being rubbed, fondled and cuddled. A bit like a sex worker, really. For a man who started life as a keen angler in a remote Palestinian fishing village, he has come a long way.

Eli and I stroll through the streets. There is pilgrim pop everywhere; kids with toy bagpipes compete with each other to be the most annoying child in Santiago; there are office workers on vacation from Santander and San Sebastian with brown felt Santiago hats and useless pine walking sticks with plastic scallop shells tied on with red string that wouldn't last five paces on the Meseta; there are marching bands of pilgrims, some with Templar crosses, carrying flags and singing songs. All this religiosity is spooking me. I have only just got here but already I have to get out of town.

At a restaurant we talk to an Australian couple. Born here in northwest Spain, they now live in Balmain in Sydney and are members of the Australian Galician Society. 'It's frustrating,' they say. 'When people find out we're from Spain, they all think it is flamenco dancing and Real Madrid. They don't realise this is just Ireland with olive skin.'

Eli's bare feet in her Birkenstocks are a mess of bandages. She looks like a leper in a Monty Python film. A schoolboy stops her in the street and asks if he can take a photo of her feet for a school project he's doing on pilgrims. She poses for him and he is pathetically grateful.

Eli has been serene since we reached here. She has proved something to herself. I guess she has proved something to a lot of people.

I wonder now, if I had been on that hospital gurney as she was six years ago, would I have had the strength or the desire to get up? Where is the line between character building and soul destroying? At this moment the separation between these two states seems membrane thin; I mistrust anyone who thinks they know.

Perhaps we need to travel great lengths to find out what that difference is. At least eight hundred kilometres.

Day 36
Finisterre

Colin: *To the ends of the Earth*

I always wondered where Finisterre was. I remember hearing the name on the BBC weather forecasts when I was a kid. There was always the chance of a force 9 gale, apparently.

Finisterre is actually a cape on the northwest coast of Spain, eighty kilometres from Santiago. It is the westernmost point, on the Costa da Morte, the Coast of Death, and in Roman times it was the last redoubt of the known world. The ancients believed it was where the world of men met the world of the gods and the tradition of homage to this place was hijacked by the Spanish church when Jimmy the Fish's remains were conveniently discovered in a hillside tomb just short of the coast.

Finisterre itself is a tatty, moth-eaten fishing village, but its crappiness holds incredible charm for me. Fishermen sit in their garages under their flats mending nets, waitresses serve *café con leche* with their thumbs in the cup, washing hangs from the balconies of waterside flats. Old men sit around outside and drink espresso and play cards and wonder if it's their month to shave. It is a blessed relief after Santiago: no chanting scout groups, no Tour de Santiago cyclists in bright yellow lycra clutching pilgrim passports in one hand and their bulging gonads in the other, no Sunday strollers with plastic *peregrino* walking sticks.

Mist creeps around the headland that fingers into the sea. Gulls cry like babies. Red and blue and green fishing boats jog on the spot in the harbour. Peugeots drive too fast through the narrow streets. A man in a wheelchair eats his lunch in the middle of the roundabout. And there are seafood restaurants everywhere. Spaniards will eat anything but plankton and waves. The blackboard menus advertise lobster, shrimp, clams, prawns, monkfish, deep-fried lighthouse and flotsam in shellfish sauce.

There is a legend that the Virgin Mary came here once in a stone boat to encourage James in his preaching. Encourage him how, I wonder. Maybe with a hug—he likes those. Or did she just give him a good slapping? Five converts in nine years. Ace it up, stupid! I want to see results or you can go back to catching herring!

I walk the short distance out to the cape. It nestles on the peninsula like a child hiding in its mother's skirts. There is a statue of a boot over a small stone fire pit where modern pilgrims burn their shoes to mark the end of a pilgrimage. (Of course in Roman times they could not do this, they had to turn around and walk home in theirs.)

I climb down the cliffs to the edge of the world for my own private ceremony. A veil of rain sweeps in from the heavens and sets me shivering, cooling the sweat on my back. I have written some words on a piece of paper and I put it in an empty wine bottle and send it to the gods with a private prayer. The ceremony is quickly done and I don't linger.

This time the prayer is for me. Why is it harder to send a prayer for myself than someone else? It might seem noble, but now I have worked out the answer and I can assure you it's not.

I can understand how the ancients concluded this was the end of the world. It does feel like the gods or goddesses are just out there, where the pearl grey horizon meets the sea. I hope when my bottle gets there and they read what's inside, they don't just laugh and decide to play more practical jokes. God's great banana skin is not even funny the first time; a second time would be pushing the friendship.

Here's a thing. If you're ever in Muxia, immediately go somewhere else.

I walk that morning from Finisterre on pine needle paths through conifer forests and ratbag hamlets with dry stone walls overgrown with brambles. It is a rotting eternal world of donkeys, compost heaps, stone ruins, corn, cats, barking dogs, cow shit, rusting ladders and washing machines falling to bits in the ruins of crumbling stone houses.

I walk with a couple of smiling Spanish boys. Unfortunately they don't have much English and I don't have much Spanish.

'Do you hab beezahs for your country?' one of them asks me as we walk along.

'Visas? No.'

'Oh very good.'

'We had to have them five years ago but not anymore.'

He looks puzzled. 'You hab beezahs for five years but you don't hab now?'

'It doesn't matter to me. I have dual nationality.'

He looks truly worried. 'What you beezah look like?'

'Well, like a stamp. It goes in your passport.'

'Here the beezah yellow and black. One just bite me on the ear, I think.'

Ah, that sort of beezah.

We stare at each other in mutual dismay and abandon any further attempts at conversation.

Out here on the road to Muxia it's like being back in the early days of the Camino. There are no tramping hordes, because there is no cathedral and no remission of sins. Here people come on private pilgrimage. They know they will still have their sins when they leave: they just hope not to commit so many of them from now on.

I've come to Muxia for a purpose. I have with me a photograph and a prayer that have accompanied me the whole way from Sydney, and I intend now to deliver them. It is the same prayer to the Madonna that I have repeated at every church, every shrine, that was open to receive me.

The church of María de la Barca stands on the cliffs at the tip of the peninsula. Its doors are so close to the waves you can feel the salt spray on your face as you look through the grill at the Queen of Heaven. But for the first time it occurs to me that the prayer is just another intricate manipulation. I am trying to manipulate God into giving me what I want, and manipulate the creator of the prayer into thinking I am the one who can answer hers. There are no victims here. Just authors of their own disasters.

I go to the back of the cathedral and without prayer or ceremony leave the photograph and petition behind, secreted in the church. For all I know, they are still there.

I sit on the rocks and stare at the sea. From my backpack I remove a cigar case I have brought with me from home, even though I don't smoke. It is engraved: *To my lover and best friend.*

Sometimes it seems there is not room enough in the world for all our regrets. And yet when even the smallest lesson is learned, or glimpsed, what can you do but regret that you had not learned it sooner, and wonder at how things might have been different if you had?

I had thought to toss the cigar case into the sea; the inscription rang hollow to me now. But I didn't. I returned it to my pack as reminder of a more innocent time.

I could blame a lot of people for the mess in my life. In the last thirty-six days I probably have, as we have walked in silent contemplation of the past. But I will be honest with you, I now suspect that the person responsible is sitting right here, right now, on these rocks below the María de la Barca. I was the one who wanted to be everyone's saviour, so why complain when someone thanks me for saving them and then moves on? Who denied anyone a free choice, who insisted they see it his way, and that was the only way there was to look at things? Is this how I have killed love in my life? Do I destroy love by closing my fist around it and trying to grasp it?

And yet I could have avoided all this. I could have stayed with the devil I knew. It was safe there. I would never have had to face all this, could have told myself that I was a good man by never stepping outside the walls of the castle I had built. Looking good, going nowhere.

Eli has done something no woman has yet done. She called my bluff without scooping up the pot and walking away from the table. By my observation, she needed neither my physical nor emotional support to walk to Santiago. And I suspect she knew this all along. But she still apparently saw something in me that I did not.

This is not Hollywood. I don't have a trite denouement where a last minute miracle shows me the way. Out there beyond the horizon, the gods have taken my bottle from the ocean and are studying my prayer, and Eli's, and perhaps yours also. And in a day, or a year, I will have back their answer.

I have walked my pilgrimage and I cannot dictate if the gods beyond the sea will listen or laugh at my feeble attempts to control my own destiny. But out here I have felt, if only for a time, small and humble, and have heard in ancient stones the prayers of pilgrims long since dead. I have felt—if for a moment—a part of eternity, and a greater plan, at the end of the Earth.

All I can do when I walk away from here is shrug on my smile, like Eli's pack—*doof!*—and take each day back, each step at a time.

Eli: And beyond

We arrive in Finisterre in the early evening as daylight fades beyond the horizon. Though views of the surrounding township are filtered through a thick haze of ocean spray, I can't shake a persistent sense that I have been here before. In appearance it's unique, like nowhere I've seen. I've never bought a print of it or received a postcard from Finisterre. Yet everything about this charming fishing village is somehow familiar: the coloured masts of the tiny sail boats painting a picture on the harbour, the labyrinth of narrow winding streets, the ruined castle turrets dripping into the ocean below, and the concrete pier. Déjà vu in each direction; either I have been here before or I have lived the feeling this place inspires.

The following morning, I wake to find Colin has already left. It is just after seven and he has gone to spend the day and night in Muxia. It's something that he needs to do.

With the day to myself, I visit the local supermarket around ten before returning to the *albergue*, where I lay a picnic out across a table in the communal dining room. As I take notes and snack on a spread of Spanish tapas, a Swedish traveller who's recently set up home here in Finisterre joins me at the table. He tells me he finished the Camino seven months ago and realised in the process that his life at home had lost relevance, so he stayed.

'I go home to an office job in a call centre with a boss who gets paid to stand over my shoulder and make me feel like mud. He doesn't even know my name. But still, I must answer to him and he must answer to the company and the company must answer to the government, who I pay tax to. It is all around and about in circles going nowhere,' he says.

I tell him I understand. Life here is a far cry from the rat race of cities everywhere. Bills, mobile phones, *Sex and the City*, nine-to-five working days and the general dog-eat-dog mentality of everyday life are rendered inconsequential when each day is stripped to its essentials. Priorities change.

What I appreciate most about Camino life, however, is time. Time to think, to breathe, to talk, to ponder, to explore, to learn, to interact and grow, to enjoy food and wine and moments and views. Time to give thanks for what you have, identify what you don't have and work on things you need. Time. And as much of it as you like. I'm going to miss it and I know, in time, I will miss the person I am with it.

After lunch I begin the trek alone out to Cape Finisterre, the final destination on my itinerary. There I'll sit at what was once believed to be the end of the Earth, on the western edge of the European continent, and look out into the vast ocean knowing that there is not a single step left to take. The prospect of a seven-kilometre hike now is like a wander down the driveway to collect the mail. I never thought I'd see the day. It's a short yet significant little trip. And the last I plan to make on foot for quite a while.

Walking out of the township along the roadside, I peel off the sealed path, deciding to take a secondary trail up the cliff face and along the ridge. I have no map or arrows to guide the way, and am not sure where it leads but I have four hours of daylight to find out.

The path zigzags all the way to the top and at the crest of the hill the land pans across a windswept plain dotted with the mushroom caps of boulders. The ocean lies like a lake in the distance. I look ahead to try to spot the lighthouse but can't see through my tears. I'm surprised. I've cried a lot since Santiago. It seems for every step I've walked a tear has been stored, waiting to be released. I'm not sure what they all mean. But it feels right, so I let them go.

As I wander across the sparse terrain towards the water, I think about Colin walking out here earlier this morning, stumbling through the dark of dawn, doing what he needs to do to bring his journey to an end.

I can't tell you what an experience it has been to watch him fall and rise beside me. Both fascinating and heartbreaking. I once heard him say, 'to be a better man there has to be some sort of spiritual connection made'. Before we came to Spain, he admitted he had none. But the fact that he has left today to send a message to the gods or goddesses across the sea tells me that, if nothing else, he has at least found that much here.

I guess it's only when we're open to receiving answers that we stand any chance of finding them. And it's typically at our weakest or most vulnerable that we seek them. Perhaps *this* is what pilgrimage is about. To cast aside your possessions, discard your ego and to push yourself beyond your limits. Essentially, to surrender your wants and trust that what you do find will be exactly what you need.

My wish for Col today is not that his prayer will be received but that he will find peace for having sent it.

I arrive at a knoll overlooking the lighthouse, which itself hangs on a cliff edge overlooking the vast Atlantic. Clambering onto a rock, I perch myself in line with the horizon. There I take a moment to write a note that I hope to go back and read if and when I ever doubt myself again. Having come this far, I've decided self-doubt is nothing more than a bad habit I can break. The Camino has been the first step in that process, a kind of cleansing; a spiritual detox. I have my evidence now.

Nearing the lighthouse, I notice that, like the cathedral in Santiago, there are many more tourists than there are pilgrims. I ignore the attention as I pass, edging my way beyond the barriers to the steep cliff face. Descending closer toward the spray of breaking waves, I use my stick to tread carefully down the jagged rocks, reminding myself of the irony of a slip to death at a time like this. Though he'd never admit it, I'm sure Col would manage a great laugh at my expense. Arriving at the farthest point, I take my place on the flat surface of an overhang—feet dangling directly above the notorious waters, the Coast of Death. My stomach sinks with flutters of fear and for a pleasant change I can't feel my feet.

I have arrived at the end of the Earth. The western tip, a place recognised throughout the ages for its spiritual significance and ethereal energy. And the last place where the sun sets over European shores each day to be reborn the next. It's here that the journey Col and I have taken together is finally complete.

I spend close to an hour gazing out across the ocean, giving thanks and wondering what might now lie ahead. Standing, I secure my footing in the mud and pitch the stick that has helped carry me here into a crash of waves below. And prepare to walk back to Finisterre unaided to begin the journey home.

Looking back a final time over my right shoulder, I marvel at the courage of the sailor brave enough to set out across uncharted waters in the hope of proving that there was, in fact, something out there—beyond the sea—worth finding and fighting for. Pegging his hope and belief against a world full of sceptics, he pursued his dream regardless, and in 1492 Christopher Columbus discovered land and indeed changed the world. Who said it can't be done?

In doing so he also proved that what we think we know

is not always what is real. That we are only bound by our own imagination. And that sometimes, what may appear to be the end is, in actual fact, the beginning of something even better.

Acknowledgments

A big thank you to Tim Curnow, our agent, for helping us both see this book through to completion and to our wonderful publisher, Jude McGee, for her faith in this book and in us. You are both golden. Thanks to everyone at Allen & Unwin who has shown such enthusiasm for our little book, to Clara Finlay and Jane Alexander and all who worked behind the scenes to get our little baby out there into the world.

There are others we would like to thank: Sylvie Traechslin, for getting Col to a doctor in time. Simon and Mercedes for helping El down off the bridge when she really wanted to catch the tram back to Saint Kilda. The mad nun in Santo Domingo who helped Col through his writer's block and gave him a whole chapter of material. The many doctors and nurses who helped patch Eli together on a daily basis. And to the manufacturers of Betadine and Mercurochrome for their wonderful products. Last, but not least, sincere thanks to Saint James himself, for staying unshakably cheerful through the whole experience.

Elizabeth Best & Colin Bowles

theyearweseizedtheday.net